LUTHER AND THE RADICALS

ANOTHER LOOK AT SOME ASPECTS OF THE STRUGGLE BETWEEN LUTHER AND THE RADICAL REFORMERS

by

HARRY LOEWEN

0-88920-008-4
(paper)
0-88920-009-2
(cloth)
© 1974

Wilfrid Laurier University
Waterloo, Ontario, Canada

For

Gertrude

H. Harry, Charles

and

Jeffrey

TABLE OF CONTENTS

FOREWORD 7

PREFACE 9

Chapter
- I   BACKGROUND FOR THE CONFLICT BETWEEN LUTHER AND THE RADICAL REFORMERS   13
  - Luther's Conversion   13
  - Luther's Early Writings   16
  - The Dissenters   21
  - Origin of the Dissident Groups   24
  - Reasons for Opposing the Reformer   26

- II   LUTHER AND THE WITTENBERG RADICALS   29
  - Moderation Versus Radicalism   29
  - Increasing Radicalism and Luther's Reaction   33
  - Order Restored   37
  - The Sacramental Controversy   40

- III   LUTHER'S STRUGGLE WITH THE REVOLUTIONARY RADICALS   47
  - Luther and Authority Prior to 1525   47
  - Thomas Müntzer and Luther   50
  - Müntzer's Increasing Radicalism   54
  - Luther and the Peasants' Revolt   59

- IV   LUTHER AND THE EVANGELICAL ANABAPTISTS   67
  - Origin and Spread of Anabaptism   67
  - Luther's Early Contact with Anabaptism   70
  - Anabaptism and Revolutionary Radicalism   73
  - Infant Versus Adult Baptism   79
  - State Church Versus Free Church   85
  - Dogma Versus Morals   89

- V   LUTHER AND THE REVOLUTIONARY ANABAPTISTS   95
  - The Anabaptist Kingdom in Münster   95
  - Luther's Attitude Toward the Münster Episode   98
  - Anabaptism and Münsterism   102

VI	LUTHER'S ATTITUDE TOWARD THE SPIRITUALISTS, ANTINOMIANS AND ANTITRINITARIANS	109
	The Spiritualists: The Inner and the Outer Word	109
	Luther and the Antinomians	126
	Luther and the Antitrinitarians	130
VII	LUTHER AND THE RADICALS ON TOLERANCE AND RELIGIOUS LIBERTY	135
	Luther and Religious Liberty	135
	The Radicals and Tolerance	143
VIII	CONCLUSION	151
ABBREVIATIONS		160
NOTES		161
BIBLIOGRAPHY		191
INDEX		207

FOREWORD

In this book Professor Loewen has presented us with a fresh treatment of the subject on which there is already considerable literature. Major contributors to the discussion have been Karl Holl, Karl Gerhard Steck, George H. Williams, John S. Oyer and others. A new book on the subject of Luther and the radicals will therefore need to justify its appearance. There is no question that Professor Loewen's book meets the test.

The publishing of this book can be justified on several grounds. First, the work is discriminating. Lutheran writers on the subject have had difficulty in carefully distinguishing the various groups of radicals from one another. This is especially true of the distinction between what Loewen calls "evangelical Anabaptism" and Thomas Müntzer. The author makes careful and well-grounded differentiations, finding five separate groups of radicals. Such discrimination introduces order and fairness into the discussion which has sometimes been lacking.

Secondly, the work is comprehensive, providing the reader with a fine overview of the responses of Luther to the radicals from his own writings. Loewen shows how, because of Luther's theology and especially his view of the two kingdoms, he was actually more tolerant of dissenters than other Protestants and Catholics. The author shows how Luther's attitude toward Anabaptists hardened after Münster, but that even then he was reluctant to agree to the death penalty for them.

Thirdly, the book is marked by a sympathetic view of Luther throughout. The author seeks to understand Luther's stance and the reasons for his actions. Such sympathy for Luther is, of course, not new in the literature. What is new is that the author is a Mennonite, writing from within a firm commitment to a historical tradition which is one of those discussed in this book. Moreover, as Professor Loewen implies in the preface, it is the one that least deserved Luther's hostility.

All this is not to say that Mennonite historians have been unsympathetic to Luther. It is to say that it has been a major concern of the author to seek to understand Luther without glossing over or excusing his sometimes violent words and actions. Professor Loewen is determined to show that Luther acted mainly from worthy motives, namely his convictions about the nature of the Gospel, and that his actions were consistent with his own experience of redemption.

Looking at Anabaptists from the direction of Wittenberg, they do not appear as harmless and innocent as Mennonite scholarship has sometimes insisted they were. Independently Loewen has arrived at views supported strongly by a book like *Anabaptists and the Sword* by James Stayer. He does this primarily by carefully reinterpreting the letter of Conrad Grebel to Thomas Müntzer.

The author expresses strong caution on making claims for Anabaptists as champions of religious liberty. I confess that at this point I have some reservations regarding Professor Loewen's conclusions. While it is true that Anabaptists shared in the basic intolerance of the time the fact remains that with the exception of Münster no Anabaptist ever exiled or dispossessed or executed another man because of his faith. True, they disagreed with everyone else and consigned men who believed other than they did to the wrath of God. However, when it came to dealing with deviance in their own midst they used brotherly exhortation and ban as methods of church discipline. It is important, however, to question the excessive claims sometimes made at this point.

In his new book the author has fully achieved his purpose. This, in his own words, is "to remind scholars of Anabaptism that in their zeal to correct the image of the radical reformers they sometimes become one-sided and less than charitable toward the mainline reformers who in good faith could not tolerate what they considered alien views."

Walter Klaassen

PREFACE

The purpose of this study is to take another look at some aspects of Luther's struggle with the radical reformers of his time. The Reformer's struggle with the radicals may be likened to King Lear's confrontation with his daughters. At the height of his anguish Lear exclaims, "I am a man more sinn'd against than sinning" (III, 2, l. 60). King Lear in his haste, rashness and blindness had obviously sinned against his daughters, especially against Cordelia who loved her father dearly. Later, however, two of Lear's children turned with such malice against their father that their sins against the old man outweighed those of the king. Similarly Luther had in a sense provoked his spiritual children, the Protestant radicals of the sixteenth century, to turn against him, but in their radicalism they not only caused their spiritual father much grief but some of them went so far as to attempt to destroy him altogether. There were those children, the so-called evangelical Anabaptists, who, like Cordelia, suffered innocently at the hands of their father. But again as in Lear's case, the more radical children and certain issues blinded Luther's eyes to such an extent that it was almost impossible for him to differentiate properly between those of his children who merely wished to be honest with themselves and go their ways independent of their father, and those who sought to destroy him and that which he had so laboriously built up. Whether Luther in his struggle with the radicals was like Lear "a man more sinn'd against than sinning" depends on the point of view one wishes to take, but the question will be kept alive throughout the study.

There was a time when the story of Anabaptism was either ignored by historians or else distorted because it was seen through the eyes of the mainline reformers, the enemies of the movement. This has changed. Most of the radicals of the sixteenth century have been "rehabilitated" by scholars sympathetic to the radical reformation. Anabaptism is now generally seen as a movement which complemented the emphases of the mainline reformers, stressing such issues as voluntarism in church membership, separation of church and state, non-violence, and religious liberty, principles largely neglected by Luther and Zwingli. However, in their zeal to tell the true story of sixteenth-century radicalism, some sympathizers of the movement have portrayed the once maligned individuals and groups as innocent, pious people who suffered cruel persecution at the hands of more or less wicked state-churchmen. Their side of the story is thus often as one-sided as was the story of the enemies of the Anabaptists. The study before us seeks to understand the reasons for the clash between Luther and the radicals, a point often neglected when one or the other side is emphasized. However, the study keeps Luther in a central position, exploring the issues which led to the Reformer's attitude toward the radicals and analyzing the principles that were at stake in his struggle with the various dissident individuals and groups.

The radicals included in this monograph are those men and groups who at first hailed Luther as a great reformer of the church but later dissented from him because they felt he did not go far enough in his reform drives. They include the Wittenberg radicals, the Zwickau prophets, Thomas Müntzer and the peasants, the Spiritualists, the Antinomians, and the revolutionary and peaceful Anabaptists. Luther's encounter with some of them was personal, violent and dramatic; with others it was indirect, impersonal and judicial. Whether Luther confronted the radicals personally or whether he pronounced judgment on certain dissident groups when asked about them, he always acted from conviction and after some deliberation. Luther's struggle with the radical reformers thus throws light on his views concerning God and man, sin and redemption, church and state, Scripture, the sacraments, and tolerance and religious liberty.

This study does not wish to give the impression that in the struggle between the sixteenth-century reformers the only alternatives offered were those of Luther and the radicals. The fact is that the Roman Catholics and the Reformed advanced other positions. However, inasmuch as there are many studies of Luther's relations with the Roman Catholic and Reformed positions, I have largely ignored these and concentrated upon the Luther-radical relations.

I should like to acknowledge the following persons who encouraged me in writing this book. Professor Walter Klaassen of the University of Waterloo (Conrad Grebel College) read the manuscript and kindly supplied the Foreword. Professor Aarne Siirala of Waterloo Lutheran Seminary offered many helpful suggestions; his encouragement was much appreciated. With Dr. Otto W. Heick, Professor Emeritus, Waterloo Lutheran Seminary, I discussed several issues raised in the book. Mrs. Margaret Barber typed the first draft of the manuscript and Mrs. Doreen Armbruster typed its final form—to both my thanks. I appreciate the help of Elfrieda Bensler who read the manuscript for style and grammar. Dr. Norman Wagner, Director of Graduate Studies and Research at Wilfrid Laurier University, arranged and directed the technical details of publication. As much as the above were involved in the preparation of this book, I am solely responsible for its contents, weaknesses and errors. The book has been published with the help of a grant from the

Humanities Research Council of Canada, using funds provided by the Canada Council.

H.L.

CHAPTER I

BACKGROUND FOR THE CONFLICT BETWEEN
LUTHER AND THE RADICAL REFORMERS

At the basis of Luther's attitude toward the dissident sects of the sixteenth century lies his conversion in the monastery and his subsequent theology. Luther's conversion and theology led to his early writings and rebellion against the dogma of the Roman Catholic church. The Reformer's example and writings influenced profoundly other men and groups who also for various reasons were first led to rebel against Catholicism and then in turn against the originator of Protestantism. Remaining true to himself and his theology, Luther could not help but oppose those who dissented from him. The issues between Luther and his dissenters were thus locked, often to the point of mortal combat.

Luther's Conversion

Countless men and women before Luther had entered the monastery to make satisfaction for sin, to fulfill a vow, or to dedicate themselves to the love of God. Countless monks and nuns before Luther had gone through the agonies of soul, but through the media of prayer, the sacraments, or even mysticism they had resolved their spiritual problems. Luther, for some reason, failed to find peace. Heinrich Boehmer comments: "The one thing ... that distinguishes Luther from the great mass of ascetics is simply the fact that all the means of quieting such doubts provided for by the old monastic teachers not only failed but rather had a completely opposite effect; that is, they merely increased his inner distress and anxiety."[1] In his commentary on Galatians in 1531, Luther reflected on his years in the monastery. While devoting himself entirely to fasting, vigils, prayers, the reading of masses, and other disciplines, he constantly fostered mistrust, doubt, fear, and hatred.[2] Christ was for Luther a fear-inspiring judge, sitting on a rainbow ready to execute judgment upon the wicked. Luther feared him more than the devil. He could not call upon his name, he wrote in 1537, "nay could not even bear to hear his name mentioned."[3]

Several factors may have contributed to Luther's fear and sense of worthlessness. The Brethren of the Common Life, with whom Luther had studied in Magdeburg (1497-1498), intensified his belief in the sinfulness of man; St. Augustine's doctrine of man and predestination may have added to his feeling of despondency; and his unsuccessful attempts to find peace of soul in the monastery may have contributed to his belief in the bondage of the human will.[4] It was Luther's spiritual superior, the mystically inclined Vicar General Staupitz, who pointed the struggling man to the love of God in Christ. Luther confessed later that it was Staupitz who had helped him through his trying years.[5]

Luther's inner breakthrough occurred probably in 1514 when he lectured on the books of the Bible. The idea of God's righteousness caused him much anxiety until he read in Habakkuk 2:4 that "the just shall live by his faith." From this passage Luther concluded that spiritual life must be derived from faith; all human attempts to find peace are thus in vain. It is God, according to Luther, who imputes divine righteousness to sinful man without man's participation in any sense, solely on account of Christ's substitutionary suffering and death.

It would be wrong to imply that with his experience in the monastery Luther had discovered the concept of grace as opposed to the "law" of Roman Catholicism. The Catholic church had a highly developed doctrine of grace, but the difference between Catholicism and Luther's experience was that while the church had the power to bring down the grace of God through the channels of the sacraments, the Reformer experienced God's grace directly, without, as he put it, "the works of man." It is thus a Christo-centric experience that lies at the basis of Luther's theology of the cross and God's working in the hearts of men.

Luther's sense of having grasped the full truth concerning man's redemption by grace alone was so strong that there was no doubt in his mind that it was the heart of the gospel.[6] Whoever did not accept the doctrine of justification by faith alone could not be saved. In a letter of December 21, 1525, to Duke George of Saxony, Luther wrote that no one, including the hostile Duke, would succeed in quenching his gospel. It would accomplish its divine work in the hearts of men, for the gospel was not his own, Luther pointed out, but God's.[7] On August 5, 1530, Luther wrote to Chancellor Brück that the Reformer's cause was God's cause, and that God could never forget those who had made God's cause their own.[8] In view of Luther's *sola fide* principle it is thus not surprising that he was unable to tolerate any person, group or system which tended to deviate from this theology.

Luther's dramatic conversion not only emphasized the biblical doctrine of justification by faith alone, but it also led to the formulation of the principle of *sola scriptura*. Since Luther had found the answer to his spiritual anguish in the Bible, it followed that Scriptures became his absolute authority in matters of faith and morals. It must be added, however, that in interpreting the Bible,

Luther's experience of justification by faith alone held a central position. In essence this meant that a Christian had the right to interpret the Word of God according to his understanding of it. The individual conscience, enlightened by the Holy Spirit, thus became in addition to the Bible man's highest court of appeal. In 1521 Luther pronounced at the Diet of Worms that to act against conscience is not allowed.[9] Neither bishop nor pope, nor any man whatever, according to Luther, has the right to prescribe a single syllable to any Christian. For the Reformer conscience was freed from obedience to anything contrary to the Bible. But in emphasizing this point, Luther lay himself open to the charge that he and his followers interpreted the Bible subjectively, according to their experiences and points of view. Luther, however, was convinced that he interpreted Scripture by the spirit of the Word of God. He emphasized time and again that he had no wish to be known as a man more learned than others, and that he wished Scripture to be sovereign and not interpreted according to his mind or the mind of another, but interpreted by itself in its own spirit.[10] Luther's quarrel with the Catholic church was that it did not interpret the Bible according to its plain sense; and the plain sense of Scripture, according to Luther, is its teaching concerning the inadequacy of man before God, and man's salvation through the substitutionary death of Christ. The right of interpretation Luther granted to all Christians, but he seemed to believe that all men of good-will would of necessity arrive at his own interpretation of the Bible.[11]

Luther's principles of *sola fide* and *sola scriptura* led without premeditation on his part to all his subsequent activity, to the internal organization of the Lutheran church, and to questions with regard to church and state. If these newly-acquired principles were contradicted by any man, authority, or sect, Luther did not doubt for a moment that he was right and all others wrong. For him the doctrine of justification by faith alone was to the end of life the sum and substance of the gospel, the heart of theology, the central truth of Christianity, the article of the standing or falling church. According to Luther, only those who understand and teach the article of justification by faith alone may be considered true theologians.[12] In his lectures on Galatians in 1531 Luther pointed out that if the article of justification is lost, all Christian doctrine is lost at the same time. People who do not hold to this justification are either Jews, Turks, papists, or heretics.[13]

Luther's sense of having grasped the heart of biblical theology was so strong that his central doctrine became the standard of value for all the biblical books. Some critics have charged Luther with deliberately carrying a Protestant spirit into his version of the Bible.

The word "alone" was inserted in Romans 3:28 in spite of all outcries to the contrary. Those books of the New Testament which seemed to contradict the doctrine of justification by faith alone were not regarded as fully inspired. The books of Hebrews, James, Jude and Revelation belonged to this group. Particularly the epistle of James, which seemed to stress the importance of "works," was a stumbling block for the Reformer. He called it "an epistle of straw"[14] and wished to exclude it from the New Testament canon. He wrote that someday he would use James to heat his stove. In his *Preface to the Epistle of James* the Reformer gives his reasons for not wishing to include this book in the biblical canon.[15] According to Luther, it directs opposition to St. Paul and all the rest of the Bible, it ascribes justification to works, and it declares that Abraham was justified by his works when he offered up his son. Moreover, not once, according to Luther, does James give Christians any instruction or reminder of the passion, resurrection, or the spirit of Christ. For Luther it was impossible to reconcile St. Paul, who emphasizes the doctrine of faith, with St. James, who advocates works in addition to faith. If someone could reconcile the two for him, Luther challenged his table companions, he would consent to being called a fool.

Luther's Early Writings

On October 31, 1517, Luther nailed his Ninety-five Theses to the door of the Castle Church in Wittenberg, thus giving expression to his radical experience and his newly-acquired theology. The stir his theses created was great. Eager students took hold of them, translated them into German, and published them without the Reformer's consent. In a dedicatory letter to Pope Leo X in 1518[16] Luther stated that his theses were intended for disputation only and not for the public; since they were written in Latin only the more scholarly people were to discuss them. He then went on to explain to Pope Leo that the theses were not doctrines, and had he known or foreseen the commotion they would stir up, he would have taken the necessary precautions.

However sincerely Luther may have believed that the purpose of his theses was purely academic in character, there can be little doubt that he intended that his rediscovered gospel should penetrate to the people. He must have known that the substance of his proposed disputation would become public knowledge. That Luther must have had these thoughts in mind seems to be borne out by the fact that on the same afternoon he preached in the historic church itself on the substance of his contention: Indulgences and Grace. Then also, once his theses had become a public issue, the Reformer threw himself with zeal and vigour into the fray, not tiring of writing, teaching, preaching, and disputing. He soon kept three printing presses entirely occupied. By 1521 Luther had progressed to such an extent in his opposition to Rome that his earlier humble submission to the pope had given way to outright rebellion against the ecclesiastical structure of his time.

In 1520 Luther published three major pamphlets which were to become destructive to the established authority of the Catholic church and influential in the formation and strengthening of various sects. The first of these pamphlets, *To the Christian Nobility of the German Nation*,[17] was completed on July 20, and before August 18 more than four thousand copies—an enormous number for that time—were published and a new edition was called for. The influence this booklet had on the various groups connected with the reformation movement will be more fully appreciated after a brief summary of its salient points.

Luther begins by stating that since the clergy cannot bring about the much-needed reformation of the church, the German nobility should be moved by the plight of Christendom and do something to relieve it. Luther then proceeds to destroy what he calls the "three walls" of the papacy: that the spiritual power is above secular authority; that the pope alone may interpret the text of the Bible; and that the pope alone may call a general council. The "first wall" Luther attacks by saying that all Christians, whether clergy or laymen, are spiritual in the sight of God; they have all received baptism and the gospel of Christ. The only difference between the laity and clergy is that of function. Since God has ordained the secular powers to punish the wicked and reward the pious, it is the magistrates' right and duty to discipline wicked popes as well. Luther attacks the "second wall" of the papacy by asserting that all Christians may interpret the Bible, for the Spirit of God resides in all those who belong to Christ. The "third wall" falls automatically with the first two. Since all baptized Christians are in truth priests and bishops, Luther states, and all have the right to interpret the Bible, the pope, it follows, cannot hold a special position above all others. If the pope is evil, as Luther implies that he is, the magistrates have the right to call a council for corrective measures in the church.

There are other statements in this tract which became dynamite in the hands of various social and religious groups. If we fight the Turks, Luther argues, and thieves and murderers are being hanged, why then should we tolerate the wickedness and robbery of the papacy. God has made us free from all human laws which contradict God's law and our soul's salvation; in spiritual matters Christians need not recognize any authority above themselves. The clergy should have the freedom to marry, for to prohibit marriage is contrary to all natural law; all pilgrimages to Rome ought to discontinue; private masses, the interdict, and all festivals, except Sunday, must be abolished. The Word of God must be taught to the people. Universities are gates of hell if they do not train young people in Holy Scriptures. Other passages which later were to encourage the formation of sectarian groups pertained to the autonomy of Christian groups and local churches. If a little group of Christians, Luther argues, were taken into exile where there was no ordained priest, and if they were to elect one of their number, married or unmarried, they could confer on him the authority to baptize, say mass, absolve, and preach, and he would be as true a priest as if ordained by all the bishops or popes. This argument which Luther applied primarily to himself and his immediate followers who with him rebelled against Rome was later taken up by his dissenters and applied to their situation against the Reformer.

The pamphlet *To the Christian Nobility* was a firebrand. Some feared that it might lead to a religious war. Some of Luther's friends, especially John Lang, were fearful of the consequences and warned the Reformer not to publish the tract. The pamphlet did not cause a war at the time but its influence on the public was great. The destruction of the "three walls" of the papacy and Luther's idea of the "priesthood of all believers" led of necessity to the emancipation of the laity from churchly control and to their direct involvement in the affairs of the church. The first evidence of this was seen in the attempted reforms in Wittenberg during Luther's absence at the Wartburg, and later this lay movement found expression in the radical reformers in general. Many of these radical groups believed, as Luther did, that they were forsaken and persecuted for the sake of their Christian faith, and since they also had the Holy Spirit they too were priests who had direct access to God. Luther believed that the opposition and persecution he and his followers met were visible signs of God's favour upon their faith and action; the dissenting groups interpreted the hostility of both Catholics and Lutherans toward them similarly. Thus, ironically, the very arguments which Luther had used against the Catholic church were later used against him by those who broke away from the Lutheran cause.

Luther concluded his *To the Christian Nobility* with an announcement that he had "another song" to sing against Rome. In October, 1520, he published another booklet, *The Babylonian Captivity of the Church*.[18] It was primarily this piece of writing which initiated the sacramental controversy in sixteenth-century Protestantism. Luther begins his tract by denying that there are seven sacraments; he feels there should be three only, namely, baptism, penance, and the last supper. He doubts, however, whether according to the usage of Scripture there could be more than one sacrament only—the eucharist. The other two should possibly be reduced to "sacramental signs." He then goes on to insist that the cup in the last supper should not be withheld from the laity, as the practice was in Roman Catholicism. If the people desire to partake of the cup as well, it is tyrannous to withhold it. Luther adds, however, that no one should attempt to seize the cup by force; he is merely instructing Christians that they may endure the tyranny of Rome, knowing that they have been forcibly deprived of their right in the sacrament.

The mass, Luther continues, ought to be abolished on the basis that it has become a good work and a sacrifice, thereby annulling the sacrifice of Christ. External things in the worship service, such as vestments, ornaments, and all the pomp of visible things, should be done away with because they detract from the essence of worshipping God. Vows and religious orders are unscriptural and show contempt for the common things in life. Extreme unction, according to Luther, is ridiculous and invalid, for it rests on no proper biblical foundation. On the question of baptism the tract is somewhat confusing. Luther seems to recognize baptismal regeneration, although he also speaks of baptism as a "symbol" of a person's death and resurrection in Christ. Luther also adds that if baptism is to be valid, a person must continue to believe in Christ's merits for sinners. In speaking of masses for the benefit of others, Luther categorically rejects the idea of human substitution, for everyone must believe for himself. In connection with infant baptism, however, Luther states that infants are aided by the faith of others, namely, the faith of those who bring them to baptism. This confusion in Luther's thinking was soon to be evident in others. Both the Anabaptists, who demanded personal faith before baptism, and the believers in pedobaptism later appealed to the teachings of Luther on baptism.

The pamphlet had an immediate impact on Luther's followers who, during the Reformer's hiding at the Wartburg, sought to advance the reformation in Wittenberg. Men such as Melanchton and Carlstadt attempted to spiritualize the mass by abolishing vestments and by administering holy communion in both kinds. It is to be lamented, however, that these radical reformers went to excesses in their zeal to implement Luther's teachings. True, they felt bound in their conscience to bring about reform, and it is not surprising that they seemed to have misunderstood Luther in his references to the tyranny of Rome, but the fact remains that even in these red-hot reformation writings the Reformer counselled moderation and patience. With regard to the sacraments in this pamphlet, the issues are more blurred. Luther cast doubt on the validity of most sacraments, retaining in the end baptism and the last supper. Why should he later be greatly surprised when the sacramentarians, also on the basis of Scripture, repudiated all the sacraments, including baptism and the last supper which they reduced to so-called "ordinances" or "signs"?

In November, 1520 Luther published his third major reformation pamphlet, *The Freedom of a Christian*.[19] In a letter to Pope Leo X the Reformer wrote that this tract contained the sum of a Christian's life. In this pamphlet Luther teaches that man is unable to fulfill the demands of the Old Testament law and that he therefore in despair comes to accept in faith the divine mercy provided through Christ. This faith in Christ releases a Christian from the demands of the law and thus makes him perfectly free in Christ. It is faith only, not works, that justifies man before God; good works, or the good life, are the result of man's justification and an expression of his gratitude to God. According to Luther, good works do not make man good, but a good and pious man will do good works. Luther thus rejects good works as a means of salvation, but he does not state that good works are not necessary. As far as the Christian's relationship to God is concerned, only faith matters; as far as his relationship to his fellowmen is concerned, faith must express itself in love, hence in good works. The freedom in Christ is, then, a freedom from sin and from the demands of the Old Testament law; it is not freedom from Christian responsibility and morality. In fact, an important point in *The Freedom of a Christian* is Luther's teaching concerning the priesthood of all believers, which should dispel all notions about possible license in the Christian's walk. The Christian, according to Luther, is both king and priest before God, positions which carry dignity and a high degree of moral responsibility. It must be admitted, however, that when Luther in his zeal emphasized the importance of man's justification by faith and not by works, certain individuals within the Lutheran camp began to live without the ethical restraints of Christianity. The result was, as will be seen in another chapter, the antinomian controversy, which led Luther to modify some of his earlier views on the relationship between law and freedom.

The implications and effects of Luther's example and early writings must not be forgotten if one is to understand the men and groups who turned away from Luther and the Reformer's later attitude toward the dissenters. Luther's radical break with the mediaeval church and the enunciation of his reformation principles had a powerful influence on both the clergy and laymen. The

Reformer's example and writings had awakened in the layman particularly an entirely new conception of his obligations with regard to the existing order. As a member of the priesthood of all believers he could not sit idly while the church was held in bondage; he felt he had to act and correct the abuses. The principles of *sola fide* and *sola scriptura* with their dissolving effects on all constituted authority were applied, and often misapplied, to suit all thought and action. Luther's treatment of the biblical canon undoubtedly encouraged doubts with regard to the inspiration of the Bible and the spreading of rationalism (The Antitrinitarians and Luther's reaction to them will be treated in a later chapter). The Reformer's writings of 1520 had a direct influence on the Zwickau prophets and Thomas Müntzer. When Luther encountered these "enthusiasts," as he called them, he had to modify somewhat the idea of the universal priesthood of all believers, or at least differentiate more clearly between those who were truly believers and those who were believers in name only. Whether Luther's judgment was always correct will be investigated in subsequent chapters. Nevertheless, the Reformer's intense religious experience and theological convictions, coupled with various circumstances, made it impossible for him to tolerate his spiritual children who dissented from him; the radicals, bound in turn by their own conscience and their understanding of the Bible, found it impossible not to oppose their spiritual father. To the men and groups who dared to disagree with Luther we now must turn.

The Dissenters

The men and groups who dissented from Luther and other leading reformers were all lumped together and called "enthusiasts," "rebels," "fanatics," "visionaries," "baptists," or most commonly "anabaptists." The diversity of these groups makes it difficult to decide as to which group or individuals should be included in a study of the so-called Anabaptist movement. However, to lump them all together is not only inaccurate but highly unfair to those who sincerely sought to implement the teachings of the Reformer. Most of the radicals did not wish to be called Anabaptists, for they did not regard infant baptism as a true baptism. Although most dissenting groups opposed infant baptism, not all accepted adult baptism; baptism was not the most essential thing with some of the sects. For some groups baptism was merely an expression of their concept of the church, which, according to them, consisted of baptized believers only. For others, baptism was an act of initiation whereby new members were received into their community. For still others, the

Mennonites, for example, baptism was a symbol of an inner transformation and dedication to Christ. However apparent some of their differences may have been, in one respect the sects were alike: they were all radical with regard to reform. Compromise, moderation, and consideration of other institutions and viewpoints were largely foreign to them. They sought to reform, sometimes by violent means, all existing orders, be they social, economic, political, or religious. In their quest for new institutions they disregarded all tradition and historical development. Some groups attempted to re-establish the primitive church, whereas others felt called to inaugurate the Kingdom of God as it had never existed before. The designation "radical reformers" has thus been applied to all individuals and groups who dissented from the leading reformers and at the same time opposed Roman Catholicism.[20]

Because of their diversity it is difficult to classify the radicals of the sixteenth century. Even their contemporaries found it almost impossible to differentiate between the dissenting groups. Sebastian Franck, a Spiritualist, writes with some slight exaggeration: "There are many more sects and opinions, which I do not all know and cannot describe, but it seems to me that there are not two to be found who agree with each other on all points."[21] Luther looked upon this confusion and division among the Anabaptists as a clear sign of their ungodliness.

Some historians have attempted to classify the dissidents according to their conception of the church. There were those who believed in a restored and gathered congregation of baptized believers under strict discipline and separation from the world and state. Generally, the Swiss, the South German, and Mennonite Anabaptists belonged to this group. Then there were the Hutterian Brethren who believed in a church-community, holding all things in common. Thomas Müntzer and the Münster Anabaptists believed in a church-kingdom as the ideal church. Lastly, there were men like Sebastian Franck, Caspar Schwenckfeld, and Hans Denck who held to an inward, invisible, spiritual, and universal church. Others classify the radicals on the basis of their theological views: There were those who denied the real presence in holy communion; there were those who denied the validity of infant baptism; there were those who denied the authority of the Old Testament; and there were those who opposed the doctrine of the Trinity. Ludwig Keller differentiates between three main parties among the radicals.[22] Between 1525 and 1530, he states, the peaceful movement under the leadership of Hans Denck predominated; between 1530 and 1535 the

Background for the Conflict

Münsterites under the guidance of John of Leyden dominated the scene; after 1535 Menno Simons became the recognized leader of the Anabaptist-Mennonite movement. The Baptist church historian A. H. Newman differentiates between chiliastic, biblical, pantheistic, mystical, and antitrinitarian Anabaptists.[23]

Today most historians generally agree on a threefold division within the radical movement, differentiating between the Spiritualists, Anabaptists, and Rationalists. According to Mennonite historians, there was a marked difference between the Spiritualists and the Anabaptists. The Anabaptists generally looked to the past, seeking to recreate original Christianity along New Testament lines; the Spiritualists generally gazed to the future, seeking to establish an entirely new church. The Rationalists, who were greatly influenced by Renaissance humanism, tried to explain the mysteries of Christianity according to common sense and reason. These three groups are further subdivided. Among the Spiritualists there were three distinct groups. First, there were the revolutionary Spiritualists who were largely inspired by Thomas Müntzer. They experienced the spirit as a driving force, drew largely upon the books of Daniel and Revelation, and emphasized the cross, or the bitter Christ, in opposition to Luther's "sweet Christ." Secondly, there were the rational Spiritualists who contemplatively philosophized on the mysteries of religion. Thirdly, there were the so-called evangelical Spiritualists who advocated a middle-way position between Lutheranism and Catholicism.

The Anabaptists are also divided into three groups. The so-called revolutionary Anabaptists looked consistently to the Old Testament as the standard for their ethical life and behaviour. The contemplative Anabaptists, such as Hans Denck and Ludwig Hätzer, stressed the importance of the "inner word" in contrast to the "outer word," or biblicism. The evangelical Anabaptists, as Mennonite historians like to call the Swiss Brethren, the Hutterites, and Mennonites, stressed the New Testament as the standard of all teaching and morals and subordinated the ethics of the Old Testament to the New Covenant. They repudiated the use of the sword and capital punishment, and applied the ban rigorously to their erring members. The Rationalists may be divided into two groups for the sake of convenience rather than accuracy: the Antinomians and the Antitrinitarians. In his later life, as will be seen, Luther came in touch with these last two groups as well.

In view of the above differences of beliefs and practices among the dissident sects, it has been asked whether Luther was justified in lumping the radicals together and fighting them indiscriminately. Perhaps Luther should have taken the pains to investigate the various groups more thoroughly before passing judgment upon them, but as far as he was concerned, the many dissident groups had certain important things and ideas in common. One writer states that the only thing the radicals had in common was their opposition to Luther and the Catholic church.[24] While opposition to Luther and Catholicism was shared by all dissident groups, Luther soon discovered that important doctrinal considerations separated him from the radicals, all of whom, in varying degrees, adhered to some basic theological points. Most of them emphasized, in one way or another, the principle of communism, a point which may account for the popularity of the Anabaptist movement among the lower classes. Almost all groups opposed Luther's teaching on the will and good works, believing, again in varying degrees, in the freedom of the will and emphasizing the necessity of good works as evidence of salvation. Luther felt, with some justification, that this emphasis would of necessity lead to legalism as opposed to his concept of Christian freedom. Most radicals sought to establish a visible church, while Luther leaned more toward an invisible church consisting of all the redeemed, past, present, and future. The idea of a visible church led the radicals to deny infant baptism. A visible church, they held, consists of voluntary believers. Almost all radicals regarded the centuries between Constantine the Great and the sixteenth century as a period of spiritual apostasy. Müntzer even went so far as to believe that the true church had disappeared immediately after the death of the last apostles. Lastly, all the radicals repudiated the real presence in the last supper. For Luther this was the weightiest characteristic of all the fanatics. As far as he was concerned, people who denied the presence of Christ in the bread and wine of holy communion were of the devil.

Origin of the Dissident Groups

It is still not clear whether the radicals owe their origin to some mediaeval heretical sects, or to the Reformation of the sixteenth century, or to both. Some historians insist emphatically on their mediaeval origin, connecting them with the Wycliffites, Waldensians and Hussites. R. A. Knox, for example, points to the following similarities of views between these former sects and the radicals: Both held that the church is for saints only; both believed that the progress of iniquity in the world must be actively opposed; and both insisted on the correction of existing sin and crime. Other characteristics, such as opposition to warfare, the taking of oaths, and the service in the state, coupled with an undue emphasis on enthusiasm, were part of both the mediaeval heretics and the Anabaptists.[25] Others connect the radicals with the mystics such as Tauler, Eckhard, Suso, and the Brethren of the Common Life under whose influence many of the fanatics had come.[26] Some writers have pointed out that the *Devotio Moderna* formed the basis for the piety of the Anabaptists, giving them the idea of a conventicle-like separation from the world.[27] Some of the Anabaptists believed themselves to be the spiritual descendants of the Waldensians.[28] Lindsay simply states: "... the whole Anabaptist movement was medieval to the core."[29] Although no historical connection between the radicals and the mediaeval sects has as yet been found, it has been established that Anabaptism flourished in areas where Waldensians had existed in large numbers in the fourteenth and fifteenth centuries. Moreover, the teachings of the "Zwickau prophets" and Thomas Müntzer showed considerable dependence on Taborite views, and Tauler's sermons were venerated and cited by these enthusiasts.

With regard to origin there is also the question of whether humanism may be held responsible for the rise of the radicals. Huizinga held with Walter Köhler that Erasmus was the father of Anabaptism. Robert Kreider in a study of the lives of the leading evangelical Anabaptists concludes that most of them had studied under humanists.[30] According to Kreider, the theological emphasis of the Anabaptists, such as the freedom of the will, non-resistance (in the case of the peaceful groups), the separation of church and state, and the stress of ethics rather than dogma, were similar to the principles advocated by the Christian humanists. Kreider insists, however, that Anabaptism went beyond humanism in that it fixed its eye not on man but on God. While the question of whether humanism had appreciable influence on the Anabaptist movement may be debatable, there seems to be little doubt that such rationalistic radicals as the Antitrinitarians actually belonged within Renaissance humanism. They not only fixed their eyes on man, but also applied reason, not faith, to their theology and way of life. Yet even the religious rationalists may never have come boldly to the open had they not been stimulated by the Reformation.

While the origin of the radical sects of the sixteenth century needs to be further investigated, the view that most of the radicals were actually children of the Reformation seems to correspond with some important facts. Many of the dissidents, such as Carlstadt,

Müntzer, Melchior Hofmann, Hans Denck, Balthasar Hubmaier, B. Rothman, and others, were former Lutherans. Some of the radicals had been close associates of Luther; some had been for some time Lutheran ministers; and most of them had at one time or another taken courage from Luther's teaching and writings. Moreover, although the radicals deviated from Luther in many points, they adhered essentially to the principles enunciated by the Reformer: Like Luther, they rejected the authority of the Catholic church in favour of the principles of *sola fide* and *sola scriptura*; like Luther, they stressed the place of the Holy Spirit in the life of a Christian; like Luther, they believed in personal faith, in freedom of conscience, in the priesthood of all believers, and in the active involvement of all Christians in the concerns of the church. The difference between Luther and the dissenters was often a difference in interpretation and emphasis rather than a difference in essential beliefs. Whatever the connection between the radicals and Luther may have been, it was the Reformer who caused the various radicals of the sixteenth century to come boldly into the open and encouraged their growth by his own example of rebellion and his provocative early writings. Whether the various radical groups would have appeared without the emergence of Luther cannot be answered; that the radicals appealed to the teachings and example of the Reformer is a fact. We tend to agree with Ernst Troeltsch who concludes: "Although greatly assisted by some lingering traces of the influence of the Waldensians and other sects ... at bottom ... the whole movement belonged to the Reformation. It was caused by the Reformation; it appealed to its principles and ideals, and it remained in closest touch with it."[31]

Reasons for Opposing the Reformer

Why did the early followers and admirers of Luther turn against their spiritual father? Concerning the dissident children of the Reformation Franklin Littell states: "In their records they refer to Luther half in praise and half in sorrow, as a leader whom they first followed but who did not carry them through to as thorough a reformation as they had anticipated."[32] An unknown Anabaptist expressed himself in 1538 as follows:

> While yet in the national church, we obtained much instruction from the writings of Luther ... concerning the mass and other papal ceremonies, that they are vain. Yet we recognized a great lack as regards repentance, conversion, and the true Christian life. ... I waited and hoped for a year or two, since the minister had much to

say of amendment of life, of giving to the poor, loving one another, and abstaining from evil. But I could not close my eyes to the fact that the doctrine which was preached . . . was not carried out.[33]

Some dissenters, then, felt that Luther was not as radical with regard to reform as they wished him to be, while others became impatient with Lutheranism because of its seeming gap between teaching and ethical practice.

Writing in his *The True Christian Faith* (1541), Menno Simons states that Lutherans overemphasize the doctrine of justification by faith to the point that anyone who also preaches the necessity of good works is considered a heretic. When one points the Lutherans to Christ and his blameless example, Simons continues, and that it is wrong for a Christian "to boast and drink, revile and curse, then he must hear from that hour that he is one who believes in salvation by good works, is a heaven stormer, a sectarian agitator, a rabble rouser, a make-believe Christian, a disdainer of the sacraments, or an Anabaptist!"[34] In a reply to Gellius Faber, a Lutheran, Menno Simons wrote in 1554 that the governing principle of the Reformation, namely, the rejection of all unbiblical institutions in favour of scriptural doctrines and practices, had not been carried through by the reformers. Referring to infant baptism, Menno Simons continued: ". . . although they and their writers have in the past condemned unto hell all the institutions and commands of men, and have written one volume after another against them, yet they, alas, altogether continue to cling to this rude abomination, because they do not want to assume the cross, nor the reproach of the world."[35] A similar view is expressed in an anonymous booklet, written between 1525 and 1535. The writer acknowledges his debt to the "evangelical preachers" for pointing him to divine truths, but then goes on to accuse them of speaking "the truth of Christ partly" and of not wanting "to pass through the narrow gate" of suffering and consistent Christian living.[36]

The writer of *Die älteste Chronik der Hutterischen Brüder* accuses Luther and other leading reformers of having succeeded in breaking down Roman Catholicism, but failing to build a better church. Moreover, they have attached themselves to magistrates and princes, trusting in human strength rather than in God. They have retained infant baptism; they are defending their doctrines with the sword; and they live contrary to the teachings of the New Testament. Their greatest merit, the writer concludes sarcastically, is to eat meat, take women to wives, scold the popes, monks and clerics, and to live as they please.[37]

Some radicals dissented from Luther for social, economic, or political reasons. Thomas Müntzer's political ideas were radical and destructive of all established institutions; the peasants in southern Germany, claiming to be free from all feudal restrictions, resorted to violence in the name of Luther's reformation principles; the Anabaptists in Münster, claiming to live by the Word of God, instituted polygamy, theocratic rule, and other unorthodox practices; and even the more peaceful Anabaptists held views on the economic and social institutions of that time which ran counter to tradition and accepted practice.[38] Add to this the splintering nature of Protestantism, caused by the principles of *sola scriptura* and the priesthood of all believers, with the right of each individual to interpret the Bible according to his understanding of it, and the reasons for the clash between Luther and the dissident sects become quite clear.

We shall turn now to an examination of the conflict between Luther and the radicals, focussing our attention primarily on Luther's reasons for opposing those who dissented from him.

CHAPTER II

LUTHER AND THE WITTENBERG RADICALS

After Luther had successfully defended his position and writings at the Diet of Worms (April, 1521), he was taken secretly into solitary confinement at the Wartburg. Luther was absent from the reformation capital, but the spirit that he had called up was still at Wittenberg and could not be idle. Men such as Gabriel Zwilling, Justus Jonas, Philip Melanchton, and Andreas von Carlstadt threw themselves wholeheartedly into the work of reform. It is the purpose of this chapter to sketch the nature of the new reform movement in Wittenberg and Luther's subsequent attitude toward the men and issues involved in it.

Moderation Versus Radicalism

The man who has been held most responsible for the violent outbreaks at Wittenberg in the winter of 1521-1522 was Andreas Bodenstein von Carlstadt.[1] He was born in Bavaria about 1480. In 1499 he enrolled at the University of Erfurt where he studied until 1504. In 1504 he came to the newly-established University of Wittenberg where he became famous as a teacher of philosophy. He clung tenaciously to scholasticism, believing in the supreme authority of Thomas Aquinas. By 1510 Carlstadt had acquired all the higher academic degrees, and in that year he also became archdeacon at a church in Wittenberg. As archdeacon he was required to preach, to say mass once a week, and to lecture at the university. In 1515 he went to Rome where he studied law and took a degree with the intention of becoming dean of the Castle Church in Wittenberg. Since all this was done without the permission of the university and the Elector of Saxony, Carlstadt was not given the desired position when he returned.

It was during this time that Luther acquainted Carlstadt with St. Augustine, whose writings he began to read with great interest. Carlstadt broke with scholasticism and accepted Luther's views on the schoolmen. In 1516 Carlstadt published 151 theses which contained the fundamental traits of his later theology. In these theses he combatted Aristotle and the scholastics and pondered the question, no doubt stimulated by Luther, whether the human will was capable of attaining to God. Carlstadt shared the Reformer's hostility toward Roman Catholicism, but there never existed a personal friendship between the two men.

The differences between Luther and Carlstadt soon became apparent. After his disputation with Dr. Eck in June and July, 1518, Carlstadt increasingly began to emphasize the efficacy of grace alone, writing tracts against indulgences and the justification through works. Luther, however, who was particularly sensitive on these points, soon detected theological flaws in the writings of his colleague. Whereas Luther strongly emphasized justification by faith alone, Carlstadt insisted that justification was only the beginning of a Christian's life and that sanctification had to follow. Luther believed that it was unnecessary to emphasize right living since it would follow once a sinner was justified. Carlstadt's lectures on justification and holy living were well attended. When Carlstadt did not agree with Luther with regard to the book of James, but instead was attracted by the strict discipline and emphasis on holiness that breathed from its pages, the Reformer began to suspect the soundness of his colleague's theology. Sensing a dangerous legalism in his colleague, Luther, according to Hermann Barge, sought to detract the students from Carlstadt's lectures.[2] When King Christian II of Denmark asked for assistance with the reformation in his country, there is reason to believe that Luther and Frederick the Wise sent Carlstadt in order to be rid of him in Saxony.[3] Carlstadt went most gladly to Denmark early in 1521, but after six weeks of fruitless activity the combined resistance of the Danish clergy and nobility forced him to leave the country. To the dismay of both Luther and the Elector, Carlstadt returned to Wittenberg.

In October, 1521, the Augustinian monks of Wittenberg, under the fiery leadership of Gabriel Zwilling, began to advocate that private masses be abolished. Carlstadt, in a dispute with the zealous monks, advocated caution in order not to give their enemies occasion for attack, but Melanchton supported Zwilling on the ground that he had the Word of God and the example of the apostles on his side. Everyone concerned knew that the mass could only be abolished with the approval of the magistrates. The Elector, moreover, counselled moderation, ordering the university to set up a commission to investigate the disturbances and then report to him its findings. This was done, and a letter expressing the more moderate views of Carlstadt was sent to Frederick the Wise.

At first Luther's sympathies seemed to be on the side of those in Wittenberg who advocated radical measures. Viewing the situation from the Wartburg, Luther hoped that the reformation in Wittenberg would be both thorough and speedy.[4] Upon learning concerning the intentions of the Augustinian monks, Luther prepared several pamphlets, *On Monastic Vows, A Blast Against the Archbishop of Mainz*, and *Concerning the Abuse of the Mass*. These pamphlets were sent to Spalatin, chancellor of Saxony, with instructions to publish them immediately. When Spalatin hesitated to do so, the Reformer became quite impatient. The tract *Concerning the Abuse of the Mass*,[5] written in October, 1521, steers skillfully between Spalatin's fearful conservatism and the Wittenbergers' radicalism.

Luther begins his *Concerning the Abuse of the Mass* by expressing joy at the zeal of the Wittenbergers in initiating much-needed reforms, but he wonders whether all of them act from motives of pure love and faith. Luther then strikes a more radical strain, evidently aimed at people like Spalatin who were afraid of any measures that might get out of hand. Luther states that he is writing this pamphlet because his earlier writings on the subject had not stirred the people to more concrete action. He is not concerned about what tradition, the saints, the church fathers, or the Parisian theologians have taught and practised; if a certain practice does not agree with Holy Scripture, it must be abandoned. Not even St. Paul or an angel from heaven may impose doctrines contrary to God's Word. The sacrifice of the Catholic mass is from the devil and hence it must be abolished. Luther's attack upon the "papists" with regard to the sacrificial character of the mass is most extreme, encouraging his followers to proceed with their reform measures in spite of the "howls and objections of their enemies." Fearing, however, that Carlstadt and the Wittenbergers might misinterpret him and resort to unwarranted violence, Luther counsels that in all reform drives the weak brethren should be considered, and faith and love should be employed at all times. Luther wrote to Spalatin, however, that he approved of the proposal to abolish masses in Wittenberg.

When rumours of the disturbances continued to pour in at the Wartburg, Luther decided to go to Wittenberg in order to investigate the situation there for himself. On December 4, 1521, he appeared secretly on the streets of the city and was generally pleased with the progress of the Reformation. The day before, however, there had been violence; students and townfolk had invaded the parish church and had molested those who worshipped before the Virgin. On his way back to the Wartburg Luther also sensed a spirit of rebellion in the air. Yet on December 5 he still wrote to Spalatin: "All I see and hear, pleases me immensely," although he added that he was concerned about the radicalism of some and that he would counsel moderation.[6] Back at the Wartburg, Luther must have thought seriously about the disturbances in Wittenberg, feeling that the situation might get out of hand and thereby jeopardize all genuine efforts at reform. This consideration compelled him to write the Wittenbergers not to proceed too hastily in their reform drives, warning them that such haste came from the devil. He was not against innovations, Luther continued, but reforms must be the result of the preaching of the Word of God. There are "many brothers and sisters in Leipzig, Meissen, and elsewhere, and these we must take to heaven with us."[7]

The letter was followed by a pamphlet *Warning to All Christians to Keep from Uproar and Sedition* (1522).[8] In this pamphlet Luther argues that only constituted secular authorities may bring about needed changes by force and destroy the power of the papacy; since it is their sacred duty to punish wickedness, their action could not be considered rebellious. In the final analysis, however, it is God who must step in to destroy the wickedness of the papacy, even through the sword of the princes if need be. The common man, on the other hand, should obey the magistrates. The papists charge us with rebellion and sedition, Luther continues, but this is a lie, for we preach submission to the powers that be. In conclusion Luther advises his followers to "teach, to preach, to speak, and to write" that all man-made laws are nothing and that they do not give money for bulls, candles, bells, tablets and churches. Luther believes that after two years of preaching there will be no pope, cardinals, monks, masses, rules, and statues. Christians may not, however, use violence and they must always have consideration for the weak in faith.

In analyzing Luther's attempt to steer between the timidity of a Spalatin and the radicalism of the Augustinian monks in Wittenberg, some writers have been very severe in their criticism of the Reformer. Henry C. Vedder states: "He had uttered sweeping opinions in favor of freedom of conscience, liberty of private judgment, the authority of Scripture, and the priesthood of all believers—opinions that contained logical implications of which he was at the time unconscious, and that he rejected as soon as others, more logical than he, attempted to realize them."[9] This is an oversimplification. True, Luther did not know what the results of his concern for the truth of the gospel would be, but to imply that the Reformer was unreasonable in expecting others to move slowly when he himself showed impatience and even radicalism is to misunderstand Luther altogether. When the various structures of the old church, such as monasticism, the mass, and absolute ecclesiastical authority, were enforced from above, without biblical authority, Luther opposed them in the name of the freedom of the spirit. Not to oppose these practices and doctrines would have meant compromising the gospel in which Luther had come to believe as the only way of salvation for himself and his followers. When the freedom of the spirit meant license and the mere subjectivity of an individual who had "swallowed the Holy Spirit, feathers and all," to use the Reformer's words, Luther had no choice but to oppose it in the name of the

Word of God. That Luther's opposition to the free spirits of Wittenberg was justified may be seen from what developed in the reformation capital.

Increasing Radicalism and Luther's Reaction

On December 17, 1521, the congregation of Wittenberg submitted to the city council six articles demanding reform. They included the demand that the last supper be administered in both kinds, that the relics in the churches be abolished, that compulsory masses be abrogated, that beer parlours and houses of infamy be closed, and that the Word of God be preached freely. Carlstadt was pleased to find that the council was well disposed toward these measures of reform; for him this was a clear sign that God's favour rested on his undertaking. Confidently he assumed the leadership in Wittenberg.

On Christmas Day approximately 2,000 people celebrated mass in the Castle Church, with Carlstadt officiating in plain clothes. The mass was recited partly in Latin and partly in German in an abbreviated form, omitting all passages which referred to the mass as being a sacrifice. With the permission of the city council and the support of the university professors, Carlstadt distributed the eucharist in both kinds, permitting the laymen to take the bread in their hands. This revolutionary celebration seemed to break the dam in Wittenberg. Priests, monks and nuns began to marry, and the tonsured let their hair grow; priests from now on wore plain clothes while celebrating the mass; the divine services were more and more recited in the German language; masses for the dead were discontinued; here and there images were smashed by zealous young men; the enrollment at the university declined considerably; and on January 19, 1522, Carlstadt himself married a young girl. When Luther heard about Carlstadt's marriage, he wrote: "I am very pleased over Carlstadt's marriage. I know the girl."[10]

During this turmoil in Wittenberg, there appeared on December 27, 1521, certain laymen from Zwickau, a town near the Bohemian border, whence they had been expelled for holding unorthodox views and advocating radical measures. Nickolaus Storch and Markus Stübner were the most outstanding among these enthusiasts who claimed to be prophets of God and who relied on the Holy Spirit rather than the Bible. Although they did not rebaptize adults, they repudiated infant baptism and advocated the erection of the Kingdom of God on earth. Stübner, a former student at Wittenberg, was quite well versed in the text of the Bible. Melanchton, while attracted to the prophet, was much disturbed at not being able to counter his arguments, which were seemingly based on Scriptures. On the day of the prophets' arrival in Wittenberg, Melanchton wrote to the Elector of Saxony: "They say wonderful things of themselves: that they have been commissioned to teach by a clear voice from God; that they see into the future; briefly, that they are prophetic and apostolic men. I can hardly say how much they affect me.... It is evident from many reasons that there are spirits in them, but no one save Martin can judge of them."[11]

Why did the prophets come to Wittenberg? Did they expect to find in Wittenberg a spiritual home, or did they believe that they had something to offer which the Reformer had neglected to include in his teaching? The latter seems to be the case. Early in 1522 the Zwickau prophets confronted Luther. When the Reformer questioned them concerning their credentials, Markus Stübner replied that in about seven years he, Luther, would see a miracle which would substantiate the divine mission of the prophets. Sensing the danger to his course from their subjective spiritualism, Luther dismissed the prophets without further disputing with them. For him they were servants of the devil.[12]

Returning to Carlstadt's relations with the Zwickau prophets, there is little evidence to suggest that Carlstadt had much in common with them. Their beliefs went too far apart. The prophets were highly mystical, believing in a sort of passive resignation to God, while at the same time advocating the use of the sword against the wicked. According to Stübner, the ungodly would be destroyed in about six or seven years. Then there would be at last one way, one baptism, and one faith. Carlstadt, on the other hand, was far from advocating the slaughter of the wicked; he wrote to Müntzer, for example, that he should abstain from all revolutionary notions. The prophets rejected on the whole the written Word of God and relied on visions and dreams; Carlstadt, while believing like Luther in a personal experience of salvation, based his faith on the written Scriptures. Yet like Melanchton, Carlstadt was no doubt at least inspired by the prophets in his activities of reform. He began to stress the Old Testament prophets in his preaching, particularly the books of Malachi and Zachariah, and to Thomas Müntzer he wrote enthusiastically that he had talked more about dreams and visions than anybody on the faculty.[13]

While Luther was concerned about the possible influence of the Zwickau prophets, he did not think it necessary to return to Wittenberg because of them. In letters, however, he warned the Wittenbergers against the teachings of the enthusiasts. "When these men talk of sweetness and of being transported to the third heaven, do not believe them. Divine Majesty does not speak directly to men.

God is consuming fire, and the dream and visions of the saints are terrible.... Prove the spirits; and if you are not able to do so, then take the advice of Gamaliel and wait."[14] In another letter he expressed the fear that the Elector might interfere with the sword to check the influence of the prophets: "I am sure we can restrain these fire brands without the sword. I hope the prince will not imbrue his hands in their blood. I see no reason why on their account I should come home.."[15]

On January 24, 1522, the Council of Wittenberg published its first ordinance of the Reformation, sanctioning most innovations in the city. The communicant was allowed to touch the host; images were to be abolished; the mass was to be conducted in Carlstadt's fashion; Luther's ideas on social reform, such as the prohibition of begging, were to be implemented; and prostitution and all manner of immorality were to be banned from the city. Carlstadt was overflowing with joy; God, according to him, had softened the hearts of the magistrates. But the excesses which accompanied the changes aroused the concern of Frederick the Wise. Duke George, a Catholic prince across the borders of electoral Saxony, complained about the radicalism in Wittenberg and accused Frederick of condoning the disorders. Some princes ordered their students to leave the university and the city. Many people in Wittenberg were confused, especially with regard to the mass, vestments, and other ecclesiastical changes. On February 13 Frederick stepped in, ordering that no further images were to be broken, that no essential parts of the mass were to be omitted, and that Carlstadt was not to preach. The Elector felt that the haste with which the reforms proceeded was detrimental to weak Christians. Melanchton submitted to Frederick's orders, but Carlstadt intended to continue with the reforms until he had reached his objectives.

Watching the events and developments from the Wartburg, Luther decided that the time had come for him to return to Wittenberg. In letters to Spalatin and Frederick the Wise he expressed concern about the breaking of images, the enthusiasm of the Zwickau prophets, and the evident intentions of the devil in Wittenberg. But in view of the political situation in Germany, the Elector was against Luther's leaving his hiding place. Luther replied that he was not afraid of Duke George or anyone else, and that he was not in need of the Elector's protection, for God was with him. The gospel of Christ suffered violence at Wittenberg and this was reason enough for his speedy return to his town. Luther, in fact, stated three reasons for wishing to return to Wittenberg: First, the church at Wittenberg and the council had invited him to return; secondly, during his absence the devil had intruded his fold; thirdly, since many people, particularly the peasants, had misapplied and perverted his gospel, there was great danger that people might rebel against all constituted authorities. In a letter to Spalatin Luther expressed the thought that he was also in favour of the reforms in Wittenberg, but he intended to bring about changes by preaching the Word of God only, not by force. On March 6, 1522, the Reformer arrived in Wittenberg, thus making good his earlier intention of not staying longer at the Wartburg than till Easter.

To restore order in the city, Luther preached eight consecutive sermons (March 9 to 17).[16] They were directed against the enthusiastic reformers, especially Carlstadt, but Luther refrained from mentioning any names. Luther in his sermons first of all accuses the Wittenbergers of having disregarded the weak brethren and of having proceeded without faith and love. Reform is good in itself, but the haste with which it has been done is clearly against God. Some preachers in Wittenberg, he continues, have not been called to preach; he, Luther, is their minister; they should have listened to him and asked him first before doing anything drastic. Some things are commanded in Scripture and others are not; to break images has no biblical support. St. Paul knew very well that images were of no use, yet he was not called upon to destroy them; nor has he, Luther, done anything by brute force. For while he slept, Luther adds, God's Word accomplished more than what mere force could have. Moses does not speak against keeping images but only against worshipping them. After all, only the properly constituted authorities have the right to abolish various ecclesiastical abuses by force. On the question of laymen touching the sacrament, Luther agrees that Christ and the apostles took the bread in their hands, but these minor things, according to Luther, are irrelevant and should not be made into a law. Above all else, Luther concludes his sermons, a Christian's freedom in Christ must be preserved, and a middle course must be followed between certain practices of the past and the innovations in question.

After preaching his eight sermons Luther wrote a pamphlet to repeat and further clarify the issues in his sermons. *Concerning the Sacrament and Other Innovations*[17] is typical of Luther's approach to reforms. With regard to external things in the church service, such as the wearing or not wearing of vestments, the touching of the sacramental bread, etc., Luther advises that a Christian follow his inner conviction; if one is convinced that the Word of God demands certain practices, then one ought not to be disobedient to that heavenly voice. Extremes and radicalism, however, must be avoided at all times. There was a time when the devil sought to make people too popish, Luther laments, but now he wants to make them too evangelical. Such practices as auricular confession and celibacy may all be contrary to God's Word, but one should never forget that the new wine may be too strong for the old wineskins. Haste is always dangerous.

Why did Luther move so decisively against the hasty reforms in Wittenberg and particularly against his colleague Carlstadt? Some have suggested that Luther became jealous of Carlstadt's popularity and success.[18] Letters have been cited in which Luther speaks of Carlstadt's ambition and his attempt to establish his rule and system on the ruin of the Reformer's authority.[19] And in Luther's *Table Talks* reference is made to Carlstadt's jealousy of the Reformer and to Luther's feeling that he, Luther, was more learned than all others, including Carlstadt.[20] While it may be true that Luther could not endure a man who acted without consulting him first and who even threatened to challenge his leadership, this explanation of Luther's reaction to the reforms of his friends in Wittenberg is too simple. The reason for Luther's caution with regard to the Reformation must be sought deeper than in the mere personality clashes of a few men. Luther's apparent change of attitude toward the Reformation, according to Walter Nigg, stemmed from the circumstances in which he suddenly found himself, as well as from the double nature of his character. According to Nigg, Luther was the greatest revolutionist that ever lived, yet in his soul he was the most conservative person there ever was. "This mighty revolutionary, who brought the world to the point of explosion, was at the same time a born conservative who drew back in dread from violence and unrest."[21] According to Nigg, Luther was a changed man after his dispute with the "enthusiasts." This is correct in only so far as this apparent change in Luther means a change in emphasis and not in substance. Luther was certainly practical enough to realize that an alliance with the lawless elements among his followers could very well jeopardize his cause. And his cause was the gospel of Christ as he had experienced it and had given expression to it in his writings. He realized that some had misunderstood what he had taught them concerning true Christian freedom and the real significance of the gospel. The events in Wittenberg following the disorders and Luther's subsequent writings bear out the point that the Reformer was primarily concerned about the gospel and the success of the Reformation.

Order Restored

Luther's appearance in Wittenberg, his sermons, and his writings produced the desired effects. As early as March 9, 1522, only three days after the Reformer's return, Hieronymus Schurf, a councillor at

Wittenberg, wrote to the Elector that with Luther now at home all would be well and that his sermons would make an end to all that the devil and his followers had wrought.[22] Carlstadt was forbidden to preach, although he was permitted to remain on the faculty of the university. The Lord's supper *sub una specie* and the elevation of the host were restored. All, except Carlstadt, repented of their rashness and radicalism. For the contritious Gabriel Zwilling Luther soon found a pastorate at Altenburg. In a letter to the former Augustinian monk Luther advises him to accept the charge and to "behave in circumspect manner, going about in an orderly priest's dress; . . . and remember that you are sent to those who must still be fed with milk."[23] When Zwilling later encountered difficulties in his new charge, Luther supported him as much as he could. Melanchton was also in full harmony with Luther again. On March 15 Schurf reported again to Frederick the Wise that Luther had managed to bring the Wittenbergers back to the truth, that the educated and the uneducated were once again full of joy, and that Carlstadt, although still dissatisfied, would be unable to do any harm.[24] Toward the end of March Luther wrote:

> I have offended Carlstadt by annulling his ordinances, although I do not condemn his doctrine, except that he has busied himself in merely external things, to the neglect of true Christian doctrine, that is, faith and charity. For his unwise way of teaching he has led the people to feel that the only thing they have to do to be Christians is to communicate in both kinds, take the bread and cup in their hands, neglect confession and break images.[25]

This summarizes Luther's attitude toward his colleague quite accurately.

Carlstadt continued to smart under his humiliation and waited for an opportunity for revenge. When he attempted to publish an article against Luther, the plot was discovered and foiled by the city council. Carlstadt became more and more inclined toward mysticism, began to despise the ministry, and went to live for some time as a peasant in Segrena, near Wittenberg, calling himself a "new layman." While he was absent from Wittenberg he continued to collect his income from the university. In 1524 he accepted a call to the congregation at Orlamünde, which was most happy to receive such a learned professor as pastor, and who was willing to lead them in their crusade against images, infant baptism, and the mass. Carlstadt was now free to write against Luther, attacking the Reformer's principle of forebearance for the weak brethren and his emphasis of justification by faith alone. Luther was annoyed. Early in 1524, he informed George Brück, Chancellor of Saxony, of Carlstadt's printing press in Jena and advised him to censor Carlstadt's writings. "Although this cannot do much injury to our ministry," Luther wrote, "still it is apt to bring dishonour upon our Prince and

University, as both have promised that nothing should be published without censorship by proper parties."[26] The authorities took the necessary steps to silence Carlstadt.

In 1524 Luther made a tour through the country, preaching against the "spirit of Alstedt," by which he meant the destructive influence of Thomas Müntzer and Carlstadt. On August 22 he was in Jena where he preached against the breaking of images, the despoilation of the sacraments, and radicalism in general. After the sermon Luther and Carlstadt met at an inn, where Carlstadt sought to justify himself by pointing out that holding different views concerning the last supper and other practices had nothing to do with the "spirit of Alstedt." He further accused Luther of stabbing him in the back instead of admonishing him like a brother, of censoring his writings, and of forbidding him to preach freely, all of which indicated that he, Luther, may be afraid that his enemy's teaching might prevail in the end. After accusing each other of jealousy and vain-glory, the interview ended with Luther giving Carlstadt the permission to write and publish against him as much as he wished, tossing to him a coin as a guarantee of this freedom.[27] After this affair the town council and congregation of Orlamünde wrote a letter to Luther, accusing him of identifying them with the spirit of Alstedt. When the Reformer later passed through the town, he discussed the letter with the council point by point, showing that there were doctrinal errors. The Orlamünders insisted that they were true Christians, and on the basis of the Old Testament they argued with Luther against the "worship of images." They also pointed out that according to Luther's earlier writings and Scripture they had the right to call and maintain their own priest. Luther reasoned with them that particularly their rashness with regard to reform was contrary to the Word of God. But Luther's words were of no avail; the resentment and hostility against the Reformer had become too intense. Fearing for his life at the hands of the Orlamünders, Luther was forced to leave the town.[28]

On September 22, 1524, Luther wrote to John Frederick of Saxony in support of the rector and minister at Orlamünde who demanded that Carlstadt, the "restless spirit," be banished.[29] The congregation interceded in vain for their pastor, his pregnant wife, and child. In his farewell address to the people of Orlamünde, Carlstadt closed with the words: "Andreas Bodenstein, expelled by Luther, unheard and unconvinced."[30] On October 27, 1524, Luther wrote to Amsdorf: "I, who myself was to become a martyr, have come to the point where I cause others to become martyrs."[31] To understand Luther's development from being a persecuted heretic to becoming a persecutor, it is necessary to look at the sacramental issue which lay at the basis of Luther's struggle with Carlstadt and the sacramentarians.

The Sacramental Controversy

After Carlstadt was driven from Saxony he went to Strassburg, Basel, Zürich, and other places, writing feverishly all the while against Luther and his doctrines, particularly against the Reformer's retention of the real presence in the eucharist. Carlstadt must be held responsible for initiating the so-called sacramental controversy which caused so much strife among the Protestants. Carlstadt's views on the last supper were shared, with minor variations, by most radicals and Anabaptists of the sixteenth century.

To understand the sacramental controversy which ensued between Luther and the radical reformers, it must be cast against the background of the Roman Catholic conception of the mass. The celebration of the eucharist was early in the history of the church designated as an "offering" or "sacrifice."[32] The church fathers Justin Martyr, Irenaeus, Tertullian and Cyprian seemed to have believed in the sacrificial nature of the mass and held either to transubstantiation or consubstantiation. Cyprian, for example, wrote: "Since we make mention of His passion in all our sacrifices, for the passion is the Lord's sacrifice which we offer, we ought to do nothing else than what He did [at the last supper]."[33] The word *missa* (mass) was apparently derived from the dismissal of an assembly after the priest had invoked God's blessing upon it. The word was soon permanently employed to designate the celebration of the mass.

According to Catholic teaching the eucharist was instituted for two purposes: It was to be the food of the soul, and it was to continue the sacrifice of Christ in the church. The mass is thus not only a commemoration of Christ's death, but a renewal and continuation of Christ's sacrifice on the cross. To put it in the words of the Council of Trent: "This new offering is necessarily also a sacrifice in its own right, but not one that has independent redemptive value, since it is nothing else than a sacramental extension of the one and only redemptive sacrifice on Calvary which the Epistle to the Hebrews had in view."[34] The sacrifice of the mass is both human and divine; it is made by Christ and the recipient. It is in the very nature of man to offer gifts to God. God accepts man's bread and wine after these elements have been transformed into the body and blood of Christ, for only the very best is acceptable to the divine Majesty. Thus the mass is not simply man's good work, according to Catholic teaching, but it contains an element of both, the divine and human. Transubstantiation was a term employed by the Lateran Council of 1215 to define the way in which the physical realities of the bread and wine were transformed (transubstantiated) into the real body and blood of Christ. The council simply explained what for many centuries had been the subject of controversy. As early as the second century some Christians believed in the real presence of Christ in the sacrament of holy communion. The belief in transubstantiation was more clearly defined by the Council of Trent: "If any man deny that in the sacrament of the Holy Eucharist are contained truly, really and substantially, the body and blood, together with the soul and divinity of our Lord Jesus Christ, and consequently the Whole Christ, but says that He is there only as a sign, figure, or power, let him be anathema."[35]

Luther first expressed his views concerning the mass in his pamphlet *On the Babylonian Captivity of the Church* (1520). In this writing he attacked holy communion in one kind (that is, the bread only for the laity), the doctrine of transubstantiation, and the sacrificial nature of the mass. When the Wittenberg radicals made a major issue of communion in one kind, Luther ceased to emphasize the importance of this first objection. The doctrine concerning transubstantiation, according to Luther, was only a mild bondage of Rome. Nevertheless, he repudiated transubstantiation because he felt that the doctrine was an attempt to reduce the importance of earthly substance; he always remained suspicious of the view which tended to underestimate the importance of the physical and material, including matrimony and worldly occupations, in favour of the "purely spiritual" life.[36] Although he never used the term, Luther seemed to believe in what was later known as "consubstantiation" in holy communion. Just as in a red-hot bar the fire and the metal do not lose their identity, he reasoned, so is Christ in, with, and under the elements of the eucharist. Or, just as God and man became one in Christ, so do the elements and Christ's body become one, both retaining, however, their distinct essence.[37] In this view Luther believed to follow the church fathers. St. Augustine's statement "the sacrament is the visible form of an invisible grace," Luther interpreted as meaning that Christ the invisible joined the visible elements of the sacrament, thus actually confirming his own position. When Tertullian called the last supper a *figura* of Christ, he did not, according to Luther, mean a figure or symbol, as some radicals believed, but a material form (*Gestalt*), something tangible and substantial.[38] Luther believed then with the Catholic church in the real presence in holy communion.

Luther's main objection to the mass was the Catholic belief that in the eucharist Christ was repeatedly sacrificed. This view struck at the very heart of Luther's experience of salvation and theology. Christ had died once and for all time on the cross; to call the mass a sacrifice would imply that Christ needed to be sacrificed again for the benefit of sinful men. If St. Augustine calls the mass a sacrifice, he simply means, according to Luther, that it reminds us of Christ's sacrifice in the past.[39] Moreover, Luther denied the human role in the transaction of the eucharist altogether, for man is completely passive in the presence of God, accepting what Christ freely offers him. Thus Luther's retention of the real presence and his rejection of the sacrificial nature of the mass were, according to H. Bornkamm, the result of the Reformer's "yearning for a reality of grace not less real than his sins."[40] Bornkamm continues: "His doctrine of Holy Communion is an expression of his faith in this reality of God in the midst of the world's reality and the reality of man's *Anfechtungen*; it is the ultimate deduction of his belief in the reality of forgiveness."[41]

Of the radicals Carlstadt was the first to be at variance with Luther on the question of the real presence; Zwingli and the Anabaptists were to follow Carlstadt. Carlstadt insisted that Christ's body and blood were not really present in the last supper, but that the elements simply represented Christ and that in partaking of them the believers merely commemorated his death on the cross. When Christ said, "This is my body," Carlstadt argued, he pointed to himself and not to the bread. In a letter to Chancellor Brück, Carlstadt emphatically stated that Christ's words of institution were most clear on this point and that they were not to be understood literally. Luther, according to Carlstadt, perverted the clear meaning of Scriptures.[42]

Luther was not slow to accept the challenge with regard to the real presence in holy communion. In the winter of 1524-1525 he wrote a most biting booklet, *Against the Celestial Prophets—Concerning Images and the Sacrament*,[43] in which he attacks the Zwickau prophets, Müntzer and, above all, Carlstadt. With this booklet Luther intends to answer all of Carlstadt's writings against the Reformer. He begins by pointing out that in dissenting from the true teaching concerning holy communion, Carlstadt has become an apostate from the faith and an enemy of Christ. Luther then turns to Carlstadt's criticism that the Lutherans call the last supper a mass, which implies that it is thought of as a sacrifice. Luther replies that there is nothing in a name as long as the mass is not regarded as a sacrificial offering in the Catholic sense. Christ's words of institution, Luther points out, must be taken literally. In fact, the text of the Bible must be taken literally wherever possible, unless it demands a symbolic interpretation. Common sense and faith must prevail in deciding whether Scripture is to be understood literally or otherwise. Concerning holy communion our faith clearly teaches us that Christ's body is literally in the elements of bread and wine. How the elements contain Christ is a divine mystery; but it is a truth, for the Word of God cannot lie. To rationalize about this mystery, as Carlstadt does, is from the devil. There is no automatic benefit in partaking of the Lord's supper, as Carlstadt interprets Luther's conception of the real presence; the recipient must have faith in Christ before he can benefit spiritually from holy communion. When the bread and wine are taken in true faith, there is forgiveness and spiritual power in the sacrament; without faith there is damnation, for the partaker is unworthy to receive the elements in which Christ resides. Luther concludes his *Against the Celestial Prophets* by pointing out that the enthusiasts have misunderstood the great truth concerning the eucharist because they have not experienced the forgiveness of God.

Why did Luther react so strongly against the sacramentarians? Three reasons may be suggested. First, he was sincerely convinced that Christ's words of institution were meant to be taken literally. Secondly, in the real presence Luther experienced the visible grace of God; the reality of forgiveness was for Luther made manifest in holy communion. Thirdly, Luther himself seems to have had profound doubts concerning the real presence. As late as 1524 he confessed how strongly he had been tempted to regard the last supper as a symbol only, but finally had to come to the conclusion that the words of Christ were against such an interpretation.[44] Luther agonized much over the sacramental issue. He wrote to Justus Jonas, a close friend: "Would that the Sacramentarians experienced for one quarter of an hour the sorrows of my heart, then I would declare they were truly converted. But now my enemies are mighty, and heap anguish on him whom the Lord chastens."[45] And in a letter to a friend in Koenigsberg Luther laments that the prophets increase steadily, thus tempting and trying all true believers, but, Luther adds, "God will expose Carlstadt in His own time."[46]

Luther's final encounter with Carlstadt came after the Peasants' Revolt in 1525. When the war broke out Carlstadt was active as minister in Rothenburg on the Tauber. When he went to pacify the peasants in his region, he made himself unpopular with them. Carlstadt had repudiated Müntzer's revolutionary views, but since Luther's writings against the revolutionary radicals had included Carlstadt as well, the former Wittenberg professor was sought by the authorities after the collapse of the war. On June 12, 1525, Carlstadt wrote to Luther from Frankfurt on the Main, asking him to forgive him for writing against him. In the letter he points out that he has decided not to write nor preach any more, and he humbly asks Luther to speak for him and his family to the Elector that he may be permitted to return to Saxony. He is willing to give full satisfaction to Luther for all that he has done to him.[47] In addition, Carlstadt wrote a tract in which he justified himself against alleged participation in the revolt, asking Luther to publish it in order to vindicate his name.

The Reformer was gracious. In a pamphlet addressed to all Christians,[48] Luther states that although Carlstadt is his foe on account of his doctrine, it is a Christian's duty to give aid even to an enemy. He expresses the hope that Carlstadt will eventually come to accept the correct interpretation with regard to the sacrament of holy communion. Moreover, according to Luther, the Peasants' Revolt was not so much the result of the activities of the fanatical preachers as the fault of the princes and bishops who had driven the peasants to such extremities that they were forced to resort to violence. Luther asks all princes to accept Carlstadt's apology and believe him for Christ's sake.

Upon the Reformer's request, Carlstadt wrote a partial recantation of his eucharistic views, which Luther supplied with a preface.[49] Luther is happy to accept Carlstadt's explanation that he is still seeking the truth concerning the Lord's supper; he also recalls that all the titles of Carlstadt's previous writings were usually in the form of questions rather than dogmatic statements. Although it is dangerous to waver in one's faith as Carlstadt does, Luther points out, it is our Christian duty to assist the erring one in brotherly love.

Luther apparently did not dare to speak to the Elector on behalf of Carlstadt, but he invited his former colleague to come and live in his house in Wittenberg. Carlstadt accepted the invitation. But the established relationship between the two men did not last for long. When Carlstadt retracted his former recantation, he and his family were again compelled to leave Saxony. His wayward life ended when he found an open door with the Swiss reformers, who joined and supported him when Luther renewed his attack on Carlstadt. In 1534 Carlstadt was called to Basel as preacher and professor at the university, a position he held until 1541 when he died during a plague. Luther was convinced that Carlstadt would suffer the penalties in hell for his views on the Lord's supper.

Herman Barge points out that Luther's return from the Wartburg nipped the lay movement of the Reformation in the bud. The priesthood of all believers, a principle the Reformer had believed in at first, did not seem to work out according to his liking. With the help of the secular arm Luther saw to it that the democratic and puritanical movement had to give way to absolutism; between God and man there was once again placed the "spiritual office."[50] While this may be true to a certain extent, Barge seems to underestimate Luther's reasons for extinguishing the flames which he himself had helped to kindle. Human considerations, such as jealousy, selfishness, and inconsistencies, no doubt played an important part in Luther's action against the Wittenberg radicals. But in the final analysis it was the cause of the Reformation which Luther saw threatened by the lawless elements within his movement. Democratic considerations were not uppermost in Luther's mind. The principle of the priesthood of all believers had nothing to do with democracy; it merely placed the responsibility of salvation on each individual and gave him the right to interpret the Word of God according to his understanding of it. This freedom, according to Luther, did not open the door to license. And as far as the "puritanical" movement was concerned, Luther saw in it a threat to his doctrine of salvation through God's grace alone. The great emphasis on the good life opened once again the door to a man-made Christianity, to a righteousness that came from works. The sacramental controversy which developed confirmed Luther in his view that the fanatics removed themselves from the written Word, placed greater importance on human insight and logic, and thus minimized the divine element in man's salvation and life. To tolerate his former friends in Wittenberg would have meant to give in to a gospel which in Luther's view was anti-Christian.

CHAPTER III

LUTHER'S STRUGGLE WITH THE REVOLUTIONARY
RADICALS

Luther's struggle with the Wittenberg radicals had not yet ended when there arose on the southern horizon a more formidable foe to Lutheranism than Carlstadt. Thomas Müntzer, the Lutheran pastor at Zwickau, whence in 1521 the Zwickau prophets had come to Wittenberg, dissented from the Reformer, advocated a dangerous millennianism, and contributed to the spreading of discontent among the peasants of southern Germany. Unlike Carlstadt, Müntzer was not content with opposing the existing order with the pen only; in his writings and sermons he advocated the destruction of the godless to make room for the reign of the saints. The vehemence with which these ideas were proclaimed greatly fanned the spreading flames of the Peasants' Revolt. There is no doubt that Luther's writings prior to 1525 had somewhat confused men's thinking concerning a Christian's relationship to the state. When the Reformer realized how his writings and example were misinterpreted and misapplied to suit the purely worldly aspirations of those who claimed to be his followers, he was not slow to turn against the rebellious elements. It is the purpose of this chapter to interpret the struggle between what may be called the status quo and millennianism.

Luther and Authority Prior to 1525

It may be pointed out at the outset that Luther's views with regard to the citizen and the state remained quite consistent to the end. In his earliest writings he emphasized that the "common man" had to submit to the magistrates at all times. Rebellion, according to Romans 13, Luther's classical Bible passage on the subject, was against the will of God, and rebels were to be punished severely. In some instances, however, Luther qualified his general position in favour of insubordination to the state. As we shall see later, in spiritual matters the state had no business to interfere in the lives of individuals or the church. It must be admitted, however, that in his spiritual rebellion against Rome, Luther often used extreme language, which sometimes left people in doubt as to how his statements against the authorities were to be interpreted. Belford Bax states: "The Lutheran Reformation, from its inception in 1517 down to the Peasants' War of 1525, at once absorbed, and was absorbed by all the revolutionary elements of the time. Up to the last-mentioned date it gathered revolutionary force year by year."[1] Although this statement is too general and certainly one-sided, it is correct to say that Luther's writings prior to 1524 at least encouraged rebellion against the status quo, especially among people who suffered economic and social injustice.

Luther differentiated clearly between two powers: the spiritual and the temporal. To rebel against the spiritual authorities when they are in the wrong is permissible, whereas to rebel against the magistrates is not allowed. In his interpretation of the fourth commandment in his treatise on good works (1520) he stated: "... one must resist the spiritual power when it does not do right and not resist the temporal power even though it does wrong."[2] Time and again, however, Luther explained that if it should happen that the temporal power and authorities should urge a subject to act contrary to the commandments of God, or hinder him in living according to them, obedience to them was to be withdrawn, for one ought to obey God rather than men. Luther's language against the spiritual powers was especially harsh. To John Lang he wrote on August 18, 1520, that he was convinced that the papacy was the seat of the true and real antichrist. As far as he was concerned, he owed the pope no other obedience than that which he owed the very antichrist.[3] Elsewhere he stated that it would be far better to kill all the bishops and destroy all monasteries and similar institutions than to allow one single soul, not to speak of all the souls, to perish on account of them.[4] In a letter to the artist Lucas Cranach (April 28, 1521) Luther recalls his humiliating treatment at the Diet of Worms where he had been asked to recant without being refuted by learned theologians. "Oh, we blind Germans," he concludes, "how childish we act to allow the Romanists to make fools of us in this miserable manner."[5] The early reformation writings, especially the booklet *To the Christian Nobility*, as we have seen, were filled with statements which were bound to incite to rebellious feelings against spiritual oppression.

The censorship of his New Testament in Bavaria gave Luther an occasion to treat more fully the question of a Christian's obedience to the powers that be. In January, 1523, he published his carefully worked out booklet *Secular Authority: To What Extent it Should be Obeyed.*[6] There are two kingdoms, Luther begins, the Kingdom of God and the kingdom of this world. The children of God, who belong to God's Kingdom, need no human laws, but the wicked people, who are in the vast majority, cannot be held in check without imposing laws and force upon them. Since a Christian is governed by the Spirit of God, he actually need not subject himself to the magistrates and their laws, but for the sake of order and as an example for the wicked, he subordinates himself freely to human governments, pays all taxes, and generally seeks the good of his fellowmen. To the question as to whether a Christian may bear arms, the Reformer replies that as a Christian he is not in need of the sword, and as far as his private life is concerned he will rather suffer pain and injustice than use force against another human being. Since a Christian, however, must seek the welfare of his neighbour as well as that of the state, he gladly bears arms for his government, for to refuse to do so would imperil the safety of society. All saints in the Old Testament used the sword, and although the Mosaic law need not be binding in the new dispensation, we are obliged to follow the example of God's people, for right will always remain right.

Having said this much in favour of obedience to the magistrates, Luther goes on to define the limits of the temporal powers with regard to spiritual issues. First, the secular princes have no jurisdiction over the souls of their subjects. No prince, bishop, or any other ruler can make laws concerning one's beliefs, and no power may compel one to believe this or that. Magistrates have power in strictly temporal matters only. They have no right, for example, to interfere with the publication and distribution of Christian literature, for to do so means interference in the strictly spiritual realm. Even heresy should be of no concern to the temporal powers; this belongs to the jurisdiction of the bishops and pastors who ought to combat adverse teachings with the Word of God. Since heresy is of a spiritual nature, iron, fire and water cannot prevail against it. Secondly, in a lord-vassal relationship the vassal must be careful to observe his obedience to the master. A vassal may never attack his lord; all he can do is implore his overlord to do the right and to shun all evil. A prince, however, may attack his own rebellious vassals, provided of course that all peace offers have been rejected by the rebels. On the other hand, should a vassal or any other man perceive that his lord or government is intent on doing evil, he need not obey in such a case.[7] If a subject, however, is in doubt or ignorant concerning the nature of the matter or issue in question, he should obey his lord or government with a clear conscience.[8] In his reasoning Luther merely followed mediaeval feudal theory on the subject.

In the same year, 1523, Luther published another pamphlet which had far-reaching consequences. In *That a Christian Congregation has the Right and Power to Judge All Doctrine*[9] he argues that bishops have no right to teach falsely, for false doctrines endanger the spiritual life of their flocks. It is the duty of the Christian congregation to determine whether the doctrines taught are according to God's Word. In taking over judgment in matters of faith and doctrine, bishops and councils act against the express command of Christ. Spiritual tyrants who rule over people contrary to the will of God are to be driven out of Christendom like wolves and thieves.

The language of this pamphlet is no doubt strong, but to construe from it that Luther advocated physical violence against spiritual oppressors is to completely misunderstand Luther's teaching on the subject of the Christian and human authority.

In his pronouncements concerning authority Luther distinguished between the two kingdoms, the temporal and the spiritual, teaching that subjects ought to obey the temporal rulers, but submit to spiritual authorities only in so far as they teach the Word of God in sincerity and truth. In these two different approaches to the two kingdoms Luther remained consistent from beginning to the end. While his statements and the vehemence with which he at times uttered them could be applied to any oppressive authority, including the secular, it is quite wrong to suggest that Luther incited men to rebel against the established institutions, be they secular or spiritual. The peasants may have been misguided in their application of Luther's principles to their own situation, and they may have misunderstood the Reformer's pronouncements concerning freedom and opposition to Rome in their favour, but men like Müntzer understood Luther's teaching concerning authority very well. Müntzer's involvement with the Peasants' War was in direct opposition to Luther, an opposition which grew out of his theology, and not out of a misunderstanding of Luther's writings. We must turn now to Müntzer's theology and involvement in lawlessness, bloodshed and war.

Thomas Müntzer and Luther

Thomas Müntzer was born in Stolberg in the Harz Mountains of Saxony about the year 1490. He received a good education at the Universities of Leipzig and Frankfurt on the Oder. He knew well the Bible and the mediaeval mystics and was acquainted with Plato, St. Augustine, and most classic Christian writers. At some date unknown, perhaps 1513, he became a Catholic priest and in 1516 he became provost of a nunnery at Frohse. Müntzer was a fluent and powerful preacher, and he soon had a reputation as a theologian. In 1519 he became assistant and supply preacher to Franz Günther of Nordhausen, a devoted Martinian, as Luther's followers were sometimes called. Although Müntzer did not belong to the circle of "Wittenberg men," it was on Luther's recommendation that in 1520 he received his most promising appointment to date, that of supply preacher at Our Lady's Church in Zwickau. The preacher at Zwickau, Sylvius Egranus, an Erasmian humanist, had taken a long leave to visit Erasmus and other scholars in the Rhineland and in south-west Germany. Upon Egranus' return Müntzer became preacher in the Church of St. Catherine, attended by weavers and generally by the poorly-paid proletariat. Influenced by the Zwickau prophets, especially by Nicholaus Storch, Müntzer soon began to quarrel with the monks in the town and thus created a general disturbance among the already restless citizens of Zwickau. When Luther was informed about Müntzer's activity in Zwickau, he more or less approved of the minister's zeal for the evangelical cause.[10] In April, 1521, the zealous reformer of Zwickau was compelled to leave the town.

Until February, 1522, we find Müntzer in Prague where he drew up his "Prague Manifesto" which became the programme for his later life. The Manifesto was a visionary document, proposing a new church of the spirit, which was not to depend on the letter of the Bible, but on direct communications from God. According to the Manifesto, God inscribes with his finger in the hearts of men his immovable will and eternal wisdom. "The script not being written with ink, no man can read it ... unless God himself opens up the human mind. This he does in his elect from the very beginning, so that they are no longer uncertain but have invincible testimony from the Holy Spirit who bears witness, with our witness, that we are children of God, Rom. 8."[11] The pure church of Christ, according to Müntzer, became a prostitute shortly after the death of the apostles and disciples due to the scholars who always wanted to be on top. God's will permitted this so that the work of all men might be exposed for all to see. The "monkish clergy shall never represent the true church. Instead, the elect friends of God's word will be instructed in prophecy, just as St. Paul was, so that they might really experience how amiably God speaks with his elect. I will, for the sake of God, sacrifice my life in order to reveal this truth."[12] Müntzer then calls upon the people of Bohemia to help him in the work of true reformation and promises the punishment of God's judgment for those who will refuse: "God will perform marvellous feats with his elect, especially in this land; for here shall begin a new church, and this nation will become a mirror to the entire world. I therefore call on everyone to assist in defending the word of God. ... If you refuse, God will have you slain by the Turks when they come next year."[13] Referring to his own mission, Müntzer states: "The time of harvest is at hand. That is why God himself has hired me to labor in his harvest. I have sharpened my sickle; my mind is honed for truth. ... Christ will give his kingdom to the elect in a little while."[14]

Müntzer wrote two versions of the Manifesto, one in German and one in Latin.[15] The German version addressed itself primarily to the plight of the common man in Bohemia, emphasizing especially the principle of the priesthood of all believers; the Latin version, in polished rhetoric, sought the support of influential noblemen and scholars. "I have entered your famous land, my most esteemed Bohemian brethren," Müntzer wrote, "desiring nothing but to strengthen the living word of God so that it might not be returned empty."[16] But Müntzer's theological arguments failed to impress the people in the land of John Huss. Stübner, who had accompanied Müntzer to Prague, was stoned and barely escaped with his life, and Müntzer was put in jail. This seems to indicate popular as well as magisterial disapproval. In December, 1521, Stübner and his fellow prophets from Zwickau turned up in Wittenberg where Carlstadt, as we have seen, began to head the radical reformation. It is likely that Müntzer also came to Wittenberg in the winter of 1521-1522.[17] Having a hard time, Müntzer moved from town to town, disappointed at not finding open minds and hearts for his gospel and programme.

Müntzer's first real success came when he was appointed, in the spring of 1523, minister in Allstedt, a small town in the Harz region inhabited by restless ore miners, always eager to promote social changes. Although the town itself had only a few hundred people, Müntzer's sermons, in which he expounded in consecutive order the books of the Bible, attracted thousands of listeners. According to the preacher, "the poor thirsty folk did so yearn for the truth that all the streets were full of people come to hear it." Müntzer conducted the worship services in the German language, distributed the last supper in both kinds, and wrote several tracts concerning the mass and against infant baptism. It was also at this time that Müntzer, like Carlstadt before him and Luther a year later, married a former nun. As late as July 9, 1523, Müntzer had still not broken with Luther, for on that date he wrote a conciliatory letter to the Reformer in Wittenberg, although suggesting that the difference between him and Luther was their different views concerning the Spirit of God and revelations. During the following winter Müntzer founded the Allstedt League, a society which was to carry out by all possible means, including violence, the Prague programme. It was at this time that a nearby Catholic chapel went up in flames. The League may have been responsible for this, although Allstedt was known for its acts of violence prior to Müntzer's coming. In any case, after the formation of the League the difference between Luther and Müntzer became apparent.

Müntzer was well grounded in Luther's doctrines of salvation and the priesthood of all believers. He was, however, more deeply steeped in the literature of the German mystics and held radical views similar to those of the Taborites of the fifteenth century. He believed that personal salvation enables man to communicate with God directly through the spirit. From Tauler Müntzer had borrowed the idea of Christian suffering, a necessary part in the life of each follower of Christ. Müntzer's doctrine concerning the "bitter Christ," as opposed to what he called Luther's "sweet Christ," grew directly out of this theology of the cross. He believed that Luther made the way to salvation too easy, telling the people simply to believe, thus making a doll out of God to be played with at will. The godless who shun all suffering and the cross, Müntzer argued, like the idea of someone suffering for them. Suffering, according to Müntzer's theology, is necessary in order to prepare the human heart for the spirit to enter it in all his glory. Müntzer had written to Luther: "A man cannot know Christ's doctrines unless he has suffered the waves and billows of great waters which overwhelm the Elect . . . so that a man hopes beyond hope and seeks the one will of God in the Day of Visitation, beyond all expectation."[18] And again in this letter, written in Latin: "No mortal understands Christ and his teaching, what is true and what is false, if he has not conformed his will to the cross."[19] Luther might have agreed with Müntzer's theology of suffering, for suffering, inner agony, and the way of the cross were part of the Reformer's life and teaching; but Luther had become suspicious of Müntzer's activities in Zwickau, Prague and Allstedt, and his mystical experience of the "bitter Christ" was foreign to Luther's view of the biblical Christ.

Luther and Müntzer were also diametrically opposed in their views concerning the authority of the written Word of God. For Luther, as we have seen, Scriptures were the revealed will of God for man, and the written Word became for him the highest court of appeal. For Müntzer this adherence to the Bible meant bibliolatry, the worship of external letters. The Bible was for Müntzer a record of God's revelation to individuals in biblical times and a testimony to that which Christians felt and experienced in their hearts.[20] Belief in the mere letter of the Bible, according to Müntzer, leads to spiritual death rather than to life. Moreover, the Bible is inadequate without a divinely inspired interpreter, that is, a man of God inspired by the Spirit of God. In his *Fürstenpredigt* before Duke John and Duke John Frederick, who came to hear the prophet in Allstedt, Müntzer stated that anyone who had not received "the living testimony of God, Rom. 8, knows nothing significant to say concerning God, even though he had eaten a hundred thousand Bibles."[21] Unless the individual is instructed by the Holy Spirit, he cannot understand the Bible, he deceives himself, and Christ becomes for him "wooden" ("dichtet sich einen hölzernen Christum").[22] Without this heavenly interpreter the Bible remains, for Müntzer, a book sealed with seven seals.

Müntzer, according to Luther, had advocated the observance of several steps before God could reveal himself directly to the individual. First, man has to get rid of all coarseness and sin (*Entgröbung*); secondly, he has to meditate and think on the new life in Christ and eternity (*Studierung*); thirdly, he has to contemplate the sinfulness of sin and God's grace for man; fourthly, he has to sorrow and repent genuinely of his former life (*Langeweile*); lastly, he must attain to a state of perfect resignation before God (*tiefe Gelassenheit*), at which point the voice of God will be heard.[23] Müntzer betrays in this his indebtedness to the German mystics; the language is that of Tauler. For Luther, as much as he too was inclined to mysticism, this experience was too subjective; it placed man rather than God in the centre. Luther needed the external Word of God and the visible sacraments to assure him of God's favour to man. But Luther never boasted of his assurance of salvation; he left the matter wholly to God, stating that man must believe in the grace of God, but remain uncertain concerning his own election and that of others.[24] For Müntzer there was no question about his election, for the indwelling Holy Spirit was a sure sign of salvation.

Toward the end of 1523, Luther wrote to Spalatin that he had begged the officials of Allstedt to beware of Müntzer's spirit of prophecy. According to Luther, Müntzer was dangerous, undermining wherever possible the work of the Reformation.[25] Müntzer felt the same about the Reformer at Wittenberg, looking upon him as the self-appointed pope of the new movement. The battle lines were thus drawn between the two men, and on the question of church and state they collided head-on.

Müntzer's Increasing Radicalism

Luther believed that the temporal powers existed as a result of sin and that the magistrates and princes were tools in the hands of God to keep wickedness in check. On numerous occasions Luther condemned the abuses of secular power, but he never preached or advocated insubordination to or abolition of all temporal authorities. Müntzer, on the other hand, was convinced that the time had come for God to eradicate all godless governments through the action of the saints. To understand Müntzer's reasoning in this regard, it is important that we consider his view of history which is expressed best of all in his "Princes' Sermon" (*Fürstenpredigt*), preached on July 13, 1524, before Duke John and his son as they passed through

Allstedt.[26]

The sermon was based on the prophet Daniel, chapter 2; it had as its object the sympathies of the Saxon authorities for Müntzer's cause. In Daniel 2 King Nebuchadnezzar has a dream which his magicians and sorcerers cannot interpret. Daniel comes before the king, and he not only interprets the dream but also tells the king what the dream was. The king, according to Daniel, saw a great image whose head was of gold, its breast and arms of silver, its belly and thighs of bronze, its legs of iron, and its feet partly of iron and partly of clay. As the king beheld the image, "a stone was cut out by no human hand, and it smote the image on its feet of iron and clay, and broke them in pieces. . . . [And the image was] broken in pieces, and became the chaff of the threshing floors. . . . But the stone that struck the image became a great mountain and filled the whole earth" (Daniel 2:31-35). Daniel then proceeds to interpret the dream, telling the king that he is the head of gold and that the kingdoms after him will be of decreasing value, until in the end God will set up his kingdom which will destroy the kingdoms represented by the image.

Following mediaeval interpretation of Nebuchadnezzar's image, Müntzer explains that the golden head represents Babylon, the breast and arms the kingdom of the Medes and Persians, the belly and thighs the government of Greece, the legs of iron tyrannous Rome, and the feet of iron and clay represent the secular and spiritual governments of Müntzer's time. When Christ came he wanted to establish his kingdom on earth, but shortly after the death of the apostles the church of God was prostituted by godless men and false teachers. The church throughout the ages was a mixture of iron and clay, a combination of the sacred and profane. To make this vivid, Müntzer uses the image of eels and serpents sexually entwined in one lump. The clergy are serpents and the temporal rulers are eels, according to Müntzer.[27] Through all types of ceremonies and man-made ways of salvation people have been led astray from the path of truth. But the "little stone," God's Kingdom, will soon fill the whole earth, and it is the Christian's duty to assist God in his gigantic work. The wicked ones must be staved off in the fear of the Lord, for they only hinder the progress of God's cause on earth. Becoming more eloquent, Müntzer urges the Saxon authorities to wield the sword against all those who oppose the truth and hinder the gospel. If the princes will fail in this, the peasants, who perceive the truth more clearly than their temporal rulers, will take the matter into their own hands. The evildoers should not be allowed to live longer, for the godless person has no right to live when he is in the way of the pious. Some may object that the apostles did not use violence, Müntzer interjects, but it must be remembered that Peter was a timid man of whom even Christ said that he feared death. Had it been in the power of St. Paul to push his teaching to its conclusion among the Athenians, he would have broken their idols as Moses had commanded and as was practised in later history. The godless have two alternatives: they can either deny the faith in Christ or they can do away with their idols. According to Romans 13, Müntzer insists, it is the duty of the temporal powers to wield the sword against the wicked. If the Christian princes do not act according to the Word of God, the sword will be taken from them, for they confess Christ with their words but deny him with their actions. The death of the godless is the only way to bring the church back to its original purity. The godless have no right to live, Müntzer concludes, except as the elect wish to grant it to them. "Rejoice, you true friends of God, that for the enemies of the cross their heart has fallen into their breaches."

Besides advocating violence against the godless rulers and false teachers, there are other points in the sermon that run counter to Luther's teachings. Basing his view on Daniel's insight into the divine will, Müntzer stresses God's immediate revelations to the saints. In this the times have not changed; God still reveals his secrets to his friends. Teachers who teach otherwise—and here Müntzer no doubt has Luther in mind—are wrong. The Spirit of God reveals himself to those who listen to him and who are receptive to his promptings. And Müntzer believes that God has revealed the future to him. The dukes need a Daniel so that the truth might be revealed. Müntzer no doubt suggests here that he, and not Luther, should be the spiritual guide of the princes.[28] Just as Nebuchadnezzar honoured and listened to Daniel, Müntzer implies, so should the temporal authorities heed the word of Müntzer. Attacking Luther's teaching concerning the two kingdoms, without mentioning Luther by name, Müntzer points out that the princes have been fooled into believing that their only duty is to look after law and order and not to concern themselves with spiritual matters.

The Saxon authorities were thoroughly confused, asking Luther for advice. When the Reformer heard about the sermon of Müntzer, he stood aghast at the audacity of his former follower. As far as Luther was concerned, it was not the duty of the state to set up utopia on earth but to prevent earth from becoming hell. In *A Letter to the Princes of Saxony Concerning the Seditious Spirit*[29] Luther warned the magistrates against the "spirit of Allstedt" and advised them to be on guard against prophets who claim to hear voices and have visions. Why is Müntzer afraid to answer for his views to Luther? the Reformer asks in the pamphlet. Although he, Luther, had no voices from God, he was not afraid to appear at Leipzig, Augsburg and Worms when he was asked by his enemies to do so. Luther then laments that it was he who won the victory over the pope and now his deserters exploit this victory to their own advantage. His advice is to let these prophets preach and teach, as long as they do not take up arms against the governments. But as soon as they draw the sword they must be banished from the land. The spirits must fight it out between themselves, for the true doctrine, Luther is confident, will prevail in the end.

When Müntzer continued to incite his followers against the secular and spiritual authorities, the Elector summoned Müntzer to appear in Weimar in August, 1524, to account for his views and activities. The commission consisted of Duke John and Chancellor Brück, who represented the prosecution, and three professors from Wittenberg, followers of Luther. Müntzer was accused of inciting people to riot, of counselling peasants to withhold their taxes, and of despising governments. After the hearing Müntzer was informed that after due deliberations with the Elector about his case, he would be notified concerning the outcome of the proceedings. In the meantime Müntzer was to conduct himself "peacefully."[30]

Müntzer did not wait to learn what the Elector would decide in his case. Fearing the worst, he left Allstedt and fled to Mühlhausen, Thuringia, writing a vitriolic pamphlet against Luther, *Thomas Müntzer's Answer to the Spiritless, Soft-Living Flesh at Wittenberg.*[31] In this pamphlet, in which Müntzer calls Luther, among other things, "Brother Soft-Life," "Doctor Liar," "Father Soft-step," "Pope of Wittenberg," "Virgin Martin," "Educated Rascal," "Leader of the Blind," "Arch-devil," and "Arch-heathen," the writer compares himself to Christ who like himself was persecuted by the Jews and Pharisees. Luther, the Pharisee and servant of princes, knows what is good for him and thus refuses to speak out against the tyranny of the princes, which is the cause of the rebellious attitude among the peasants. When Luther advises the princes not to hinder Müntzer in his preaching, he only seeks to give semblance to Christian love and tolerance, but in reality remains a persecutor of the truth. Müntzer is not much impressed with Luther's supposed courage at Leipzig, Augsburg and Worms. When he appeared before his enemies, he had powerful friends at his side; in fact, had he faltered and yielded before the Emperor in Worms, the nobles would have stabbed him to death.

Luther in a letter of August 14, 1524, warned the Council of Mühlhausen not to receive Müntzer, for his activities in Zwickau and Allstedt had shown that he was a murderer. Müntzer, Luther suggested, should be asked who had called and sent him to preach, and if he insisted that the Spirit of God had sent him, he should be required to do miracles, for God always attests extraordinary activities with signs and wonders.[32] The letter was too late. Müntzer had arrived a few days earlier and had been welcomed by the town. With the help of other radicals, notably Heinrich Pfeifer, a social revolutionary, the town council was overthrown and radical reforms introduced. However, after two months of restless activity, Müntzer was compelled to leave Mühlhausen and flee to Nürnberg where he exerted some influence on Hans Denck, a later leader of the peaceful Anabaptists.[33] In November and December of 1524 Müntzer wandered aimlessly throughout southern Germany, preaching everywhere his revolutionary gospel. But his success has been overestimated. Müntzer seemed to be popular in Mühlhausen only; not even all of Thuringia accepted his ideas and Franconia rejected him outright.[34] It has also been shown that Müntzer cannot be held responsible for the revolt in the Upper Rhine regions.[35] If Müntzer was successful in arousing the peasants to action, the success was at best a limited one.

In February, 1525, Müntzer was back in Mühlhausen, whither Heinrich Pfeifer had also returned by the end of 1524. In the hope of at last rousing the discontented elements to concrete action, Müntzer wrote an explosive pamphlet, addressed to the miners of Mansfeld.[36] "Dear brothers, how long will you sleep?" Müntzer urges his readers. "How often have I told you as to how it is to be done! God can no longer reveal himself, you must act.... Get to it! It is time! The wicked despair like dogs.... You must strike now while the fire is hot! Don't let the swords cool from the blood of the princes.... It is impossible to have peace and be free while the wicked rule over you.... It is God's war and he will fight for you." The author signed: "Thomas Müntzer, a servant of God against the godless." Similarly in a letter to Duke Ernest of Mansfeld, written on May 12, 1525, Müntzer warns "Brother Ernest" not to oppress and persecute the Christians in his domain, for God will not permit such cruelty to go unpunished.[37] "The eternal living God has commanded that you be deprived of your power by force, which has been granted us." Müntzer continues: "You are of no use to Christendom; you are harmful to the friends of God.... We demand an answer at once, or else we shall move against you in the name of the hosts of God." Again the author signed: "Thomas Müntzer with the sword of Gideon." On May 15, 1525, the sword did strike in the tragic battle near Frankenhausen. The battle ended in defeat for both the fanatic Müntzer and his deceived peasants. Müntzer was captured and executed on May 27. Before he died he recanted his radicalism and received the mass according to Catholic rites. It must be said to his credit that even in the face of death this radical reformer urgently entreated the princes to deal more mercifully with their subjects and govern them according to the Word of God.

The doctrines of Thomas Müntzer did not die with their author; the sources indicate that this rebel was esteemed highly by many until the late 1530's. Not without reason did Luther continue to warn people against the "spirit of Allstedt." Shortly after Müntzer's death, the Reformer published his *A Terrible Story and Judgment of God Upon Thomas Müntzer*,[38] addressed to his "beloved Germans." In this pamphlet Luther states that he writes this story in order to show how God judges so righteously, to "warn, to terrify, and to admonish" those who are still contemplating rebellion, and to comfort and strengthen those who suffer on account of the rebels. After commenting on some of Müntzer's radical pamphlets, which are shown as being diabolical in spirit, Luther concludes his *Terrible Story* by elaborating on the false hope and confidence the peasants had placed in their leader. Müntzer had promised that one peasant would be able to kill a thousand enemies, and that the prophet himself would divert all the bullets into his sleeves. Instead, 5,000 disillusioned peasants lay brutally murdered near Frankenhausen. Luther expresses sorrow for the fate of the peasants, but he regards it as God's judgment upon them and he continues to pray for the victory of the princes. Similarly Luther wrote to John Rühel, his brother-in-law, that he was glad about Müntzer's death: "It is the judgment of God. He who takes the sword shall perish by the sword."[39] Years later the memory of Thomas Müntzer continued to haunt the Reformer. On several occasions Luther told stories about his former foe, and from time to time he referred to Müntzer's death as God's just punishment for rebellion, blasphemy and unbelief.[40]

Luther and the Peasants' Revolt

Neither Luther nor the radical reformers can be held responsible for the Peasants' Revolt which broke out in 1525 with such unprecedented fury. The war was a repetition on a larger scale of many similar attempts in the past, and the interests underlying all of them were not primarily religious—although religious considerations played an important part—but political, social and economic. Ever since the Hussite Wars of the fifteenth century, Germany had been troubled with peasant uprisings. There had been a war in Würtemberg as late as 1514, several years before the outbreak of the Protestant revolt. In our study we are not interested in the background nor in the progress of the conflagration but primarily in Luther's part in the rebellion and his attitude towards the peasants. As we shall see, the relationship between Luther and the Peasants' Revolt seemed to have far-reaching consequences for the radical reformation.

While luther cannot be accused of having caused the Peasants' War, it was no doubt due to the Reformer's influence that this war surpassed in magnitude any seen in Germany before. The conviction and vehemence with which Luther often expressed himself in his early writings left their mark on all strata of German society, including the peasants. Especially Luther's statements with regard to Christian freedom, social justice, and the limits of temporal powers became dangerous weapons in the hands of the victims of the dying feudal order. The Reformer became for many peasants the central figure of the revolutionary movement, political and social no less than religious. Luther's attack upon many features of the existing order, his criticism of the increasing luxury of the prosperous classes, his denunciation of the greed of great commercial magnates, his condemnation of the tyranny and corruption of civil rulers and ecclesiastical leaders—all this tended to inflame the populace and spread impatience and discontent.[41]

Luther's contemporaries, whether friends or foes, were fully aware of the Reformer's indirect contribution to the social discontent among the peasants. The humanist Ulrich Zasius wrote, "Luther has plunged Germany into such a state of frenzy that one must perforce regard as peace and safety the mere hope of not being knocked on the head."[42] Erasmus wrote in his *Hyperaspistes* concerning Luther and the war, "We have the fruit of your spirit—you cannot make men believe that the occasion of these tumults was not furnished by your pamphlets, especially those in German. But, O Luther, I do not yet think so ill of you as to suppose that you intended this."[43] Elsewhere Erasmus wrote, "You Luther refuse to acknowledge the insurgents, but they acknowledge you, and the instigators of this war claim the Gospel as their guide."[44]

It is certainly true that Luther had not intended the war. Luther's own example of rebellion against Rome and some of his reformation writings were no doubt revolutionary in nature, but in general the Reformer's work and pamphlets were misunderstood, misinterpreted and misapplied by the peasants. Some tracts, such as *The Freedom of a Christian*, were written for the instruction and encouragement of laymen, but the peasants used them for their own ends; others, such as *To the Christian Nobility*, were meant for the nobility only, but the peasants thought they were an appeal to them to fight against all oppression and a special assignment for them to cause a reformation of the entire old order. Luther's gospel of Christian liberty was changed from the Reformer's meaning of an inner freedom of the reborn man to mean freedom from social injustice and from the economic bondage of feudalism. This explains in part Luther's harsh attitude toward the rebellious peasants.

In March, 1525, the peasants of south-western Germany drew up twelve articles, asking of the feudal lords certain concessions and alleviations. While it is not known who authored or compiled the *Twelve Articles*, it is quite possible that some Anabaptist had a hand in the composition of the document. Some believe that Balthasar Hubmaier, the Anabaptist leader of Waldshut, was one of the authors.[45] The articles were addressed "To the Christian reader" and were highly religious in tone, with each article supported with ample Scripture passages. The demands included the following points: that the Christian congregation have the freedom to elect their own priest and that he be supported by the tithes of the community; that the status of villeinage be abolished; that there be freedom of hunting and that the woods be accessible to all; that the services due to the lords be diminished; and that the princes no longer oppress the peasants. In the twelfth article the peasants agreed to revoke any point that the princes might object to, provided it could be proved that the objectionable articles were contrary to the Word of God and reason. This was certainly in keeping with the standard of judgment which Luther himself applied in proceeding against his opponents. Some historians feel that the attitude of most German peasants in 1525 is not to be sought in the extreme radicalism of Thomas Müntzer but in the nature and tone of the *Twelve Articles*.[46] The articles were no doubt reasonable demands and seemed to express a truly Christian sentiment.

Luther at first also believed that the articles were an expression of just grievances on the part of the peasants. But when the disturbances began to increase in the south, he wrote his *Warning Toward Peace Based on the Twelve Articles*,[47] in which he addressed both the nobles and the peasants. Luther begins the first part of the pamphlet by citing Psalm 7:16, directed to the princes: "His mischief returns upon his head, and on his own pate his violence descends." Luther then proceeds to accuse the princes and bishops of opposing the gospel and oppressing the peasants, warning them that judgment is certain to come upon them, for it is not the peasants but God himself who is against them. The princes are fully responsible for the social and political unrest. Luther agrees that the demands of the *Twelve Articles* are reasonable and that they show a great deal of restraint on the part of the peasants; the princes should yield and accept them, for he, Luther, would have demanded much more. Concluding the first part, the Reformer chides the nobles for making his doctrines responsible for the disturbances; the peasants will teach the princes a lesson for such blasphemy.

In the second part of the pamphlet Luther turns to the peasants, his "beloved friends" and "brethren," admonishing them not to heed the fanatical preaching of the enthusiasts who incite them to godless action. It is against all natural law and the Word of God to oppose the powers that be, no matter how evil they may be. If the peasants cannot endure it in one place, Luther advises, they should seek refuge elsewhere, and God will deliver his children from all troubles. The peasants should not rebel against the authorities, for rebellion will retard the progress of the gospel and play into the hands of the devil. In reviewing the articles, Luther finds that the first, the one concerning choosing a pastor, is in agreement with the Word of God. The second, which deals with the abolition of tithes, is outright robbery, for the tithes belong rightfully to the government. The third article, concerning the abrogation of villeinage, is quite repulsive because it degrades the spiritual freedom in Christ to a carnal level. After all, did not Abraham and the other patriarchs own slaves? The remaining articles Luther leaves to the judgment of the lawyers, for as a minister of God he cannot advise in such mundane matters as forest laws and hunting regulations. It is his duty to instruct the consciences only. In conclusion Luther attempts to pacify both sides, stating that a good conscience must be maintained at all costs.

Luther's intentions in writing the tract may have been admirable; his exhortations, however, were no doubt imprudently expressed. The fact that Luther addressed both sides in the same pamphlet may have doomed any possibility of it being successful in stemming the tide of insurrection. The ambiguous tone of the tract was interpreted by the peasants to their advantage and served to stimulate rather than to pacify the insurgents. In fact, the document strikes one as definitely more favourable to the rebels than to their opponents. Be that as it may, Luther's train of reasoning did not convince the peasants. As far as they were concerned, he first seemed to state their case well and then decided to withdraw, telling them that unbearable as their lot might be, as Christians they had no right to overthrow the oppressive order because Christ taught submission to all authority, however tyrannical. As far as the nobles were concerned, the pamphlet seemed to them to strengthen their position considerably by admitting their right to rule over their subjects. On the one hand Luther thus merely threatened the nobles with the judgment of God, something which was not taken too seriously by the princes, and on the other counselled the peasants to be patient in the face of oppression. While the peasants were confused, the nobles saw clearly their course of action.

The disturbances continued to spring up in various localities.

When Luther learned that he was quoted in support of lawlessness and violence, he felt compelled to act more decisively. In April, 1525, he visited Eisleben and received much first-hand information concerning acts of violence committed by the peasants. He made a tour through the region, risking his life in an effort to restore peace. The situation, however, seemed to be out of hand; Luther's preaching to the peasants fell on deaf ears. In May he wrote from Seeburg to John Rühel in Mansfeld, urging him to use the sword against the rebellious peasants, "for those who take the sword must perish by the sword."[48] Frederick the Wise, who lay on his deathbed at the time the revolt gathered momentum, was still of a different opinion, advising his brother, who was to succeed him, to do all he could to pacify the insurgents and only as a last resort were they to be attacked.[49] Returning to Wittenberg, Luther determined to write another pamphlet treating the disturbances. On May 6 he wrote his *Against the Murderous and Plundering Bands Among the Peasants*[50] for which he has been severely criticized to this day.

In his *Against the Peasants* Luther indicts the rebels on three charges: They have broken their oath to the government, hence they are subject to arrest and trial; they have robbed and murdered, therefore they have deserved death both in body and soul; they cover all their sins in the name of Christian brotherhood, thereby blaspheming God and disgracing his holy name. Luther compares the peasants to a mad dog which must be destroyed lest it contaminate a whole community. He calls upon all people to flee from the rebels as from the very devil and urges the rulers to put away all scruples about inflicting the death penalty upon the obstinate. In his previous pamphlet the princes were a set of scoundrels for the most part; now they are God's ministers called upon to restore order. The princes are told that if they fall in this war they are true martyrs, whereas whoever is killed on the peasants' side will suffer forever in hell. In conclusion Luther enjoins all nobles to stab, beat, and strangle the peasants, for such strange times have come that a prince can more easily earn heaven through bloodshed than another through prayer.

From the circumstances in which the Reformer suddenly found himself, his attitude toward the rebellious peasants can be explained, but the sharp language he used cannot be excused and the wisdom of writing the tract may seriously be doubted. Luther must have known that the princes were winning on all sides and that the peasants were fighting against overwhelming odds. The burgomaster of Zwickau felt that the princes would have punished the rebels severely enough even without Luther's encouragement to do so. Luther of course had his reasons for writing so harshly against the rebels. Carlstadt and Müntzer with their gospel of radicalism and even violence were not to be trusted. Luther sincerely believed that they held destructive opinions and acted contrary to God's Word. Luther, moreover, suffered greatly from the accusations of his enemies that he was responsible for the Peasants' Revolt, an accusation of which he wished to clear himself. It has even been suggested that Luther was fearful that in view of his previous support of the peasants the nobles would withdraw from supporting him and the Reformation.[51] Whether this consideration entered his mind cannot be established. There is, however, some evidence to suggest that Luther was not so certain that the peasants would be defeated. In his *Against the Peasants* he writes that if the peasants should win the war, the nobles would have nevertheless fought and died with a good conscience.[52] It seems certain, then, that Luther's tract against the peasants had primarily theological considerations as its basis. In view of St. Paul's teaching concerning the function of secular governments, especially Romans 13, Luther was convinced that for subjects to rebel against the powers that be was a heinous offence against God and his instituted social and political order.

Luther's treatment of the rebellious peasants had serious effects for both Luther as a person and the future of the Reformation. Not only did the peasants and the enemies of the Reformer accuse Luther of flattering and supporting the nobles against the rebels, but also some friends found it difficult to understand the Reformer. Had he not, they asked, dismissed all kindness and mercy, and encouraged the bloodthirsty princes in their cruel slaughter? Had he not, by advocating gruesome deeds to merit heaven, betrayed his principle of justification by faith alone? Had he not betrayed those who quoted him in support of their actions? In July Luther decided to explain and justify what he had written against the peasants in a tract entitled *An Open Letter Concerning the Harsh Booklet Against the Peasants.*[53] In this pamphlet Luther emphatically states that he will not retract anything in his former booklet, and that it matters little whether it displeases men or not, as long as it pleases God. Whether one should be merciful or not is of little importance when the Word of God is plain concerning a certain issue. One cannot persuade a rebel with reason, for he will not listen to sense; these peasants must be answered with the fist until the blood gushes forth from their noses. That the nobles abused their power in punishing the rebels is none of his concern, for from him they have not learned it, and, what is more, they shall have to answer for their wickedness. He is far from flattering the princes; in the near future he shall write against them as well. Had the authorities listened to his persistent warning against the fanatical preachers before the war, all the misery, cruelty, and bloodshed could have been prevented.

Before the end of 1525 the main revolt was brutally subdued. The Reformer himself assumed that a word from him would have gone far to turn the tide in favour of the rebels. It was he, he said, who was responsible for the death of the peasants, "for I commanded them to be slaughtered." In May Luther wrote to John Rühel, who was moved with compassion toward the suffering peasants, not to take it too hard, for had God not judged the rebels, Satan would have done even more harm.[54] In another letter Luther again assured Rühel that God knows who among the peasants is guilty or innocent. If there are innocent people among the insurgents, God will save and protect them. Most of them, however, are without any sense and therefore they must be punished. If one wishes to pray for the peasants, one should pray that they might become submissive to the authorities. If they refuse to obey, no mercy should be shown them.[55] When the nobleman Heinrich von Einsiedel was troubled in his conscience about the *corvees* and heavy dues which the peasants continued to pay after the war, he asked Luther for advice in the matter. The Reformer replied that the "common man" ought to have burdens imposed upon him, for otherwise he would become overbearing. And commenting in one of his sermons on slavery in Abraham's time, Luther stated, "It were even a good thing were it still so. For else no man may compel nor tame the servile folk."[56] In his booklet *On Whether Soldiers can be Saved*, Luther wrote in 1526: "I am almost inclined to boast that since the time of the apostles the temporal sword and government have never been so clearly described or so highly praised as by me. Even my enemies must admit this. But the sincere gratitude I have thereby earned as a reward is this that my doctrine is reviled and condemned as seditious and as striking at the government."[57]

The suppression of the Peasants' War had unfortunate effects on the Lutheran Reformation movement. By taking a decisive stand against the peasants, Luther no doubt kept the support of many nobles and thus assured the continued success of his movement. But the peasants' hope that Lutheranism would become the means of effecting a social and political reformation was blasted, and as a result the Reformation ceased to be a popular movement. The peasants and many who sympathized with the lot of the oppressed were bitterly disillusioned and hopelessly alienated from all that Luther stood for. Southern Germany, where the war had raged most, either remained faithful to Roman Catholicism or else diverted to Anabaptism, which in 1525 began to spread rapidly. There seems to be evidence that the Anabaptists used the peasants' defeat as propaganda for the furtherance of their type of Christianity.[58] It is undeniable that the failure of the peasant movement in 1525 drove many simple folk into the arms of Anabaptism. Luther had thus played into the hands of his dissenters. It must be reiterated, however, that once Luther was convinced that his attitude and actions with regard to certain issues were in accord with the Word of God, he did not consider the consequences. And he was absolutely certain that rebellion against constituted governments was from the devil. Because of his conviction in this regard, he could not apologize for what he had written against the peasants, not even for the harshness with which he had expressed himself. It is only to be regretted that Luther viewed the whole Anabaptist movement against the background of Carlstadt, Müntzer, and the Peasants' Revolt. He was no doubt aware that there was also a peaceful, a more evangelical wing of Anabaptism, but his experiences with the radicals up to 1525 prevented him from viewing the dissident groups objectively.

CHAPTER IV

LUTHER AND THE EVANGELICAL ANABAPTISTS

Origin and Spread of Anabaptism

There are three main views concerning the origin of sixteenth-century Anabaptism. The oldest view is represented by Karl Holl who believed that Anabaptism originated with the Zwickau prophets and Thomas Müntzer. It has been shown that while these prophets advocated the abolition of infant baptism, there is no evidence to suggest that they rebaptized adults.[1]

Another view holds that Zürich, Switzerland, was the cradle of the Anabaptist movement. It has been established that the first adult (believer's) baptism during the Reformation was performed in Zollikon, near Zürich, on January 21, 1525. After a group Bible study, George Blaurock asked Conrad Grebel to baptize him with what he called the true Christian baptism. Grebel, although not ordained to the ministry, performed the rite, and Blaurock in turn baptized Grebel, Felix Manz, and others. On the same night the first Anabaptists were banished from Zürich.

A third, more recent, view sees the beginning of Anabaptism in both Switzerland and Germany, pointing out that the German Anabaptists were more radical and fanatical than the Swiss Brethren, who were more quietistic and pious. In 1526 Balthasar Hubmaier, who had been in close contact with the Swiss Anabaptists, baptized Hans Denck of Nürnberg. In the same year Denck baptized his friend Hans Hut, who had been influenced by Thomas Müntzer's apocalyptic views. In the fall of 1526 the representatives of both Anabaptist wings met for a conference in Strassburg where their differences became apparent. Denck, a follower of the *German Theology*, emphasized faith and love in contrast to the Swiss Baptists' stress on the external Word of God and such rites as baptism and holy communion. The Swiss *Schleitheim Confession* of 1527 repudiated the south-German group because it inclined to mysticism and stressed the inner Word. Thus the two wings of the Anabaptist movement, while having had considerable contact with each other, had sprung up and followed their courses independent of each other.

Luther has been criticized for not differentiating clearly between such militant radicals as Thomas Müntzer and the peaceful Swiss Anabaptists. This criticism is unfair, for the Anabaptists themselves did not differentiate too clearly between the various groups among the radical reformers, and it cannot be denied that there was considerable contact between the various Anabaptists. Moreover, sixteenth-century writers do not present a uniform picture of the origin of the Anabaptists, thus leaving it to individuals to decide who the Anabaptists were and where they had come from. And these individuals, be they leaders or ordinary people belonging to one or the other religious persuasion, judged the Anabaptists on the basis of their experiences or contacts with them. Since there were no outstanding leaders among the Anabaptists it was difficult for contemporary writers to know exactly what the Anabaptists in the main believed or practised. Sebastian Franck, for example, mentioned none of the Swiss leaders by name; as far as he was concerned, such south-German Anabaptists as Balthasar Hubmaier, Hans Denck, and Hans Hut were the leading men of the movement. Urbanus Rhegius named Denck only as the distinguished leader. Luther and Melanchton, as we shall see, apparently did not know the Swiss Anabaptists very well and thought of the movement as having sprung from the Zwickau prophets, Carlstadt, and Thomas Müntzer. In this chapter we are primarily concerned with the relationship between Luther and the Swiss Anabaptists, or the peaceful or evangelical Anabaptists, as they are also called.

It is not within the scope of this study to deal with the break between Ulrich Zwingli, the Swiss reformer, and the Swiss Brethren. On the surface it seemed that the schism was caused by insignificant details, such as Conrad Grebel's opposition to usury and tithes, the use of leavened bread in holy communion, the mixing of wine with water, and others, all of which Zwingli regarded as unimportant matters. Grebel and his group looked upon Zwingli's indifference as a false forbearance towards Catholic practices. From reading the Bible, the Anabaptists had come to believe that more radicalism in these matters was needed. Zwingli, and Luther before him, considered it wisdom and prudence to move ahead slowly for the sake of the weak in the faith; Grebel looked upon this hesitation "as a spiritless slipping along, as a compromising yielding which was bound to result in serious danger to the cause of the Gospel."[2] But the fundamental issue in the dispute between the Swiss Anabaptists and the reformers was the question of a voluntary church composed of adult believers, which the Anabaptists advocated and the reformers rejected. Coupled with this was the conviction of the Anabaptists that the church was to be free and independent of the state, a principle which today has found wide acceptance. As will be shown, the above principles had wide ramifications. They involved such issues as Christian individualism, religious tolerance, political considerations, military service, and church discipline.

Until recently it was held that the Anabaptists came from the lower strata of society. While this may be true as far as their later history was concerned, in the initial stages of their development this was not so. Attempts have been made to trace the social background of the evangelical Anabaptists and it has been found that many of them came from the cities and that the leaders consisted of leading humanists (Grebel), priests (Menno Simons), monks, evangelical preachers (Michael Wüst), scholars (Felix Manz), and a few noblemen.[3] Economic considerations did not play an appreciable part in the rise of evangelical Anabaptism; in its inception the movement was purely religious. Even the first peasants, baptized by Anabaptist leaders, were more concerned about their relationship to God than earthly goods.[4] This is seen from their powerfully emotional conversion experience which resembled that of Luther and which was the direct result of the preaching of the first Anabaptists.[5] As a result of persecution the movement was soon deprived of its spiritual and intellectual leadership, thus leaving the radical reformers with largely uneducated lay preachers who, although sincere in their attempt to propagate the gospel, were unable to cope with the various burning issues affecting sixteenth-century Anabaptism. Furthermore, after the defeat of the peasants, the disillusioned masses listened eagerly to any preacher who promised them redemption in this world and the next. There is thus no doubt that in time the passionate preaching of the "hedgepreachers," as Luther called them, resulted in many instances in hatred of the nobility and the magistrates.[6] The culmination of this socio-religious movement was the erection of the Anabaptist kingdom in Münster.

Two forces caused the Anabaptists to spread rapidly in all directions. Persecution and the socio-economic element have been referred to already. Felix Manz was the first to be drowned by order of the Zürich authorities and with the approval of Zwingli. The rest of the early Swiss Brethren were able to escape death by fleeing, propagating their gospel wherever they went. The other force which caused the Anabaptists to spread was their inner urge to evangelize all men. In spite of persecution, suffering, and death, they felt God's call to convey their views and experiences to others. Luther himself had encouraged his followers to suffer and if necessary to die for the sake of the Christian gospel. In 1522 he had written: "The greatest work that follows from faith is that with my mouth I confess Christ, sealing that confession with my blood and, if it is to be so, laying down my life for it."[7] In 1523 he had stated that if there were not sufficient ministers to preach the gospel, lay Christians were required to assume this task, for obedience to the Word of God was supreme. When God calls, Luther stated in 1528, a Christian must be willing to forsake father, mother, relatives, the government, and the church.[8] When the Anabaptists followed Luther's teaching to the letter, the Reformer opposed them on the basis that the great commission of Christ to go into all the world to proclaim the gospel applied to apostolic time only; at present all men ought to remain in their particular calling. This does not mean that Luther negated his earlier pronouncements when faced with the practices of the Anabaptists. He was simply convinced that some men were called by God to the ministry of the church while others, lay members in the church, were to testify of God's grace in their particular calling without presuming to be preachers and thereby forsaking their station in life. The success of the "hedgepreachers" was phenomenal. As early as 1531 Sebastian Franck wrote: "The Anabaptists spread so rapidly that their teaching soon covered the land as it were. They soon gained a large following, and baptized thousands, drawing to themselves many sincere souls who had a zeal for God. . . . They increased so rapidly that the world feared an uprising by them though I have learned that this fear had no justification whatsoever."[9] The evangelical Anabaptists spread eastward along the Danube River, giving rise to the Hutterian Brethren, and northward along the Rhine Valley, influencing the Anabaptists in the Netherlands and Low German territories.[10]

Luther's Early Contact with Anabaptism

As late as 1528 Luther admitted that he knew very little about the Anabaptists and their teachings. In response to the question of what he thought about rebaptism, Luther wrote an open letter, *Concerning Rebaptism, A Letter to Two Pastors.*[11] In this tract he states that electoral Saxony is still free of such ministers as Balthasar Hubmaier who teaches perverse doctrines, and that until now he has had little occasion to think seriously about the matter of baptism. Since the Anabaptists confined their missionary activities to Hesse where Duke Philip tolerated them, Luther's knowledge of Anabaptism was of a second-hand nature, derived largely from such prejudiced persons as Melanchton, Urbanus Rhegius, and certain students who came to Wittenberg. Luther's admission that he did not know the Anabaptists shows that he differentiated to a certain extent between the Anabaptists on the one hand and the Wittenberg and Zwickau fanatics, with whom he was acquainted all too well, on the other. He believed with Melanchton, however, that the Zwickau prophets, Carlstadt, and Müntzer were responsible for the rise of the Anabaptist movement.

There is some evidence that Conrad Grebel wrote Luther a letter in September, 1524. The letter has been lost, but Grebel announced his intention to write Luther to his brother-in-law Vadian, stating that he had found courage to admonish Luther for his leniency towards certain practices.[12] Grebel no doubt learned about Luther's attitude towards the radical Wittenbergers from one of Carlstadt's friends, Gerhard Westerburg, whom Carlstadt had sent to the Grebel group to announce his coming to Zürich. It is known that the Swiss resented the Reformer's treatment of Carlstadt.[13] In a letter to Müntzer, dated September 5, 1524, Grebel briefly summarized the content of his letter to Luther:

> I, C. Grebel, desired to write to Luther in the name of all of us to admonish him to desist from his forbearance which he is practising without the support of Scripture, and which he is promoting in the world and in which others are following him.... So I wrote in my name and of the other brethren to Luther and admonished him to desist from the false forbearance of the weak, which weak ones they themselves are.[14]

Luther received the letter, for Erhard Hegenwalt, a student at Wittenberg from 1524 to 1526, reported in a letter to Grebel early in 1525 that he had inquired whether the Reformer would answer Grebel's letter. Luther had replied that since he did not know how or what to answer Grebel, he did not intend to respond to the letter. Luther did, however, through Hegenwalt, convey greetings to the group in Zürich, expressing the hope that the Swiss would not think that he was "ill-disposed" toward them, although he disliked some of their ideas, no doubt their views on baptism and the Lord's supper.[15]

It was not long before the relations between Wittenberg and the Swiss Anabaptists clouded. Grebel and Hegenwalt continued to exchange letters on such subjects as the Holy Spirit, the call to preaching, the Lord's supper, and infant baptism. Hegenwalt admonished Grebel not to be radical on these issues, and began to group him with Carlstadt and other fanatics who denied the real presence in holy communion. He also announced that Luther at the time was writing a pamphlet on his understanding of the last supper which would destroy all the arguments of the enthusiasts. Then in March, 1525, Luther reported to Spalatin concerning some fanatics who had come from the Low Countries: "We have here a new sort of prophets come from Antwerp who pretend that the Holy Spirit is nothing more than the natural reason and intellect."[16] It is obvious from this account that these people were not evangelical Anabaptists, and Luther does not connect them with the Swiss or with Carlstadt. Toward the end of 1527 Luther characterized the Anabaptists as follows: "The new sect of Anabaptists is making astonishing progress. They are people who conduct themselves with very great outward propriety, and go through fire and water without flinching in support of their doctrines."[17] For Luther the good life and steadfastness of the Anabaptists was a trick of the devil to lead astray sincere Christian souls. It is not known whether Luther's description of the life of the Anabaptists came from his personal knowledge of these people or from what he had learned about them. From his letter to the two pastors it seems reasonable to assume that around 1527 Luther had very little first-hand knowledge concerning the evangelical Anabaptists.

When the Swiss reformers and the Anabaptists had joined Carlstadt in his attack upon the real presence, Luther released in 1527 a treatise entitled *That the Words "This is my Body, etc." Still Stand. Against the Enthusiasts.*[18] In this carefully argued thesis Luther laments over the fact that the various sects that oppose him pretend to base their teachings on the Word of God. As far as Luther is concerned, they are all united in persecuting Christ. All his writings, the Reformer states, are of no avail against the fanatics; they despise him and do not even bother to refute his arguments from Scriptures. Their great success in winning adherents stems from the devil who blinds the eyes of those who refuse to accept the plain truth. In writing against them he is not trying to convert them from their errors, which is impossible, but he wishes to enlighten the weak and save them from perdition, and to demonstrate to all that he has nothing in common with these enthusiasts who deny that Christ's presence is real in the last supper. Believing firmly in his heart that their doctrines are from the devil, he cannot help but condemn them. As soon as one looks disapprovingly upon the radicals, Luther mocks, they feel persecuted and heap upon themselves all the crowns of glory. It is they who begin the struggle with him and then accuse him of not keeping the peace. After all, who can keep peace when such vital issues as the real presence are at stake? Luther does not believe that the enthusiasts are wilfully evil, but as far as he is concerned, they are blind to such an extent that they cannot perceive the devil working in them. Luther feels sorry for them, for he knows that there are truly talented men among them. In conclusion Luther warns all cities which harbour such fanatics to be on guard against them, for while these people may have good intentions, they have no control over the spirit which works within them. "Müntzer is dead, but his spirit is not quenched as yet."

As late as 1528, three years after the Peasants' War, Luther still believed that the only weapon against the Anabaptists should be the Word of God. These people should not be burned or murdered; they should be allowed to believe whatever they wished.[19] Thus while Luther was convinced that all the Anabaptists had been influenced by Carlstadt and Müntzer, he was well aware of the fact that many of them rejected war and violence and were more concerned with spreading their gospel than with effecting social change by force. He believed, however, that the peaceful intentions of some Anabaptists could not be trusted, for false teachings lead easily to civil disobedience.

Anabaptism and Revolutionary Radicalism

Was Luther correct in believing that there was a direct connection between most Anabaptists and such radicals as Carlstadt and Müntzer? There is a tendency among some Mennonite historians and theologians to disown all those radicals of the sixteenth century who failed to conform to the ideals and practices of the Grebel group and of the Mennonites of today. They become quite apologetic in discussing such "marginal" figures of Anabaptism as Hans Hut, Ludwig Hätzer, and even Hans Denck. The possible connection between Müntzer and the Anabaptists has been of the greatest embarrassment in Mennonite historiography.[20] While the reformers' assertion that the Zwickau prophets were the founders of Anabaptism has no historical foundation, it is equally unhistorical to disclaim any direct influence of the revolutionary radicals on the evangelical Anabaptists. The whole radical movement was revolutionary in nature. Both the quietistic and the more extreme groups were desperate in their defensiveness as an outlawed movement. Even the Swiss Brethren were not wholly free from excesses and violent tendencies. For example, George Blaurock, one of the acclaimed leaders of the early Swiss Anabaptists, attempted on January 29, 1525, to usurp the pulpit from a Zwinglian pastor near Zürich. The attempt failed, but on October 8, in another church, Blaurock was more successful. He entered the pulpit while the pastor of the church was absent, told the congregation that he had been sent by God to preach to them, and then delivered his sermon. Such radicalism was one of the contributing factors leading to the scattering of the Anabaptists from Zürich and the arrest of George Blaurock, Felix Manz and some baptized farmers early in 1525.[21]

As we have seen, there were direct connections between the Swiss Anabaptists and the Wittenberg radicals. When Carlstadt was forced to leave the territories in which Luther's influence was dominant, he went to Basel and Zürich where he met the Swiss reformers and the Grebel group. His writings on the mass were well known to the Swiss Anabaptists and his views on the last supper accorded with those of the Grebel group. In an apparent attempt to please the Swiss Brethren, Carlstadt wrote a pamphlet against infant baptism.[22] But Carlstadt's influence was felt in Zürich in a more concrete way. In 1523 Ludwig Hätzer published in Zürich a tract against the use of images in churches. This initiated the iconoclastic campaign in that city led by Zwingli. The tract, as Garside has shown, depended wholly on the arguments of Carlstadt's pamphlet against images, published a year earlier in Wittenberg.[23] And a few years later Grebel was attracted to Carlstadt because this radical reformer had accomplished in Wittenberg what he and his group attempted to do in Zürich.[24]

It is doubtful whether Thomas Müntzer had any appreciable influence on the Anabaptists in Switzerland. The statement of Heinrich Bullinger, successor to Zwingli, that the Swiss Anabaptists made personal contact with this revolutionist is highly suspect of falsification of facts or of gross error at best; not even Zwingli, to whose advantage it would have been to discredit the Grebel group, charged the Brethren with any such connection.[25] It cannot be denied, however, that the Swiss Brethren sought to establish contact with Müntzer after they had read some of his theological writings on faith and baptism. In the name of the radical group in Zürich, Grebel wrote on September 5, 1524, a most interesting letter to Müntzer,[26] at the time minister of Allstedt. Although the letter did not reach Müntzer, the fact that it was written at all has been of considerable embarrassment to those who wish to disassociate themselves from this revolutionist. Opponents of the Anabaptist movement, on the other hand, have pointed to passages in the letter which seem to confirm their assumption that all radical groups were affected by the "spirit of Allstedt."

Harold Bender, in his excellent biography of Grebel, has quite conclusively shown that there is no substantial evidence to suggest that Conrad Grebel and his group ever met Müntzer personally. In interpreting Grebel's letter to Müntzer, however, he becomes somewhat emphatic in his attempt to show that "this source [the letter] is sufficient to decide once and for all" that even Müntzer's literary influence on the origin of the Swiss Brethren was non-existent.[27] Bender states further: "Those who insist on a close relationship between Grebel and Müntzer point to a few *isolated expressions* in the letter, in which Grebel praises Müntzer as a 'true and faithful herald of the Gospel', and as 'his faithful and dear fellow brother in Christ'."[28] Elsewhere in the biography Bender writes:

> The epistle has a peculiar double character. On the one hand it pays homage to Müntzer "together with Carolostadio" as "the purest

heralds and preachers of the purest, divine Word." On the other hand—*and this is its primary purpose*—it constitutes a *strong criticism* of Müntzer. In fact the whole epistle, except for the short introduction and the similarly short conclusion, is cast in the form of an admonition and instruction to Müntzer.[29]

Summarizing the relationship between the Swiss Brethren and Müntzer, Bender concludes:

> The best understanding of the relationship to Müntzer would be somewhat as follows: When the persecuted Brethren in Zürich who had been cast off by their "unfaithful shepherds", looked out of the darkness of their circumstances into the World and saw there other men such as Carlstadt and Müntzer, who had also been cast off by their leader Luther and had yet not lost heart, they likewise took new courage and hastened without much consideration or careful examination to make friends with them. Their reaction to their discovery of these men was primarily an emotional (not theological) reaction, and one that is easily understood psychologically in the light of their situation at that time.[30]

In an examination of Grebel's letter to Müntzer, the following questions should be kept in mind: Does the letter in fact prove that Müntzer's writings had no influence on the origin of Anabaptism? Was the letter "in essence a criticism of Müntzer's position"? Are Grebel's praises of Müntzer only a few "isolated expressions in the letter?" And if Grebel's response to Müntzer was "primarily an emotional reaction," why then should the letter be full of theological considerations and interpretations of certain biblical passages? A brief summary of Grebel's letter may indicate that the Swiss Brethren wished to convey more to Müntzer than mere instruction and criticism.

Grebel addresses Müntzer as follows: "To the sincere and true proclaimer of the Gospel, Thomas Müntzer at Allstedt in the Hartz, our true and beloved brother with us in Christ."[31] Having established the spiritual kinship between the Grebel group and Müntzer, the author proceeds to state the purpose of writing the letter: First, he desires to establish contact with the minister in Allstedt, requesting him "like a brother" to communicate with the Swiss Brethren by writing. Secondly, Grebel states that Christ, who is the master of all true believers, "has moved us and compelled us to make friendship and brotherhood" with Müntzer. Thirdly, he wishes to bring certain points to Müntzer's attention. And fourthly, Müntzer's "writings of two tracts on fictitious faith has further prompted" the Brethren to write the opponent of Luther. Grebel then points out that he and his group had deplored the "false forbearance" of the reformers before they knew Müntzer, but by his writings they were "more fully informed and confirmed," and it rejoiced them "wonderfully that we found one who was of the same Christian mind with us and dared to show the evangelical preachers their lack."

Grebel then objects to Müntzer's German version of the mass and the use of hymns in the worship service. Since the apostles nowhere in the Bible command us to sing, we ought not to do so; only those things should be observed which were taught and practised in Scripture. Detailed regulations are then given as to how the last supper is to be administered. Not in priestly garments; not by a minister but by a lay brother; not in "temples" but in houses; only worthy members may participate; ordinary bread is to be used. "The bread is nought but bread. In faith, it is the body of Christ and the incorporation with Christ and the Brethren . . . for the Supper is an expression of fellowship, not a Mass and sacrament." Apparently looking up to Müntzer as his spiritual superior, Grebel adds somewhat apologetically: "Let this suffice, since thou are much better instructed about the Lord's Supper, and we only state things as we understand them. If we are not in the right, teach us better."

Commenting on Müntzer's and Carlstadt's opposition to the Wittenberg reformers, Grebel has nothing but praise for the radicals: "Thou and Carlstadt are esteemed by us the purest proclaimers and preachers of the purest Word of God." Their opposition to Luther, and Müntzer's devotional pamphlets have, according to Grebel, fortified the Swiss Brethren and have instructed them "beyond measure us who are poor in spirit." Grebel continues: "And so we are in harmony on all points, except that we have learned with sorrow that thou has set up tablets, for which we find no text or example in the New Testament." The reference to singing and stone tablets containing the ten commandments, which Müntzer had set up in his church, indicates again the importance which some of the Anabaptists attached to seemingly insignificant practices.

Of greater significance is Grebel's reference to Müntzer's "opinion and practice" with regard to war. But strangely enough, this matter does not take up nearly as much space in the letter as the points concerning Müntzer's opposition to the evangelical preachers and the biblical teaching on baptism. According to Grebel, the gospel and believers are not to be protected by force of arms; the followers of Christ are sheep among wolves; they must suffer persecution; with the New Testament all killing has ceased among Christians. In a postscript to the letter Grebel states that he has heard that Müntzer has preached against the princes, "that they are to be attacked with the fist." If the report is true, Grebel admonishes Müntzer to cease from all such notions, particularly if he should fall into the hands of

Luther or Duke George of Saxony. "Then wilt thou be completely pure, who in other points pleasest us better than anyone in this German and other countries."

In conclusion Grebel rails against Luther who has made of the Bible "Bible, Bubel, Babel," encouraging Müntzer to defend himself with the Bible "against the idolatrous caution of Luther." "May God give grace to thee and us," Grebel ends his letter. "For our shepherds also are so wrath and furious against us, rail at us as knaves from the pulpit in public, and call us *Satanas in angelos lucis conversos*. We too shall in time see persecution come upon us through them." Grebel and his group sign the letter: "Thy brethren, and seven new young Müntzers against Luther."

Although Grebel's letter did not reach Müntzer, the fact that it was written and the nature of its content call for certain conclusions. It must be stated at the outset that in many important points Grebel and Müntzer were theologically far apart. On the question of a Christian's position with regard to physical force and war, Grebel and Müntzer stood diametrically opposed to each other. The realization that their beloved brother in Christ might in effect have advocated the killing of the godless filled the Grebel group with grave misgivings concerning their spiritual superior, hoping, however, that these reports might be rumours only. In reading the passages in the letter which address themselves to the question of the sword, one gets the feeling that the possibility of Müntzer's militaristic position is treated as a hypothetical problem. In the postscript to the epistle Grebel mentions that a "brother" has written about Müntzer's sermon against the princes, and then adds: "Is this true? If thou art willing to defend war—then I admonish thee by the common salvation of us all that thou wilt cease therefrom—." And in the letter itself the question of war is treated as a theological problem, alongside such subjects as suffering and persecution, the use of tablets and singing in the church, the Lord's supper, and baptism. In fact, the matter of baptism, for example, on which Müntzer had written and which pleased the Grebel group so well, takes up much more space in the letter than the concern that Müntzer might have unsound opinions about the Christian and bloodshed. After a lengthy explanation of what the Swiss believe concerning baptism, Grebel encourages Müntzer and Carlstadt to write forcefully against infant baptism, that "senseless, blasphemous form," which Luther and other "scholars" advocate.

It would seem, then, that Grebel's letter to Müntzer was primarily an attempt to make contact with a man who, like the Swiss Brethren, had the courage to oppose those leading reformers who, according to the radicals' thinking, did not go far enough with their reforms. Grebel's criticism of Müntzer is not the primary object of the letter, as Bender would have us believe, but an expression of a hope that the reports concerning the revolutionist might not be true. The letter, moreover, expresses a feeling of oneness and fellowship of work, struggle, and suffering amidst overwhelming odds. The Swiss Brethren reach out in an attempt to grasp the hand of a resolute leader and eventual conqueror, believing that in unity there is strength and victory. Grebel writes:

> Regard us as thy brethren and take this letter as an expression of great joy and hope toward you through God, and admonish, comfort, and strengthen us as thou art well able. Pray to God the Lord for us that He may come to the aid of our faith, since we desire to believe. And if God will grant us also to pray, we too will pray for thee and all, that we all may walk according to our calling and estate. May God grant it through Jesus Christ our Saviour. Amen.[32]

As Bender rightly points out, the Swiss Brethren knew Müntzer from his writings only, and that prior to the Peasants' War in 1525. It is thus quite likely that had Grebel known Müntzer's revolutionary views better, or had he believed the reports concerning him, the letter would have taken on an altogether different tone, or else it would have been left unwritten. But here we are in the realm of conjecture. If, on the other hand, Grebel believed the reports about Müntzer's views, it comes a bit as a surprise that the peace-loving Swiss Brethren still sought the fellowship and instruction of the preacher of Allstedt. No matter how one interprets the possible motives for writing the letter, this document will continue to haunt all those who wish to obliterate all evidence that might point in the direction of influential relationships between the evangelical Anabaptists and the fanatical prophet and war-lord Thomas Müntzer. This suggestion must be even more unsettling when there seems to be evidence that many sincere people, including some peace-loving groups, continued to sympathize with Müntzer even after his defeat and death. Some years after the Peasants' War some Hutterites, a branch of the evangelical Anabaptists, continued to regard Müntzer as a great and talented man who had taught men the living Word of God and its heavenly voice against the biblicism of the mainline reformers. He was not held responsible for the uprising among the peasants, and his death was looked upon as innocent blood.[33] How could this be otherwise when Müntzer had become the mouthpiece, however radical in his expression, of all those social and religious elements in sixteenth-century society which yearned for spiritual liberty and political and economic independence? It is thus remarkable that early Anabaptism was so restrained in the face of oppression and persecution. As Lowell Zuck puts it: "A remarkable aspect of early Anabaptism is thus not so much its occasional violence, as its frequent exhibition of sobriety and good sense amidst emotional upheaval and martyrdom."[34] Luther, as we have seen, distinguished to a certain extent between radicals like Müntzer and the peaceful Anabaptists. Since all radicals, however, had many points in common, such as their views on the Lord's supper, baptism, and certain issues on reform, he remained suspicious of all dissenting groups. The struggle which had ensued between him and such fanatics as Carlstadt and Müntzer, and his firm belief that he upheld the true Word of God against the "enthusiasts" who sought to destroy the souls of men, blinded his eyes to those individuals and groups who were equally sincere in their attempt to live according to the gospel.

Infant Versus Adult Baptism

The most distinguishing mark of the evangelical Anabaptists was their rejection of infant baptism and the practice of adult baptism or, as they called it, believers baptism. With this they not only challenged the prevailing practice of baptizing infants but also the belief in baptismal regeneration held by Catholics and Lutherans alike. The Anabaptists claimed that infant baptism was an invention of the pope, but this merely points up their ignorance of church history. The belief in the remission of sins in connection with the baptismal act can be traced as far back as the primitive church. Several fathers of the early church, including Ignatius of Antioch, Justin the Martyr, Tertullian, Cyprian, and St. Augustine, believed in baptismal regeneration.[35] Infant baptism seems to have been the rule from the fourth century on. That the practice, however, was in use before this is evident from the writings of Tertullian (A.D. 197). Since Tertullian did not believe in post-baptismal forgiveness of sins, he condemned pedobaptism, asking for a delay in baptism until adolescence or until after marriage.[36] He writes concerning the baptism of infants: "More caution is shown in earthly things. Should one entrust a heavenly possession to a person to whom one would not entrust an earthly?—Let them first understand to ask for salvation so that it may be granted to them at their request."[37]

In the fourth century several sects arose which attacked the sacraments, including baptism. The Donatists, believing that the validity of baptism depended on the moral character of the baptizer, rebaptized all those who joined them. St. Augustine called on the help of the civil power against the Donatists when his efforts to secure unity in the church failed. The Paulicians and the Jovinians rejected both infant baptism and baptismal regeneration. Baptism was to follow conscious faith in the redemptive work of Christ and was believed to be an outward sign of the inner transformation of the believer. The Jovinians were condemned as heretics by Jerome, St. Augustine, Ambrose, and by a Roman synod in A.D. 390.

In the twelfth century Peter de Bruys of France and Henry of Lousanne, a Cluniac monk, followed in the footsteps of the fourth-century heretics. Referring to the activities of these two men, Peter the Venerable lamented that wherever their influence penetrated, people were rebaptized, churches were profaned, altars were overthrown, and monks were compelled by force to marry. Arnold of Brescia, student and defender of Peter Abelard, led a similar radical movement in northern Italy. He also rejected the baptism of infants. By 1184 the Arnoldists had to some extent united with the Waldensians, who were not too clear on baptism. Some among the Waldensians rebaptized adults, others simply laid on hands instead of baptizing those who joined them, and still others practised infant baptism. Similarly the Bohemian Brethren, who arose shortly after the Hussite wars, practised both infant baptism and adult baptism.

The preceding historical sketch shows that opposition to infant baptism did not originate with the Anabaptists of the sixteenth century, and that opposition to Anabaptism was nothing new. As will be shown in another chapter, the old Justinian laws against rebaptizers were revived in the sixteenth century and enforced with the utmost severity.

The Anabaptists sincerely believed that their views on baptism were in harmony with the Word of God. For their belief they were willing to suffer persecution, exile, and martyrdom. Menno Simons, the leader of the Dutch Anabaptists, wrote: "We are driven only by a God-fearing faith which we have in the Word of God to baptize and to be baptized, and by nothing else."[38] In his booklet *Christian Baptism* (1539) Menno elaborates on three reasons for baptizing adults and not infants.[39] First, Christ commanded that faith should precede baptism; secondly, the apostles taught believers baptism; thirdly, the apostles practised adult baptism only. Conrad Grebel in his letter to Müntzer gives us a clear picture of what the Anabaptists believed concerning baptism. Before a person is baptized, Grebel writes, he must have faith in the redeeming work of Christ who forgives the repentant sinner. Water baptism is only a sign or symbol of what has taken place in the heart. "The water does not confirm or increase faith, as the scholars of Wittenberg say, and does not give very great comfort nor is it the final refuge on the death bed."[40] Baptismal regeneration is rejected by the Grebel group because it dishonours "faith and the suffering of Christ."[41] As far as unbaptized children are concerned, they will be saved without faith on the merit of Christ's death for them. Grebel condemns infant baptism as "senseless," "blasphemous," and "contrary to all Scripture."[42]

Luther did not quarrel much with the Catholic doctrine on baptism. He did not, however, believe, as the Catholics did, that after an individual had fallen into sin the effects of baptism were erased and the sinner had to perform certain works in order to come back to grace. Baptism, according to Luther, remains valid forever, for it is God's work and not man's.[43] But as far as the individual's faith was concerned, Luther emphasized time and again that baptism without faith did not save the individual. In 1522, in a sermon, he went so far as to say that baptism was "no more than an external sign to remind us of the divine promise."[44] Baptism without faith is useless, according to Luther: "It is like a letter to which seals are attached but in which nothing has been written. Therefore he who has the signs (which we call sacraments) and not faith has seals only, seals attached to a letter without any writings."[45] And in 1523 he wrote: "Baptism certainly does not justify without faith, but faith does justify without baptism; therefore no part of justification may be ascribed to baptism."[46] Moreover, since baptism signifies the drowning of the old man, Luther wrote in 1519, children should really be immersed in water. This is "demanded by the significance of baptism, for baptism signifies that the old man and the sinful birth of flesh and blood are to be wholly drowned by the grace of God."[47] While baptism, according to Luther's early views on the subject, does not automatically bring about a man's salvation, it signifies the washing away of sins and it demands that life of sanctification and faith must follow to validate one's baptism. Luther valued baptism so highly because he derived from it the principle of the priesthood of all believers. Baptism, according to Luther, makes all men equal before God, thus minimizing the sacerdotal function of the clergy.[48]

Luther's early views on baptism were modified when the Anabaptists appeared and began to erode the sacraments. Luther, as has been shown, reduced the Catholic sacraments to two, baptism and the Lord's supper. The sacramentarians attacked Luther's concept of holy communion, regarding the last supper as a mere memorial service, and the Anabaptists demoted the sacrament of baptism to a sign or symbol of what took place in a man's conversion to God. Luther began to realize that if the sacramentarians and Anabaptists succeeded in doing away with the sacramental nature of the two remaining sacraments, there would be nothing concrete or objective left to which his faith could be anchored. This is also the reason why Luther held on to the external concrete Word of God in opposition to Müntzer and other enthusiasts who stressed the spiritual, inner Word. In baptism Luther began to see more and more a means of *receiving* the grace of God, and this was best illustrated in the baptism of infants who are completely passive in this act of God. Little children cannot boast of having done anything to acquire God's gracious forgiveness; they simply receive freely what God has to offer them. On this point Luther agreed with St. Augustine who wrote: "In baptism there is remitted all our sin, not as if it no longer existed, but that it is not imputed."[49] For Luther this was a "beautiful saying," for it expressed his concept of baptismal regeneration.

The most concise and the best-known statement of Luther on baptism is that in his *Small Catechism* of 1529. Upon the question, "What does baptism give or profit?" the *Catechism* answers that baptism "works forgiveness of sins, delivers from death and the devil, and provides eternal redemption to all who believe this, as the words and promises of God declare."[50] It is not the water, the *Catechism* continues, which produces these effects, but the Word of God which is in and with the water, and faith which trusts the Word of God. Without the Word of God the water is just water and no baptism. But with God's word it is a baptism, that is, a water of life and a cleansing of regeneration in the Holy Spirit, as St. Paul states in Titus. Baptism signifies that the old man in us should, by daily repentance, be drowned and die with all sins and evil lusts, and that a new man should daily come forth and arise, who should live before God in righteousness and in purity.[51] Thus even after his encounter with the Anabaptists on the meaning of baptism, Luther maintained that there is no automatic salvation attached to the baptismal act, but that the faith and life of the baptized Christian ensured that the individual profited from the sacrament.

Upon the question of two Catholic clerics from southern Germany in 1528 as to what should be done with the Anabaptists who infested their regions, Luther found occasion to elaborate on the subject of baptism and the arguments used by the rebaptizers. In his open letter *Concerning Rebaptism* Luther accuses the Anabaptists of killing the souls of Christians by denying the sacramental value of baptism; even the papists are better in this, for they at least leave Christ to the people.[52] To baptize upon an individual's confession of faith, as the Anabaptists teach and practise, is ridiculous, for how can one be certain whether the person being baptized believes or does not believe? Such a baptism is actually a "baptism of adventure." One should not baptize upon faith but on the sure foundation of the Word of God. Luther believes that since infant baptism was practised ever since the beginning of Christianity, it should not be changed; he is certain that God would not have left Christians in the dark for so long about such an important matter as baptism. Furthermore, how can the Anabaptists say that children cannot have faith when there is no scriptural basis for such an assertion? Does not the Bible speak of young children praising God their Father, and did not John the Baptist leap in his mother's womb as a result of faith (Luke 1:41)? After all, is it not possible for Christ to implant saving faith in the hearts of infants? Infant baptism, in fact, is most beautiful, Luther continues, for little children are not required to exert any kind of effort or do any kind of work; they are completely free, sure, and blessed alone through the glory of their baptism. Just as the children of the Old Testament were received into the covenant of God through circumcision, so are the children of the new dispensation received into the covenant of Christ through baptism. Since Christ commanded his apostles to baptize all nations, he no doubt included the children as well. Moreover, just as faith remains with an adult in his unconscious condition, such as sleep, for example, in the same manner faith can begin in infants even though they are unaware of it. The objections of the Anabaptists that many priests did not believe in Christ's saving grace while administering baptism Luther refutes by stating that the validity of the sacraments does not depend on the moral character of the person administering them. It is the Word of God that is most important, not the human instruments through which the blessings flow. Since the Anabaptists must admit that infant baptism is not invalidated because children are baptized, but because, according to them, children do not believe prior to baptism, they should really work on the faith of individuals and leave the Word of God and the sacrament intact.[53] Judging from their gross errors, Luther concludes his pamphlet, it is evident that the Anabaptists are blasphemers of God and messengers from the devil. The arguments of the Anabaptists in favour of adult baptism do not convince the Reformer. Since they have no sound basis for what they believe and practice, they remain uncertain in their opinions. All they can do is hurl blasphemous names and expressions at those who believe in infant baptism, calling infant baptism "dog's bath," "a hand full of water," etc. And the devil knows that when the mad mobs hear blasphemies, they will believe more readily than when sound arguments are offered.[54]

The Anabaptists did not find Luther's arguments for the retention of infant baptism too convincing either.[55] Is it absolutely certain, they asked, that infants were baptized in apostolic times? The statement in Acts that whole households were baptized does not prove that little children were involved. Is it, moreover, true that

God would not allow gross errors to perpetuate themselves through the centuries? This, according to the Anabaptists, does not mean that the church was dead throughout the Middle Ages. There were great men of God who in spite of the general spiritual darkness lived by the Spirit of God. God honoured the faith and work of these exceptional Christians even though they were ignorant concerning the true baptism. Then came the Reformation in which attempts were made to bring back the church to its biblical foundations, including the right administration of the sacraments. The Anabaptists were in no doubt that adult baptism, in which faith precedes baptism, was the only biblical rite. Luther's argument from the Old Testament practice of circumcising all male children in support of infant baptism seemed far-fetched to the Anabaptists. And Luther's insistence that the Anabaptists could not be certain that the people they baptized actually believed, could not, as far as the Anabaptists were concerned, negate the biblical order of first believing and then baptizing, and not the other way around. Luther's attempt to prove that there is faith in infants from John the Baptist's "leaping" in his mother's womb seemed insincere or perhaps humorous at best. Menno Simons in his *Foundation of Christian Doctrine* (1539) expressed surprise at Luther's talk about a "dormant faith" in infants, of which the Bible had nothing to say: "If Luther writes this as his sincere opinion, then he proves that he has written in vain a great deal concerning faith and its power. But if he writes this to please men, may God have mercy on him."[56]

Although Luther pursued his later arguments on the subject along the lines outlined in his *Concerning Rebaptism*, there were other points which he emphasized as time went on. In his *Small Catechism* (1529) the Reformer stated, as we have seen, that it is not the water which saves the individual, but the Word of God which is attached to the sacrament and the person's faith which accepts the Word. In 1530 he wrote that if adults only should be baptized, most people would live like pagans until the time of their death before asking for baptism. Throughout their life they would thus fail to come to hear the Word of God, for non-Christians are indifferent to spiritual things. St. Augustine is for Luther a good example of this. This church father was not baptized until he was thirty years old, falling as a result into the grave heresy of the Manichaeans and other sins.[57] When the Anabaptists denied the sacramental nature of baptism, Luther in 1535 argued to the contrary, stating that baptism has all three requirements of a sacrament. It has the external element (water); it has the Word of God attached to the element; and, most important of all, it is backed by the command of Christ to baptize all people.[58] Since this is so, our faith or our unbelief do not affect the sacrament of baptism in any way. If the candidate for baptism believes, well for him; if he does not have faith and if he refuses to believe after his baptism, he will have received the life-giving sacrament for his own damnation. In a letter of December 17, 1534, to Prince Joachim of Anhalt, Luther asked the prince to stand sponsor on his daughter's baptism in order to help "the poor little heathen out of her sinful state by nature into the most blessed new birth."[59] This reference, together with statements in the *Small Catechism*, indicates that Luther believed in what has been termed baptismal regeneration. However, he never pressed this point, stating time and again, as we have seen, that a living faith is the best evidence of a regenerate life.

In Luther's struggle with the Anabaptists' position on baptism, two considerations need emphasis. First, Luther's quarrel with the Anabaptists was not primarily over the issue of infant versus adult baptism. We have seen that the Reformer himself had at first his doubts about infant baptism, and only later when the Anabaptists made a big issue over "believers' baptism" did Luther begin to defend the practice of baptizing infants. As we have seen from his pamphlet *Concerning Baptism*, he had not spent much time studying the Anabaptist position. Indeed, he may not have deemed the issue too important. His at times weak arguments in favour of infant baptism seem to support this assertion. Secondly, in Luther's arguments against what he considered to be errors in Anabaptist thinking with regard to baptism, the sacramental nature of baptism was more important to him than the question of whether one should baptize infants or adults. While still an Augustinian monk, Luther wrestled for assurance of certainty of salvation. Eventually he found this certainty in the promises of the written Word of God and in the sacraments which conveyed to him the grace of God. In all his doubts and spiritual struggles he came back to these external means of grace, claiming divine pardon and assurance of salvation. The Zwickau prophets and Thomas Müntzer had devalued the written Word of God, emphasizing in contrast the inner or spiritual Word; the sacramentarians had attempted to demote the sacrament of the Lord's supper to a mere memorial of Christ's death; now the Anabaptists considered the sacrament of baptism a mere sign of what happened spiritually in the life of believers. For Luther all this was a devilish conspiracy designed to rob Christians of their salvation and thus destroy the work of the Reformation and Christianity itself.

State Church Versus Free Church

While the right administration of baptism was important to the

Anabaptists, there was more to Anabaptism than mere adult baptism. More important than baptism was their concept of the church which of course was closely tied to adult baptism. From reading Luther's edition of the New Testament and from the Reformer's own teaching on the subject, the Anabaptists had come to the conclusion that the church must be composed of voluntary believers and hence separated from the state. Infant baptism was opposed to this concept of a free church, for it included all of society in the body of the church.

In his defence of the thirteenth thesis against Dr. Eck in 1519, Luther asserted that the church, the *Una Sancta*, is the communion of saints; those who truly believe belong to the church of Christ.[60] In 1520 he wrote that Christ is the head of the church and only believers are true members of the church. Although all things, including evil people, are subject to Christ, "Christ cannot be the head of an evil community," that is, Christ is the head of a holy community only.[61] In his "Lectures on Romans" Luther had spoken of the church as a persecuted remnant. Between 1522 and 1527 Luther even attempted to establish a church composed of earnest Christians, who not only professed the gospel but also lived it. He thought at first of entering the names of God-fearing people in a special book, thus separating them from the nominal Christians. He then proposed to be the minister of such a saintly group while someone else would serve the larger body of professing believers. Luther concluded, however, that he would not have a sufficient number of such dedicated people to realize his ideal.[62] It is difficult to say whether the princes would have tolerated such a church within the church.[63]

The idea of a separate church remained with Luther throughout his life. As late as 1538 he declared in a sermon that church and state must remain severed and separated from each other if the true gospel and the true faith are to be preserved. For the nature of the Kingdom of God is very different indeed from that of temporal government committed to princes and lords.[64] To carry out this principle Luther would have had to renounce all assistance from the secular princes, however well-meaning their motives, and rely completely on the power of the gospel in his reform drives. But to assure the course of the Reformation, particularly after the Peasants' War, Luther was compelled to accept the offered help of his followers among the nobility. The idea of such an alliance was not new. Ever since Constantine the Great church and state worked together off and on; the *Eigenkirchentum*, against which the church reformers of the eleventh century had fought, was a clear case of the church's subjection to the state; and the humanists' conception of a Christian state seemed to sanction the idea of the government's involvement in church affairs. Luther, however, was never quite at ease about the surrender of the evangelical church to the state. To explain somehow his awkward position, he began to call the evangelical princes "emergency-bishops" who were expected to assist in the work of the Reformation not because they were princes but because they were also members of the Christian church with special powers and authority. As soon as the circumstances would be more settled, these princes would step back from their involvement in church affairs and leave the spiritual government to the clergy.[65] This position led Luther to speak of an "invisible church" which manifested itself in the preaching of the pure gospel and in the right administration of the sacraments, and not necessarily in the faith and redemptive life of a Christian community. His early ideals concerning a church composed of believers only had given way to practical considerations.

In contrast to Luther's "invisible church" and his increasing co-operation with secular authorities, the evangelical Anabaptists sought to follow the Reformer's ideal of separation between church and state to its logical conclusion. They desired to establish a concrete, visible, and pure church composed of voluntary believing members. According to the Anabaptists, Constantine the Great had brought about the fall of the apostolic church by uniting it with the state. Most of the Anabaptists agreed that Luther and the other mainline reformers had begun to restore the early church; however, the task was abandoned by them and then taken over by the radical reformers. The signs of a truly restored church, according to Anabaptist sources, are the following: a community of voluntary believers who have become members of that community by repentance, faith, and adult baptism; an unadulterated pure doctrine; a scriptural administration of the sacramental signs (the ordinances of baptism and the Lord's supper); true discipleship (*Nachfolge*); willingness to suffer persecution and martyrdom; a brotherly love for each other which sometimes manifests itself in a community of goods; and complete withdrawal from the state and the world.[66]

The Anabaptists' withdrawal from the world and the state drew upon them the suspicion of the mainline reformers and magistrates who accused them of conspiring against the secular powers. The Peasants' War, the fact that most of the later Anabaptists belonged to the lower strata of society, and the Anabaptist kingdom in Münster seemed to give ground for believing that at heart every Anabaptist was a rebel. The evangelical Anabaptists were most submissive to the secular powers, basing their obedience to the state upon the teaching of the New Testament. They believed that God had instituted secular governments in order to preserve law and order, and that all true

Christians are indebted as children of God, for love's sake, to give to the outward powers all obedience and submission. As one Anabaptist treatise put it: "All outward matters, even life and body, are subject to the outward powers, only the true faith in Christ may not be compelled or conquered."[67] When the Swiss Brethren were accused of disturbing the peace, Grebel and his group denied it categorically. And from Grebel's letter to Müntzer we have seen how the Swiss Anabaptists felt about violence and war. A document written in 1529 by one Clemens Adler gives some reasons why the Anabaptists did not take up arms against others:

> For the love of Christ they [Christians] love their enemies, do good to them and pray for them, as Christ teaches them, and thus hearken to the voice of their shepherd. Even if the world rises up against them, yet they rage and storm against none; and if the world lifts up its sword against them, yet they take no sword against it nor against anyone, for they have made their swords into plow shares and their spears into pruning hooks.[68]

Even for self-defence many Anabaptists refused to carry a weapon. Luther is reported in his *Table Talks* as saying: "The Anabaptists are desperate and wicked fellows. They do not carry weapons and they boast of their great patience."[69]

Having surrendered some of his early ideals to practical necessity, particularly in the realm of church-state relations, Luther began to look with contempt upon the Anabaptists' attempt to maintain a free and pure church. "Where they want to go," Luther said of Anabaptist church discipline, "I am not disposed to follow. God save me from a Church in which are none but the holy."[70] In a sermon on the wheat and tares from Matthew 13:24-30, Luther compared the Anabaptists with the Cathari and Donatists of old who also had attempted to establish a pure church. This, according to Luther's interpretation of the parable, was quite impossible. The saints from Adam on have always had wicked people within their ranks; even Christ had tolerated Judas among the twelve disciples.[71] Although Luther's changed position with regard to church and state matters is understandable in view of the circumstances, his attitude toward the Anabaptists who worked hard toward establishing a New Testament church as Luther himself had at first envisioned it and who were willing to pay for their ideal with their lives can hardly be justified. The least the Reformer could have done was to maintain a discreet silence on the subject. It may have been his uneasy conscience which caused him to justify his position and negate the Anabaptists' teaching and practice in this regard.

Dogma Versus Morals

The Anabaptists believed that Luther's great emphasis on justification by faith alone frequently led to loose morals among the Lutherans. The evangelical Anabaptists agreed with the Reformer that man is saved by the grace of God, but they repudiated his idea of an enslaved will and maintained that a justified person had to bring forth good works to make good his salvation. This gave Luther occasion to brand the Anabaptists as Romanists, but it was for him difficult to deny that there often was a marked difference between their ethical life and that of his followers.

Luther was not indifferent to the practical life of his adherents. As early as 1521 he wrote to the Wittenbergers that it was necessary to live according to one's faith and not only to talk about it.[72] From time to time he stressed that to teach the right doctrines will be of no avail if the godly life did not follow. In a sermon of September 14, 1538, Luther declared: "Believe me, Christ did not come that you might remain in your sins and damnation; for you will not be saved if you do not stop sinning. To be sure, sins are forgiven; but you must stop being a miser, an adulterer, or a fornicator."[73] In 1546, shortly before his death, Luther emphatically declared that it is impossible to reach heaven without having seriously striven for sanctification here on earth.[74] A good case could be made that all of Luther's theological studies and sermons were directed to man's practical living of the gospel. Luther was against "works" only in so far as they tended to minimize the grace of God in man's experience of salvation.

Luther believed that the Catholic church had neglected to teach salvation by grace alone and instead had emphasized "works of men." In 1520 he wrote Pope Leo X that he had no dispute with anyone concerning morals but only concerning the word of truth. In 1521 he wrote concerning his Catholic opponents: "Whether you are good or bad does not concern me. But I will attack your poisonous and lying teaching, which contradicts God's Word."[75] In 1524 he wrote to certain princes that he would have had little to do with the papists had they taught aright; their wicked life did not matter to him.[76] Luther believed that if justification by faith were stressed a sanctified life would follow, for a justified person was sanctified by Christ and empowered to live a holy life. Luther knew that even after his justification in Christ, man remained sinful. But according to the Reformer this sinfulness was not held against the individual whose sins were forgiven and who now lived in a state of Christ's grace. To put it in the words of Luther: "Our doctrine is pure because it is a gift of God. But in our life there still is something sinful and punishable. However, this is forgiven and not imputed. It is not put on the books against us; but *remissio peccatorum* (remission of sin) is placed over it, and the sin is wiped out."[77]

It is undeniable that Luther's followers often negated with their lives what the Reformer believed and taught, and it is possible that Luther's strong emphasis on the principle of justification by faith alone contributed to a lack in the realm of Christian ethics. In 1522 the Bohemian Brethren were much interested in the Reformation in Germany, but they found fault with the discipline and the moral life among the Lutherans. When they complained to Luther about this, the Reformer was annoyed at their plain speaking but promised to do something about the moral laxity among his followers.[78] In 1524 Staupitz wrote to Luther, pleading with him not to disregard the moral aspect of Christianity: "I see that countless persons abuse the gospel for the freedom of the flesh." The poet Hans Sachs, a strong supporter of Luther, addressed the Lutherans in 1524 as follows: "There is much cry and little wool about you. If you have no use for brotherly love, you are no disciples of Christ. If you were really evangelical as you profess to be, you would lead a godly life like the Apostles."[79] Melanchton pointed out in 1525 that the "common people adhered to Luther only because they think that no further religious duty will be laid upon them."[80] In 1530 Luther blamed his "lazy and indifferent" ministers for the people's utter disregard for the sacraments. "The longer we preach the gospel," he lamented, "the deeper the people plunge into greed, pride and luxury."[81] These examples and quotations could be multiplied. The bigamy of Philip of Hesse and Luther's embarrassing involvement in the case are well known and need not be recounted.[82] In some instances even ministers were permitted to divorce and to remarry with the Reformer's consent. Michael Kramer, for example, married three times "because he could not be without a wife."[83] The Luther principle of justification by faith alone was admittedly often abused by those who had no desire to follow the Christian principles of living. An evangelical divine wrote in 1871: "Justification by faith is made to cover, in advance, all sins, even the future ones .... Hence we see not seldom the justified and the old man side by side, and the old man is not a bit changed."[84] This was no less true in the sixteenth century than it was in the nineteenth. For Luther, however, this was a perversion of the gospel and of his teaching.

Luther knew that the moral life of some of his followers left much to be desired, and he did not find it difficult to acknowledge the well-meant criticism of his friends. But when the Anabaptists began to attack not only the life of the Lutherans but also the doctrine of justification by faith, which they believed underlay this moral laxity, Luther defended his position and in doing so went at times to extremes. The Anabaptists' attack on the dogma and morals of Lutheranism is best of all represented in the charge of Menno Simons. He wrote: "For with the same doctrine [justification by faith alone] they have led the reckless and innocent people, great and small, city dweller and cottager alike, into such a fruitless, unregenerate life, and have given them such a free rein, that one would scarcely find such an ungodly and abominable life among Turks and Tartars as among these people."[85] Alfred Coutts, interpreting the Anabaptists' opposition to the Reformation, writes: "Just as Luther had traced all the moral chaos of his time to the errors of Rome, so the spiritual reformers found the explanation of the moral and spiritual degeneration of the Reformation age in the doctrinal errors of the Reformed Church."[86] The criticism of the Anabaptists, according to Luther, was a sure sign of their lack of the Holy Spirit, for the Spirit condemns false doctrines only and is patient with those who are "weak in the faith."[87] In a sermon in 1533 Luther warned his listeners against the apparent godly life of the Anabaptists. The Anabaptists are like wolves in sheep's clothing. They do not curse, they despise the outward necessities of life, they pray and read the Word of God, they are patient in suffering and not vengeful against their enemies. All this is good and worthy of emulation. But one must be on guard against thinking that their outward piety is proof that their doctrines are correct. Luther lists what he considers are their errors. They rely on their good works; they make God a liar by negating their first baptism and by baptizing again; they teach that in holy communion there is nothing but bread and wine; they destroy the concept of marriage by insisting that the believing partner separate himself from the unbelieving spouse; they teach that it is sinful to own property; they despise the governments as non-Christian institutions. In summary: they turn upside-down and destroy the three divine orders: the church, the state, and the household.[88] In another sermon in the same year Luther states that the Anabaptists deny both the Christian faith and good works. According to the Reformer, they do not believe in the sacramental value of baptism and holy communion, thus withholding from themselves and others divine forgiveness, and in their zeal to preach their gospel they forsake their wives and children, thus robbing themselves of all good works, for whoever casts off his own has no one to show his Christian love to.[89] It is significant to note that Luther did not accuse the Anabaptists of fanaticism, murder, and other crimes, as did the Swiss reformers. Luther thus differentiated between people like Müntzer and the Anabaptists. He acknowledged the outward piety of the Anabaptists, but believed that this piety was intended to lead astray sincere and unsuspecting Christians.

The piety of the sixteenth-century Anabaptists is reflected in many documents. Philip of Hesse wrote to his sister, the Duchess Elizabeth of Saxony: "I found more goodness in those so-called 'Enthusiasts' than in those who are Lutherans."[90] Erasmus wrote to the Archbishop of Toulouse in 1529: "The Anabaptists are to be commended above all others for the innocence of their lives." And again: "This sect so hated contains many persons of better life than the separated factions. They preach repentance; they summon all men to amendment of life; they follow the example of the Apostles."[91] Franz Agricola, a Roman Catholic, wrote in his *Against the Terrible Errors of the Anabaptists* (1582): "As concerns their outward public life they are irreproachable. No lying, deception, swearing, strife, harsh language, no intemperate eating and drinking, no outward personal display is found or is discernible among them, but only humility, patience, uprightness, meekness, honesty, temperance, and straight-forwardness in such measure that one would suppose that they have the Holy Spirit of God."[92] Yet the irony of it all is that the Christian life of the Anabaptists was held against them, and that Luther and the other evangelical ministers condemned in the Anabaptists those traits which they themselves had at first advocated. As the Swiss Brethren lamented:

> The ministers of the established church at first have taught this evangelical doctrine, and some of them teach it even today, that one should abstain from sin, lead a pious, irreproachable Christian life, be born of God and regenerated, manifest Christian love, follow Christ, bear the cross . . . forsake home, property, wife, children, etc. . . . And now, when we by God's grace desire to do, believe, teach, and live, in accord with their first teaching, we are to them an abomination, they cannot tolerate us, they defame and reproach us in this our Christian faith . . . as if it were heretical and erroneous.[93]

Luther, as we have seen, was not indifferent to the question of ethics among his followers. He had preached and written concerning the necessity of "good works" in the life of those who claimed to have experienced the grace of God, as the Anabaptists themselves admitted. In the light of this it is sad that he failed to appreciate the sincere attempt of the Anabaptists to put that into practice which he himself preached. And Luther had to agree that in the realm of discipleship the Anabaptists often put the Lutherans to shame. To believe, however, that Luther deliberately misrepresented the motives of the Anabaptists in an attempt to either justify the often loose living of his followers or to warn people against what he considered their errors is to misunderstand the Reformer and the real issues involved. Just as Luther in his break with Rome was not primarily concerned with the alleged lack of ethics among Catholics, so he was not overly impressed with the pious living of the Anabaptists. He realized that doctrine led to conduct; but he also knew that right conduct was not necessarily a sign of right doctrine. And right dogma mattered to Luther more than right living. Thus when he examined the beliefs of the Anabaptists and found that they contradicted his understanding of the Word of God on the most vital points in his theology, he did not doubt for a moment that the devil used the piety of the Anabaptists to lead astray sincere souls. The Anabaptists' emphasis on discipline and good works detracted, as far as Luther was concerned, from the cardinal doctrine of the New Testament: justification through God's grace alone. Luther feared that as soon as the human element received priority in the Christian life—and in Anabaptism he believed that it did—it would lead to pride and to minimizing God's work in the life of individuals. That Luther's emphasis on *sola fide* often contributed to a disregard of discipline and good morals among Lutherans, and that his belief in the enslaved will was sometimes used as a pretext for carnal living, cannot be denied. Luther castigated this carnality among his own. But on the issue of doctrine and works Luther remained clear and consistent to the end. Man is saved and sustained by the grace of God; good works are evidence of the grace of God in individual lives and expressions of gratitude for what God has done in Christ. Ironically, the Anabaptists believed similarly, but they tended to emphasize the necessity of Christians to live for the glory of God. This difference in emphases between Luther and the Anabaptists blurred the issue of dogma versus practical living. Had both sides been patient with each other they would have been able to see that the Lutheran and Anabaptist positions were not mutually exclusive.

CHAPTER V

LUTHER AND THE REVOLUTIONARY ANABAPTISTS

When the Anabaptists erected their kingdom in Münster, Westphalia (1534-1535), Luther's response seemed to be that of "I told you so." He regarded the developments in Münster as the logical outcome of what most Anabaptists believed and practised. Linking the Münsterites with Carlstadt and Müntzer, his attitude toward all Anabaptists and dissidents began to harden. Luther regarded the revolutionary activities of the dissident groups as God's punishment for the sins of Germany and the devil's attempt to destroy the Reformation. The Münster episode is important to our study in that it contributed to Luther's final assessment of the entire Anabaptist movement. Up to 1534 Luther still seemed to differentiate between revolutionary enthusiasts like Müntzer and the more peaceful Anabaptists. After Münster he tended to lump all Anabaptists together and began to counsel severe measures against them. Luther's final assessment of the Anabaptist movement persisted till the mid-nineteenth century when the Catholic historian C. A. Cornelius disentangled the threads and showed that the Münster episode was not characteristic of all the Anabaptists.[1] It is the purpose of this chapter to briefly sketch the development of the Anabaptist kingdom in Münster, to show Luther's attitude toward the Münsterites, and to consider any possible connections between the fanatics of Münster and the evangelical Anabaptists.

The Anabaptist Kingdom in Münster

The Anabaptist movement in Münster stood in closest relation to the unrest of the time in general and the revolutionary tendencies within the city in particular. With a population of about 15,000, Münster was a major city in Westphalia. The Bishop of Münster was also civil ruler in his bishopric. Since the city enjoyed a large measure of self-government, radical changes were possible almost at any time. As early as 1525, during the time of the Peasants' War, the populace of Münster began to demand improvements in economic, social, and religious conditions. The craftsmen and merchants of the city, organized in seventeen guilds, were properly represented in the council. Being quite powerful, no important measures could be passed without their consent. It was the guilds with the support of the city mob who later gained control over the council and the bishop.

One of the priests of the city, Bernt Rothmann, began in 1530 to advocate anti-Catholic reforms. He had been educated with the Brethren of the Common Life at Deventer, where he had also become acquainted with the New Testament. In 1531 he visited Wittenberg, the headquarters of Lutheranism, and thence he went to Strassburg where he was the guest of some Zwinglian reformers. Upon his return to Münster, Rothmann began to preach with great success, so that the St. Maurice Church became too small to hold the audiences and a pulpit had to be erected outside the church. The council gave Rothmann strict orders to preach inside the church only, but the enthusiastic preacher disregarded the council's ruling. When the bishop outlawed Rothmann on January 7, 1532, the preacher asserted his Catholic orthodoxy. A few weeks later, however, he published a confession in which he defended Lutheran doctrines and advocated the establishment of a new state church along Lutheran lines. Hermann Knipperdolling, a cloth merchant and prominent member of the council, and a mob supported Rothmann in his defiance of the council and the bishop. On August 10, 1532, all the churches of the city, with the exception of the cathedral, were in the possession of the Lutheran radicals.

Before the close of the year 1532 a split occurred in the ranks of Rothmann's followers. The preachers began to favour Zwinglian and Anabaptist views on the last supper, whereas others continued to uphold the Lutheran standard. Luther in a letter to the Council of Münster warned against tolerating Zwinglian and similar heresies,[2] but it was no longer in the power of the magistrates to silence Rothmann. Through the influence of Heinrich Roll, who had come to Münster from nearby Wassenberg, a Melchiorite[3] centre, Rothmann's faction began early in 1533 to advocate certain Anabaptist views. Infant baptism was repudiated and adults were rebaptized. Within a brief period of time approximately 1,400 people submitted to baptism. According to C. A. Cornelius, the newly baptized renounced all worldliness, practised communion of goods, led good moral lives, and lived simply and piously.[4] However, the Anabaptist principle of non-resistance was absent; the factions warred with each other, opposed the established order, defied the council and the bishop, and, like the Wittenbergers before them, insisted on the layman's right to participate in church reform. With the assistance of the ever-increasing number of refugees who flocked to Münster from all parts of the empire, the city was by the end of 1533 in complete control of the radical reformers.

Jan Matthys, from Haarlem in the Netherlands, had kept for some time an eye on the affairs in Münster. Similar to Thomas

Müntzer, Matthys claimed to be directly inspired by God and to receive divine revelations. After the example of Christ, he sent twelve apostles into the world, ordering them to baptize and to preach that no Christian blood ought to be spilled any longer, for the Kingdom of God was at hand. On January 5, 1534, Bartholomaus Boekebinder and Willem de Kuiper, two of Matthys' followers, arrived in Münster. On their way from Amsterdam they had preached about the worthy example of the faithful in Münster who had taken matters into their own hands. In their preaching they encouraged the people to look forward to the great salvation and peace on earth when none would be persecuted for practising adult baptism. Rothmann was greatly strengthened by the arrival of the prophets. On January 13 another apostle of Matthys, John of Leyden, a tailor, arrived in Münster, and in February Jan Matthys himself appeared. The council at this time still feebly urged moderation and tolerance, but on February 23, at the regular election of the council, Knipperdolling was elected burgomaster. Fearing the worst to come, many Catholics and Lutherans left the city.

For Jan Matthys the time had come to disclose his plans for the defeat of the remaining unbelievers in Münster. Knipperdolling warned him that these rash measures would prove fatal for the new movement. Matthys was finally persuaded to lengthen the days of grace to March 2, giving the "godless" an opportunity to leave the city. Many fled; others received baptism, not from conviction but as a matter of expediency. By March 2, 1534, it was believed that the city was free of all opposing elements, and church and state were united with Matthys at the head. A blacksmith who dared to call the prophet a deceiver was killed by Matthys himself. While the Münsterites established their kingdom within the city, Franz von Waldeck, the Bishop of Münster, led the siege outside the city walls. Believing that he had received a vision from God, Matthys led a small band of warriors against the besiegers on April 5, 1534. He died in the attack.

After the death of Matthys, John of Leyden assumed the desired leadership of the faithful. The city council was abolished and twelve men were ordained to be "the elders of the twelve tribes of Israel." The city was turned into a well-organized military camp, with John of Leyden looking after the details of operation. The new Zion proved its strength when the besiegers, on May 25, 1534, made an attempt to take the city by storm. The attack failed, with many of the bishop's forces killed while the Münsterites lost only a few men. Militarily strengthened in his position, the youthful prophet introduced polygamy, married the widow of Jan Matthys, although he was married at the time, and soon was the husband of seventeen wives. The innovation was looked upon with horror by the better elements of the city, but the prophet argued from the practices in the Old Testament that polygamy was biblical, and threatened to punish those who opposed him on the matter. Rothmann, who practised polygamy on a slightly more moderate scale than John of Leyden, also defended the excesses on the grounds of the Old Testament. On July 29, 1534, 200 men seized the prophet, Rothmann, and Knipperdolling, demanding that they abolish polygamy in the city. The men were overpowered by John's friends, the prophets were set free, and a terrible bloodbath followed. Once again in command of the situation, and after another success against the enemies outside the city, John of Leyden proclaimed early in September, 1534, that he was to become the new King David in Zion. He surrounded himself with an imposing court, converted priestly garments into regal robes, erected a throne in the market place, and made his favourite wife, the widow of Jan Matthys, the queen. People sank to their knees wherever the king appeared; his authority was complete and unopposed.

Toward the end of 1534 fate turned increasingly against the Münsterites. The bishop and his allies fortified their position and disease and famine caused untold hardships within the city. The new king promised salvation from above, tried to amuse the hungry people with dances, music, and theatrical performances, but all to no avail in the long run. In the spring of 1535 old men, women and children began to leave the city for the enemy camp where many were executed while others were pardoned after recanting their errors. On July 24, 1535, the city was betrayed and taken by the combined forces of the bishop, Cologne, and Hesse. Approximately 4,000 Münsterites, including Rothmann, were slaughtered. John of Leyden, Knipperdolling and others were imprisoned only to await torture and execution half a year later. The kingdom of the Anabaptists had come to a tragic end.

Luther's Attitude Toward the Münster Episode

At first Luther was not too perturbed about the rising unrest in Münster. Rothmann's reform drives, his views on church and government, and the declining influence of Catholicism in Münster must have given the Reformer great satisfaction.[5] When Rothmann, however, inclined to the Anabaptists' views on the last supper, Luther became suspicious of the developments in Münster. On December 21, 1532, he wrote a letter to the Council of Münster in which he warned against the Zwinglian and Anabaptist teaching concerning the sacrament of holy communion.[6] With reference to

Rothmann he wrote: "God has given you fine preachers, especially Bernhard Rothmann; yet they need to be admonished, for the devil can lead astray good, pious, and scholarly preachers." Such people as Müntzer, Hätzer, Huth, and Hubmaier have been punished by God for their erroneous views concerning the sacrament, Luther stated, and many have deviated from the faith by becoming Zwinglians, Anabaptists, and rebels against the secular authorities. But the news from Münster continued to be discouraging. The Münsterites denounced both the pope and Luther as "Twin Prophets of Wickedness." Luther began to conclude that "Münster was reaping the whirlwind of all the storms which the older fanatics had unleashed."[7] Luther's personal letter to Rothmann on December 23, 1532, in which he pleaded with the preacher to be moderate and to guard his congregation against the influence of the sacramentarians, was to no avail.[8]

Luther wrote two missives against the Anabaptists of Münster in the form of prefaces, one to Rhegius' *Confutation of the Münster Confession*[9] and the other to *News from Münster*.[10] In the first preface Luther refers to the charges of the Anabaptists that he is a false prophet, worse than the pope, and to the charge of the papists that he is the cause of the existing sects. The devils, Luther points out, were also angels at one time, yet God cannot be held responsible for their apostasy, and just as the bees suck honey from a rose and the spiders poison, so does the church produce both pious and wicked people. And it should be remembered, Luther states, that all heretics came out of the church of Christ and not from paganism. Luther thus acknowledges to a certain extent his responsibility for the rise of the dissident sects, while showing that he and the radicals are basically strangers to each other.

In his preface to *News from Münster* Luther both censors and ridicules the Anabaptists' folly at Münster. The devil who attempts to set up a kingdom in Münster must be very inexperienced, an ABC devil who has not yet learned how to have success. In order to succeed, the devil should have put on a pious front, proclaimed days of prayer and fasting, taken no money from the people, eaten no meat, regarded all women as poisonous, shunned worldly amusements, and repudiated all recourse to force and violence. But to act as the devil does in Münster will deceive no one; the intent and the excesses of the evil one are too obvious. Of significance is Luther's comment on how the Anabaptists in Münster should be combatted. Luther feels that the best way to fight the devil is with the sword of the spirit, for the devil is a spirit and is thus not impressed with physical might.[11] The bishops and princes, however, instead of preaching the Word of God and thus winning the hearts of men, strangle and kill the bodies of their opponents and leave the souls to the devil. In conclusion Luther attacks the doctrinal errors of the Münsterites. First, he holds it against them that they deny the human nature of Christ, believing that Mary was simply the channel through which the divine Christ came into the world.[12] Luther points out that the Bible is clear on this issue, for we read that Mary was "pregnant" and Christ was "born," thus clearly implying that Christ was also a human being. Secondly, they condemn the sacrament of infant baptism, making of it a human and pagan institution. It is strange, Luther concludes, that the same people who despise all that is human at the same time enjoy the gold of the godless, as the Anabaptists do in Münster. Thirdly, they hold perverted views concerning marriage and polygamy. If the marriage of the "godless" is prostitution, as the Münsterites believe, it follows that the Anabaptists are all illegitimate children. Fourthly, their "kingdom of the rats" is so obviously rebellious that there is no further need to speak of it. Luther believes that Münster is God's means of chastising Germany for the purpose of needful repentance; but God is gracious and will not allow the devil to destroy the land.

The Münster tragedy confirmed Luther's suspicion he had had concerning the whole Anabaptist movement. It proved to him beyond all doubt that every heretic and fanatic was also a rebel in disguise. They first sow lies, he argued, and later seal these lies with civil disobedience and murder. Münster also confirmed his belief that every Anabaptist, no matter how pious he may seem, is a devil concealed. Münster had as it were opened the eyes of the governments by the revolt of the Anabaptists, and thereafter no one would trust even those evangelical radicals who claimed to be innocent. Luther's sermons and writings after 1535 are filled with references to the Anabaptists' attempt to establish a kingdom on earth. In a sermon of November 2, 1539, on Matthew 24, Luther brushed aside the dream of such people as Müntzer and the Anabaptists that Christ would set up an earthly kingdom in which the saints would reign. And what moved these people to harbour such notions? Luther asks. He answers that it is the fact that the ungodly are so fortunate in the world, possess kingdoms, power, and wisdom while the Christians are of no account in comparison with them. So they believed that the ungodly will be rooted out so that the pious may live in peace.[13]

While Luther's assessment of Münsterism generally applied to the revolutionary radicals, it missed the mark with regard to the evangelical groups who believed that the Christian life was filled with persecution and martyrdom, and that a follower of Christ was called to suffer patiently rather than take up arms against the oppressors.

But Müntzer and Münster blinded Luther's eyes to evangelical Anabaptism. For Luther the case of Anabaptism was closed; the Anabaptists had been tried and found wanting.

What happened in Münster cannot be justified, but it is possible to understand the excesses in the Westphalian capital. As a result of severe persecution the apocalyptic expectations had become very strong among the Anabaptists. Most Anabaptists considered themselves at a crucial point in history, believing that God assembled his people "for the decisive attack, but Satan, too, arms with all his forces for the great counter attack. All the forces of the *Civitas Diaboli* are let loose now upon the *Civitas Dei*: the old dragon and the great beast, the Anti-Christ, and the false prophets."[14] These eschatological visions were much stronger among the Dutch Anabaptists than among the Swiss Brethren. Most of the radicals, however, looked upon the end in spiritual terms, expecting a heavenly kingdom, not an earthly. Only a strong minority, influenced by the economic, social, and political conditions of the time thought of an earthly establishment of Christ's kingdom.

Luther himself believed that he was living at the end of an age. In 1520 he identified the pope with antichrist who according to Scripture was to appear in the last days.[15] In view of the dark prospects of his cause, Luther wrote in 1521: "Oh, how truly these are perilous times, worthy of the last days," of which the prophet Daniel spoke.[16] In his *On the Misuse of the Mass* (1522) Luther wrote that the Lord was beginning to destroy the antichrist with the spirit of his mouth, and that Christians are waiting for the return of Christ when the antichrist will be finally defeated.[17] Luther expected that Christ would return soon and encouraged all Christians to pray that God would soon utterly destroy the antichrist and his sinful ways.[18] In 1532 he expressed the opinion that the last day would come before the close of that year. In 1534 he expected to see certain signs which would precede the coming of Christ. For a time Luther even felt that the Turks should not be resisted, for God would use them to usher in the end of the world. At one time he felt that the world would not endure beyond the year 1548.[19] The Anabaptists, then, were not the only ones in the sixteenth century whose apocalyptic views were an ever-present reality. Luther's views concerning the end of time, however, seemed to correspond with those of the New Testament writers who also believed that Christ's second coming was imminent. The revolutionary Anabaptists believed that God had chosen them to usher in the Kingdom of God. This, according to Luther, is where they deviated from the biblical teaching on the subject.

It must also be noted that not only the Münsterites but also Luther and other leaders of the Reformation held some unorthodox views concerning the plurality of wives. Luther agreed hesitantly to the bigamy of Philip of Hesse, justifying his position on the basis of Old Testament practices, and in 1531 he advised the Queen of Henry VIII of England not to consent to the proposed divorce, suggesting rather that Henry VIII take another wife after the example of the Old Testament patriarchs. Similarly Melanchton believed that polygamy was not prohibited by divine law.[20] Some of the radical reformers, other than the Münster Anabaptists, were also charged with immoral living.[21] When Rothmann wrote his *The Restitution* in which he defended the practice of polygamy, he was no doubt aware of the various opinions and practices in this regard.[22]

Anabaptism and Münsterism

There are those who in spite of the evidence to the contrary still follow the traditional line of thinking that there was little difference in the beliefs and practices of the various Anabaptist groups. R. A. Knox, for example, states that there is a contradiction between the Anabaptist doctrine of non-resistance and the blood-drenched history of their course. He attempts to resolve the problem as follows: They preach non-resistance since they regard the state as a part of the kingdom of darkness with which they have nothing to do. But when it comes to fighting the ungodly under "perfect" rulers or generals, such as Müntzer or John of Leyden, they become more bloodthirsty "than is the common wont of 'psychic' men."[23] It is true that no historian of the Anabaptist movement can claim the absence of all lineal connection between the south-German Brethren and the Münsterites. There was in a way a direct succession from the followers of Hans Denck in Strassburg, where Melchior Hofmann was baptized, through the latter by way of Jan Matthys and John of Leyden.[24] But as C. H. Smith points out, "the mere fact that Leiden can trace his baptism through direct lineage to the non-resistant Anabaptists at Strassburg does not commit the large body of peaceful Anabaptists to the evil practices and the fanatical theories that found their first inception in the fertile though diseased brain of that ill-advised revolutionist."[25] The peaceful Anabaptists were no more responsible for the excesses of John of Leyden than was Luther for the radicalism of Carlstadt, Müntzer, and Rothmann. Writers such as Knox ignore all historical differentiation between the teachings and practices of the evangelical Anabaptists and the revolutionary trends in other groups. It is also often overlooked that Münster was not the inevitable and final development of Anabaptism. Münsterism was only an excrescence of the Anabaptist movement, brought about by the appearance of certain elements which were entirely foreign to the principles and ethics of such evangelical groups as the Swiss Brethren and most Dutch Anabaptists.

What were these unfortunate elements and how can they be accounted for? First, it must be noted that the violent suppression of the Peasants' Revolt had not destroyed the seeds of discontent among the peasants and workers; the lower classes remained as dissatisfied as ever, and the governments expected further uprisings after 1525. Münster was one such uprising. While the religious element played an important role in the Münster episode, the socio-economic factor hid behind the Christian front.[26] The only thing that the Münsterites and the evangelical Anabaptists had in common was the outward form of baptism. Secondly, the kingdom at Münster was preceded by a steadily mounting persecution of the Anabaptists in the Low Countries and to some extent in Germany. This is significant. When able leaders such as Denck, Grebel, Hubmaier and others were gone, the Anabaptists were left without effective leadership with the result that the radical movement was in some instances sidetracked from its New Testament ideals. Thirdly, the rapid expansion of Anabaptism sometimes introduced elements into the movement which had not become truly saturated with the essence of what these people stood for. Having quickly organized a congregation in one place, the Anabaptist evangelist left for another, often leaving the immature but eager group of converts to inexperienced leaders. Fourthly, the episode in Münster was not characteristic of the whole Anabaptist movement; it was the result of the ambitions of a few fanatical leaders. As we have seen, even in Münster John of Leyden was unable to maintain his authority without the use of physical force. Münster was an isolated example of the worst aspect of radical Anabaptism; it was a caricature of the movement.

The above considerations are borne out when the beliefs and practices of the Anabaptists and Münsterites are compared. The Münster fanatics forced baptism upon all people in the city; the Anabaptists baptized only after there was evidence of genuine repentance and faith. The Münsterites believed in a state-church with a king who combined the functions of both church and government; the Anabaptists advocated a free and separate church and generally refused to serve in governmental offices. The Anabaptists' principle of liberty of conscience was foreign to the fanatics of Münster; like Müntzer they advocated the use of force and violence which the evangelical Anabaptists repudiated. The Münsterites practised and defended polygamy; the Anabaptists generally adhered to strict church discipline, excluding those from their fellowship who offended on moral lines. Whereas the Münsterites, like Müntzer, exalted the Old Testament above the New Testament, the Anabaptists were known for their adherence to the New Testament, particularly to the principles of the Sermon on the Mount. In his *The Restitution* Rothmann ignored the Swiss Brethren completely. He pointed out that the restitution of Christianity was begun by Luther, "but through our brother, John of Leyden ... the truth has been gloriously established."[27] The Anabaptists in turn disavowed the Münsterites, pointing out that there was no bond between them. The Hutterian Brethren, for example, fought both Luther and the Münster fanatics as false prophets. But the most outspoken enemy of Münsterism was Menno Simons (1496-1561) of Friesland in the Netherlands after whom the Mennonites are named.

Ordained to the priesthood when he was about twenty-eight years of age, Menno's first doubts came in connection with the celebration of the eucharist. At first he tried to dismiss the question of how the bread and wine could turn into the actual body and blood of Christ as a temptation of the devil. He began to study the New Testament with the Catholic doctrine of transubstantiation in mind, and came to the conclusion that on the question of the Lord's supper he had been following the "teachings of men." It was Luther who taught Menno that "man-made laws do not bring about eternal death." Luther's influence on Menno was profound in his early years as a priest. He read several works of the Reformer,[28] adapted the various issues raised to his own needs, quoted from Luther's works in his own writings, criticized the "learned theologian" wherever he thought he erred, and followed an independent course from Luther. Menno accepted, for example, Luther's principle of justification by faith alone, but believed that the Lutherans were so one-sided in their teaching of this doctrine that they neglected to stress the importance of Christian ethics. It is ironic that on the question of baptism Menno learned from Luther to doubt the validity of infant baptism.[29] We have seen that Luther in his earlier references to baptism had stressed the necessity of faith, and in his later works he had shown that even children were capable of having faith. Menno's study of Luther's works and of the New Testament on the question of baptism and his contact with Anabaptist views led him to reject infant baptism and to embrace believers' baptism. In addition, the suffering and martyrdom of the Anabaptists made a lasting impression on him; he decided to join the despised sect in the Netherlands, becoming their teacher and leader. When the authorities after Münster intensified their persecution of the Anabaptists, Menno Simons felt called to defend and support them. He purged the minds of many Anabaptists of the "apocalyptic fancies taught by many of their leaders... inculcated the old ideas of non-resistance, of the evils of state control over the church, of the need of personal conversion, and of adult baptism as its sign and seal."[30]

At the height and in the aftermath of the Münster fanaticism Menno Simons became the champion of peaceful Anabaptism. Opposed to what Münsterism stood for, Menno attacked particularly the teachings, pretensions, and practices of John of Leyden. In a pamphlet entitled *The Blasphemy of John of Leyden* (1535), Menno sought to invalidate the prophet's claim that he was the new King David. In the introduction of the tract Menno states that necessity compels him to write against the Münsterites, "because we cannot tolerate the shameful deceit and blasphemy against God that a man be placed in Christ's stead."[31] Christ is the king of all; no man can usurp the divine throne. "Greater antichrist there cannot arise than he who poses as the David of promise."[32] On the question of physical force, Menno states that if Christ fights his enemies with the sword of his mouth, "how can we, then, oppose our enemies with any other sword."[33] Christ had no desire to be defended with Peter's sword. According to Scriptures, Christ will not destroy his enemies before the time of his coming, but John of Leyden proposes to destroy the enemies here and now. Warning his fellow Anabaptists, Menno concludes: "Let every one of you guard against all strange doctrine of sword and resistance and other like things which is nothing short of a fair flower under which lies hidden an evil serpent which has shot his venom into many. Let everyone beware."[34]

In other writings, Menno tried his utmost to cause the authorities to become aware of the differences between true Anabaptism and Münsterism. Writing in 1539 in his *Christian Baptism*, Menno states: "Therefore I say, if you find in me or in my teachings which is the Word of God, or among those who are taught by me or by my colleagues any thievery, murder, perjury, sedition, rebellion, or any other criminal act, as were and are found among the corrupt sects—then punish all of us."[35] The tragedy of Münster, however, stigmatized all Anabaptists as rebels and criminals, and Menno's pleas for clemency for his co-religionists were not heeded. It has been estimated that in the ten years following the disaster at Münster, no fewer than 30,000 Anabaptists were executed in Holland and Friesland alone,[36] and in such southern areas as Moravia and Hesse where Anabaptists were tolerated before 1535, the radicals were exiled and persecuted. Menno himself became a fugitive, finally fleeing the territory of Charles V and finding refuge in Holstein under the protection of Count Bartholomew of Ahlfeldt. There he was left free to preach, publish his works, and counsel both his followers, who regarded him as their patriarch, and Lutherans.[37]

Perhaps one should not be too critical of Luther who saw the connections between revolutionary radicalism, doctrinal error, and the excesses at Münster, and failed to appreciate the biblical sincerity of many Anabaptists. In view of the circumstances and considering Luther's position within the Reformation we can understand the Reformer's attitude toward Münster and Anabaptism, but his judgment of Anabaptism on the basis of a vocal and violent group of fanatics is certainly historically unsound. The great mass of Anabaptists, as we have seen, were moderates; they consistently acknowledged the civil governments as from God, paying their respect, submission and taxes to them; they wished to be left alone in exercising their faith and conduct as they understood the teaching of the Bible; and they were quite consistent and largely successful in upholding their principle of non-violence and peace. Ironically, the Anabaptists were charged with rebellion and bloodshed by those who did not adhere to the principle of non-resistance. Both the Zwinglians and Lutherans did not shrink from using violence when it came to supporting their cause. For example, the leading Lutheran princes, John Frederick of Saxony and Philip of Hesse, invaded in 1542 the Catholic province of Brunswick, drove out the rightful ruler, Duke Henry, and forced the Lutheran creed upon the people.[38] The Anabaptists were not blind to these inconsistencies. Menno Simons wrote:

> Why do they indiscreetly accuse us of uproar while we are wholly innocent and clear of all uproar and they never pay attention to their own destructive, bloody murdering uproar. Again what bloody uproars the Lutherans have for some years made to introduce and establish their doctrine, I will leave to them to reflect upon. Nevertheless we, although innocent, must be accounted the tumultuous heretics and they the God-fearing, pious, peaceable Christians.[39]

It is also ironic that in other matters the Münsterites and Lutherans had more in common than the Anabaptists and the Münster fanatics. In matters of morals the evangelical Anabaptists placed the New Testament, particularly the Sermon on the Mount, above the Old Testament; the Lutherans and the Münsterites regarded both the Old and New Testament as authoritative in the realm of ethics. In fact, in some important beliefs and practices, such as relations between church and state and the sanction of capital punishment of heretics, both Lutherans and Münsterites appealed to the Old Testament. Some go as far as to state that the Münster radicals were more imbibed with Lutheran ideas than with Anabaptism.[40] To lay the offences of the Münsterites to the charge of the Anabaptists on the ground that both practised adult baptism is, as Menno Simons pointed out, "as unreasonable as to accuse the Lutherans of the crimes of which some of the popes became guilty, on the ground that both were pedobaptists."[41]

CHAPTER VI

LUTHER'S ATTITUDE TOWARD THE SPIRITUALISTS,
ANTINOMIANS AND ANTITRINITARIANS

*The Spiritualists: The Inner and the
Outer Word*

The mysticism of the Zwickau prophets had been so pronounced and Thomas Müntzer's use of Scripture so radical that Luther had no difficulty in detecting in these enthusiasts the work of evil spirits. According to Luther these radicals clearly violated the will of God as expressed in the written Word of God. But when sane and educated men, who appeared to be sincere in their attempt to follow Scripture, stressed the inner Word or the inner light as being more important than the written Word, Luther was compelled to re-examine his own position with regard to this issue.

We have seen that for Luther the principle of *sola scriptura* was of utmost importance. On the basis of this principle he opposed the theology of the Middle Ages, the decisions of councils, the Catholic interpretation of Scripture, the position of the papacy, and the decrees of the emperor. He was bound in his conscience not to act contrary to God's Word. Some believe, however, that for Luther the Word of God and the Bible were not identical and that he began to stress the importance of the written Word only when he encountered the Spiritualists who de-emphasized the external Word. Alfred Coutts points out that the young Luther inclined heavily to mysticism, admiring particularly the *Theologia Germanica* (1500), which he edited several times and recommended it to all Christians. Coutts finds this striking; it "shows the strong leanings of Luther to the mystical side of the Christian life, when it is remembered that in the *Theologia Germanica* there is no mention made of the supreme authority of the Scriptures, nor of justification by faith alone—foundation principles of the Reformation. Salvation is attained by the loss of Self in the Divine."[1] Commenting further on Luther's conception of God's Word, Coutts writes:

> For Luther himself, there was a twofold witness of the Holy Spirit for the authority of Scripture—the witness of the written Word itself, and the witness of the believing mind. But it is evident that he put the witness of the believing mind first, for everywhere the inspiration of Scripture was tested by the place it gave to Justification by Faith, which was really the testimony of his own religious experience. The real authority Luther set up, though he did

not clearly see it, was not the Scripture, but his inward experience of Justification by Faith which he found in Scripture, and to which Scripture gave witness. Where he did not find that doctrine, he found neither inspiration nor authority. He selected as the touch-stone of Scripture a fact of subjective Christian experience which for him was undeniable, and by that he judged the value of Scripture, and sought to discover, by its aid, what should be accepted as the authentic Gospel.[2]

There are no doubt references, particularly in Luther's early works, which seem to lend substance to the view that the Reformer was most subjective in his interpretation of Scripture.[3] But Aarne Siirala rightly insists that to charge Luther with subjectivism is to misunderstand the Reformer's view of Scripture.[4] The fact that Luther fought those radicals who stressed the inner Word above the written Scripture underlines the difference that existed between the Reformer's conception of the Word of God and that of the Spiritualists. It is thus necessary to first sketch the views of some important Spiritualists concerning the Word and then show Luther's position and his reason for opposing the Spiritualists.

Among the more prominent men who in Luther's time strongly advocated the inner Word were Hans Denck, Sebastian Franck, and Caspar Schwenckfeld. The most attractive of the three was Denck, rector of St. Sebald's Church in Nürnberg. A humanist and scholar, he had been greatly influenced by the mediaeval mystics, Luther, and Thomas Müntzer.[5] Having become disillusioned with what he considered the unregenerate life of the Lutherans in Nürnberg, Denck was increasingly drawn to Anabaptism which to him seemed to stress Christian discipleship with great success. His individualism and mysticism, however, and his emphasis on the inner Word set him apart from the mainline evangelical Anabaptists whose approach to faith and conduct, according to him, was too biblicistic and legalistic. In contrast to Müntzer, Denck abstained from all recourse to violence; no one practised the principle of non-resistance as well as he. His life and writings spoke of God's love; he wrote reluctantly in answer to his enemies; and he confessed that he loved even those who persecuted him. "Persecution has severed me from a few men," he wrote, "but my heart has not been severed from them."[6] In the autumn of 1523 the Council of Nürnberg had decided for the Lutheran Reformation, with the minister Andreas Osiander becoming the spokesman of the new religious movement. When toward the end of 1524 some "godless artists" were denounced, Denck was also mentioned in connection with some heretical views. In January, 1525, Denck had to submit a confession to the city council which proved to be less than satisfactory to the Lutherans.

He was banished from Nürnberg and forbidden "for ever" to return within ten miles of the city on pain of death.

Denck's *Confession to the Council of Nürnberg* (1525)[7] leaves no doubt as to what the author believed about the inner Word and external things, including the Bible and the sacraments. Writing in his *Confession*, Denck "feels" that he is a sinful man, but he also "feels" that there is something within him which opposes his sinful nature and inclinations. There is something in him which compels him to believe Scripture; this is Christ within him, of whom Scripture witnesses. Scripture is a lamp unto our feet, but since it is written by men it cannot remove the darkness completely. Only Christ in the heart of the believer can remove all darkness. Scripture can only be understood and interpreted through the Spirit of God in the heart of man. Similarly, outward baptism cannot remove the sins of men, but the inner baptism is necessary, for it is written that whoever believes and is baptized shall be saved. The external eating and drinking of the sacramental bread and wine may strengthen the outer man, but the spiritual eating of Christ gives strength to the soul. In fact, the partaking of the invisible cup and the love of God "deify the individual and humanize God" in the individual.[8]

In a booklet *What Does it Mean when the Scripture Says God Does and Works Good and Evil* (1526),[9] Denck gives more details on what he means by the inner and outer Word. The Kingdom of God, according to Denck, is in man and he who searches for it outside of man will never find it, for apart from God no one can either seek or find God, and he who seeks God already has him. But it is not enough that God is in man; man must also be in God, that is, he must partake of the life of God. It is an illusion to believe that God is within if one does not honour him; it is of no avail to call oneself God's child if one does not behave like a child of God.[10] Denck thus stresses the free will of man in salvation. Man hears the voice of God within himself and from the pages of Scripture and then decides whether he will accept or reject the salvation of God. But the truth in the heart is above Scripture, for Scripture testifies of the truth. "Therefore, whoever deems the testimony of greater importance than the truth itself, reverses the order, which is an abomination in the eyes of God."[11] The light of God shines in all people; the Word of God is in all of God's creatures. Man has no excuse if he does not see the light or if he does not hear God's Word; he has the ability to atune himself, if he will, to his inner light and inner Word.[12] The only evidence that one is obedient to the inner Word is the doing of the will of God. "For those who hear the law of God and do not fulfill it with their deeds, are not righteous before God."[13] Answering the objection that we are enjoined to come to Christ and learn of him, Denck states: "The Word of God is with you before you seek; God gives before you ask; and he opens before you knock."[14]

Denck's idea of the inner Word is most clearly expressed in his *Widerruf* (1527), a work in which he summarizes his theology.[15] Denck holds the Holy Scripture above all human treasure, but not as highly as the Word of God, which is living, powerful and eternal. The Bible is letter and not spirit; while it is useful to read the Bible, salvation is not tied to it. The outward Word cannot improve a wicked heart; but a pious heart, that is, a heart in which there is a "genuine spark of God's enthusiasm,"[16] is improved through all things. While it is useful to preach and to read the Bible, an individual can be saved without preaching and Scripture. Outward ceremonies are of no avail. Such things as outward baptism and the breaking of bread in communion are superstitions if one believes that they can lead to God. Infant baptism is merely a man-made law. Christians are free to practise it if they wish, but baptism in itself is of no importance, for it is the life of a Christian which matters most of all.

Salvation, then, for Denck is wholly an inward process, initiated by God through the divine Word, the Christ within, whom we know outwardly as the historical Jesus and inwardly as the revealer of light, love, and faith. "But however audible the inner Word may be; however vivid the illumination; however drawing the Love, there is never compulsion, the soul itself must hear and see and feel; must say *yes* to the appeal of Love, and must co-operate by a continuous adjustment of the personal will to the Will of God and 'learn to behave as a child of God.'"[17] Rufus Jones concludes his study of Hans Denck as follows:

> In an epoch in which the doctrine was new and revolutionary, he succeeded in presenting the principle of the Inward Word as the basis of religion without giving any encouragement to libertinism or moral laxity, for he found the way of freedom to be a life of growing likeness to Christ, he held the fulfilling of the law to be possible only for those who accept the burdens and sacrifices of love, and he insisted that the privileges of blessedness belong only to those who *behaved like sons.*[18]

It may well be argued that Denck's mysticism was held in balance by his insistence that the Christian life must express itself in practical living. Like Luther before him, Denck was able to combine within himself perfect freedom in Christ and the discipline and subjection to the Christ who had redeemed him. Moreover, Denck's differentiation between the inward and outward Word of God was, as we shall see, at least in a small measure in line with Luther's approach to the subject. For Luther, however, the Spiritualists' view of Scripture, the inner light, and the sacraments was filled with dangerous heresies. Hans Denck was expelled from Nürnberg on January 21, 1525, and the "godless artists," the brothers Sebald and Barthel Beheim and G. Pentz, on the twenty-sixth or twenty-seventh. On February 4 Luther wrote J. Briessmann in Nürnberg: "Satan has carried it so far that in Nürnberg some persons are denying that Christ is anything, that the Word of God is anything, that the eucharist is anything, that the magistrates are anything. They say that only God is."[19] For Luther it was the spirit of Müntzer and Carlstadt which made its influence felt in Nürnberg. On the same day Luther wrote to Lazarus Spengler,[20] who seems to have been the person in Nürnberg who sent Luther the information concerning the city council's proceedings against Denck and the artists. In this letter Luther expresses joy and sorrow at the news from Nürnberg. He is happy to hear that Christ is able to protect his own from the wolves in Nürnberg, and he is sad to learn that the devil's messengers had succeeded in creating doubt concerning some articles of faith. It is good, however, Luther adds, that these things are exposed and then corrected. In answering the question as to how the heretics should be dealt with, Luther feels that they should not be treated as blasphemers, which would mean the death sentence upon them, but as Turks or misled Christians. However, if they should refuse to obey and to acknowledge the temporal powers, which would expose them as rebels and murderers, the secular authorities should not hesitate to proceed against them.

It may be argued that Luther knew little about Denck and other Spiritualists in Nürnberg, and that his judgment concerning these men was based on hearsay only and thus unfair. From the two letters it is evident, however, that Luther was well informed about the Spiritualists in Nürnberg and that he understood their theological position quite well. When Luther referred to the spirit of Müntzer and Carlstadt in Nürnberg, he was not entirely wrong about what Hans Denck and other Spiritualists believed. While Denck repudiated Müntzer's programme for establishing God's Kingdom on earth, he was influenced by the revolutionist's mysticism and view of the inner Word. And as far as the spirit of Carlstadt is concerned, Denck was in agreement with the Wittenberg radical on the question of the Lord's supper, a point of utmost importance to Luther. Furthermore, when Luther wrote that in Nürnberg some persons deny that Christ is anything and that the word of God is anything, he was quite serious in making these statements. Denck's differentiation between the historical Jesus and the inner Christ was no doubt confusing and could be interpreted to mean that the inward Christ was of greater importance than the historical Jesus who died for the redemption of mankind. Similarly Denck's stress on the inner Word in a sense denied the importance of Scripture, which, according to the Spiritualist, merely gives witness to the voice of God within the heart. Moreover, the Spiritualists' individualism and stress on freedom must have seemed to Luther as an attempt to put man and his experiences in the centre, thus denying any human authority over him. It may well be, as Rufus Jones points out, that in Denck's case the principle of the inward Word did not encourage libertinism or moral laxity and that his freedom was the freedom of a follower of Christ. But Luther was not as optimistic about human nature as Denck was, and in 1525 he saw on all sides how the principle of individualism and freedom was abused by men who were not governed by the ideals of Christian humanism.

Another Spiritualist who collided more directly with Luther than Denck was Caspar von Schwenckfeld (1489-1561), a Silesian nobleman from the duchy of Liegnitz. Having studied in Cologne, Frankfurt-on-the-Oder, and probably at the University of Erfurt, he threw himself into the life of a courtier, intending to make his success in a worldly career. Luther's struggle against the Roman Church and his proclamation of justification by faith changed Schwenckfeld's life. Schwenckfeld became a fervent follower of Luther and an active reformer in Silesia. As late as 1543 Schwenckfeld admired Luther and acknowledged his debt to him: "I owe to you in God and the truth all honour, love, and goodwill, because from the first I have reaped much fruit from your service, and I have not ceased to pray for you according to my poor powers."[21] While being influenced by Luther's reformation writings, Schwenckfeld blazed his own theological trail, attempting to maintain a middle course between Catholicism and Lutheranism. There were several things in Lutheranism upon which he looked with dismay. He believed that Luther's emphasis on justification by faith alone was one-sided and thus led to a lax ethical life among Luther's followers. When Schwenckfeld in 1525 spoke to Luther about this, the Reformer agreed that something had to be done about the lax discipline of his people but added: "Yes, dear Caspar, true Christians are not as yet all too common. I would like to see two together. I do not know of one."[22] Furthermore, Luther's intolerant attitude toward his dissenters grieved Schwenckfeld to no end. Schwenckfeld believed that it should be possible for true Christians to resolve differences among them or at least to be tolerant toward brethren who had different views with regard to certain divine mysteries. The greatest stumbling block for Schwenckfeld was Luther's interpretation of Christ's words of institution in holy communion.

Schwenckfeld's first serious doubts concerning Christ's real presence in the last supper came when he considered the part that Judas played in the original communion service. If the elements were in any way identifiable with the body and blood of Christ, Schwenckfeld thought, then Judas must have actually eaten Christ, which was most repugnant to the nobleman.[23] Eventually Schwenckfeld came to the view that the believers eat Christ spiritually and thus receive eternal life from such spiritual eating of Christ. Particularly John 6 led him to the following conclusion: "He that eateth my flesh and drinketh my blood hath eternal life; hence Judas could not have partaken of the real Christ because that would have conferred eternal life upon him, since the body and blood are never destitute of divine power but are spirit and life; the Word is an eternal Word and the Word is Christ."[24] The Lord's supper, then, according to Schwenckfeld, is a spiritual eating of Christ, and only true believers can partake of this spiritual food. The outward celebration of the Lord's supper is, according to this view, a mere memorial act and the bread and wine remain mere emblems, reminding the communicant of the historic and salvatory facts.[25]

Schwenckfeld had discussed his interpretation of the eucharist with others in Silesia, including Valentine Crautwald, at that time the public lector and canon of the Dom at Liegnitz. Crautwald at first objected to Schwenckfeld's spiritual interpretation of Christ's words of institution on the ground that Scripture was plain on this point and that this new approach would only serve to confuse the brethren. After an extensive study of the subject and after prayer and a vision from God, Crautwald was converted to Schwenckfeld's view "that from the necessity and nature of faith the communion in the Supper was spiritual and that the sacramental elements must not be confused with the actual body and blood of Christ." [26]

While the primary occasion for the disagreement between Schwenckfeld and Luther was their different views concerning the Lord's supper, the basic issue dividing the two men was their different conception of matter and spirit. Schwenckfeld interpreted Scripture, the sacraments, the Christian life, and life itself spiritually. For him the spiritual was vastly superior to the material, an emphasis which Luther could not accept. For Luther God was the creator of both spiritual and material things, and God used the material things to convey spiritual benefits to mankind. Thus the letter of Scripture conveyed for Luther the good news of salvation to the world; in the sacrament of baptism the Word of God was joined to the element of water for the spiritual benefit of the baptized; and in eating the bread and drinking the wine in the Lord's supper the believer partook of Christ. It is these different views of reality, both spiritual and material, that must be borne in mind in an attempt to understand Luther's clash with the Spiritualists.

Having worked out his interpretation of the Lord's supper, Schwenckfeld sent Luther in the summer of 1525 twelve questions, or propositions, for investigation and possible acceptance.[27] They included among others the following points: The body of Christ is a spiritual food; only spiritual people are capable of appropriating such a spiritual nourishment, and only faith is equal to an act of spiritual eating. Christ is the eternal life, "and he distributes through his flesh and blood nothing else than he himself is, viz., eternal life. On this account our Christian faith expresses itself on this wise, that life results from eating him, and he who eats must live for his sake."[28] The blood of the New Covenant must not be confused "with alien creatures who are changeable, earthly; but it must be partaken of whether in the Supper of the Lord or on other occasions out of the Word of God alone and by a true and living faith."[29] Since Christ is the heavenly light and the eternal, unchangeable truth, no unbelievers and carnal Christians can have a part of him. Christ dwells only in the transformed hearts of Christians; he "does not abide in any kind of earthly creature in the world."[30] Hence it follows, according to Schwenckfeld, that unregenerate "persons can receive in the Supper only the bread of the Lord; but the bread which the Lord himself is and which he himself gives and distributes, they cannot taste."[31]

For some reason Luther failed to respond to Schwenckfeld's twelve arguments. Hence Schwenckfeld decided to visit Luther personally, arriving in Wittenberg on November 30, 1525. Selina Schultz writes in her biography of Schwenckfeld: "It required no small degree of courage and initiative to undertake to approach Luther at this juncture, particularly since he had ignored Schwenckfeld's letter and arguments."[32] To state that Luther had ignored Schwenckfeld's arguments is unfair to Luther, for from the time that the twelve questions were sent to Luther—about July, 1525—and the time that Schwenckfeld arrived in Wittenberg, no more than four months had elapsed. And with Luther's preoccupation with the Peasants' War and the radicals that summer, it is not unreasonable to conclude that the Reformer had not had the time to study Schwenckfeld's propositions and to respond to them.[33] Furthermore, Luther had stated in several publications his views on the Lord's supper, works with which Schwenckfeld and his Silesian followers were well acquainted. There was thus no urgency to deal with the question again. From Schwenckfeld's side it may have required courage to approach Luther on the question of the sacrament, but any apprehensions that he may have had were dispelled as soon as Luther and the Wittenbergers met the Silesian reformer. Luther was courteous, patient, and sympathetic toward Schwenckfeld's convictions. If the two men could not come to an agreement in their understanding of the sacrament, the reason for this was not obstinacy on either side. The two men could not work out their differences because they proceeded from different premises and approached reality from two different points of view, as the following encounter will show.

Schwenckfeld conferred with Luther and Johannes Bugenhagen, a Lutheran theologian and minister in Wittenberg, between December 1 and 4, 1525.[34] When Schwenckfeld asked Luther for an interview with him, the Reformer was most obliging: "Dear Caspar, I will be glad to confer with you, come tomorrow, as early as you wish, six, seven, or eight o'clock. Nothing shall hinder me. We will then give consideration to the matter [of the Lord's supper]."[35] The next morning Schwenckfeld went to Luther to discuss with him the point that "This is my body, must have quite a different sense than had been held hitherto."[36] Luther asked: "Tell me one thing, do you have a different ground than Carlstadt and Zwingli?" Answering in the affirmative, Schwenckfeld then proceeded to argue that Christ's words cannot be understood in the literal sense but must be interpreted to mean his spiritual flesh and blood. Luther, taking the Greek Testament, pointed out the words with regard to the cup and insisted that the meaning was quite clear. Schwenckfeld opposed this, pointing out that Christ could not have meant the cup or drink in the sacrament but the blood shed for mankind on the cross, although he admitted that he was not well versed in the languages. Knowing that there could be no agreement with Schwenckfeld's view, Luther did not want to engage in any further arguments on this point and said: "Dear Caspar, I will take all the material in care and send for the preacher [Bugenhagen]. We will study the problem together today, after which I will speak further with you."[37] Schwenckfeld then took his leave with a strong appeal that Luther give serious thought to the matter and take it to heart. Schwenckfeld was quite certain of his position: "By the grace of Christ we were quite fully persuaded in our own minds and wished the same for him."[38]

Since Luther wanted to discuss the question of the Lord's supper with Bugenhagen, Schwenckfeld decided to see the Lutheran preacher at once. Schwenckfeld saw Bugenhagen, and after some discussion with the Silesian, Bugenhagen was summoned to Luther to confer with him about Schwenckfeld's interpretation of the sacrament. Upon Luther's request, Schwenckfeld sent them the story of how Crautwald had received a revelation from God with regard to the spiritual interpretation of the Lord's supper.[39] Schwenckfeld attached a note to Crautwald's story which read in part:

> Dear Doctor, I beg that you will carefully study this letter, and if anything is not clear kindly put it in writing. We will, God being willing, satisfy you. It is my trust in God, that what he has begun he will also complete to his own glory and to our betterment. The overthrow of the papal power is impossible as long as this article of the flesh and blood in the Sacrament of the bread and wine remains. . . . God grant you his divine grace to complete what has been begun, for which many devout brethren pray. God be with you.[40]

The outcome of Bugenhagen's conference with Luther was discouraging to Schwenckfeld. Bugenhagen reported to Schwenckfeld: "You on your part claim a revelation. Others claim the same, and each party has a particular conclusion. There is no harmony. But the Spirit of the Lord is not the spirit of dissention. We also do not know otherwise than that we have the truth. Even if you have a good cause, you arouse suspicion since your views differ so widely."[41]

Luther's reply to Schwenckfeld, as reported by Schwenckfeld himself, shows consideration, openness, tolerance, and sympathy toward the Silesian reformer:

> I have examined your matter, but cannot give a final answer until I have considered the matter with Philip (Melanchton), who is not at home. Nevertheless, I shall be glad to speak further with you about the matter. . . . So far as I perceive the truth, I do not want to be found obstinate. I previously yielded to Carlstadt and others in regard to the intercession of saints and other articles. Why should I not yield in such an important article, if I be sufficiently instructed? . . . If anyone should convince me by substantial grounds, I would drop my opinion. But so far it has not happened. You show me a revelation. I cannot and do not wish to be against God. If we only could be sure that it was God's will thus to understand the matter. Wherefore I beg of you not to think hard of me that I cannot so soon agree with you. The matter is important. I exhort you, too, act in the fear of God, pray to him; I will do the same. He has promised me not to let me err. . . . He will not forsake me in this matter, and if it be His will thus to understand it, I hope He will grant it to me also. But that I should express myself to favor you, is not fitting. For this is a matter of faith. I must first of all have and feel it in my conscience. Nevertheless I will not condemn your opinion, although I cannot accept it, for proof is insufficient. The matter needs further study. If God grant, I will gladly agree with you. . . . Your opinion is plausible, it is very good, if it can be proved sufficiently, but you must see to that. . . . I must be convinced, particularly in such important articles, that it is to be thus understood and not otherwise.[42]

The lengthy quotation gives rise to several considerations. Luther's tolerance and sympathy toward Schwenckfeld and his view on the Lord's supper must come as a surprise to those students of Luther and the radicals who see the Reformer as an unyielding foe of all individuals who opposed him. This document, written by a man who disagreed with Luther on one of the most important issues during the Reformation, portrays the Reformer as a truly great individual and Christian who could not come to accept another man's interpretation, yet who was willing to respect another point of view. Schwenckfeld's record of what Luther said could of course be interpreted as an expression of the author's own doubts with regard to the meaning of Christ's words of institution.[43] We know that Schwenckfeld's uncertainty on this point culminated in 1526 in a *Stillstand*, a suspension of the celebration of the Lord's supper until the Lord would reveal "a right understanding and true practice of it according to his will."[44] But there is no reason to doubt the accuracy of Schwenckfeld's account of what had transpired between himself and Luther. Originally written by Schwenckfeld in the form of a dialogue, the story that has been preserved was transmitted many years later, in 1540, when the break between the two men had become final and Schwenckfeld was condemned and despised in violent language by the Lutherans.[45] "The story is charmingly told; it breathes with marked living qualities. It presents the great persons involved with a striking discrimination and with self-revelation of their dispositions and manners. Among the interlocutors one finds sweetness of temper, sometimes with a bit of dictatorial ruffling, but kindliness of expression, as well as conscientious earnestness."[46]

As pointed out before, Schwenckfeld's concept of the Lord's supper was consistent with his view of reality, including ethics, faith, Scripture, the natural man and the church. Like Denck, Schwenckfeld believed that "there is an inner and outer Word, gospel, preacher, ears, and hearing, corresponding to the inner and outer man."[47] The true, eternal Word of God is spirit and life; it is none other than Christ.

> The transitory, external letter is "word of God" only in a derived sense, whether written in Scripture, spoken in the sermon, or portrayed in symbol, picture, and sign. Once again, the internal and external word must be distinguished in separate orders: the inner Word is not conveyed by means of the outer and can brook no mixture with the external. But here again there can be a simultaneous communication, the outer word declaring, announcing, and pointing to the inner Word, Christ.[48]

The inner Word, Christ, is shown by Schwenckfeld in his various functions. The Word gives new life to the inner man; the Word is food, nourishing the reborn soul; the Word washes away the sins of the old man; the Word is spirit, not letter; life, not death; light, not darkness.[49] The elements in the sacraments, the bread, the wine, and the water, and the letter of the Bible are thus for Schwenckfeld mere outward symbols of the inner Word and life. Schwenckfeld believed that the Bible was inspired by God and is thus normative for Christian faith and conduct, but he always emphasized the demonstrative function of Scripture: "The Scriptures ... indicate, indeed, who and what the Word of God is, but do not pass themselves off for that Word. They always point beyond themselves to Christ, who must preach and utter himself into the believing heart through the Holy Spirit, and who alone is the Word, Power, and Wisdom of God."[50] Similarly Schwenckfeld's concept of the church is analogous to his theology of the sacraments and the Word. There is an internal and external church. The internal church consists of the outer establishment which includes both believers and unbelievers.[51] During his interview with Luther, Schwenckfeld stated his views concerning the church, its future, its members, and the need for discipline in the local congregations. Luther agreed that "discipline must go hand in hand with the gospel," and was sad "that no one bettered his life," but "concerning the future church he had arrived at no conclusion."[52] In Schwenckfeld, Luther, the realist, had encountered a mystic and idealist.

What was Luther's view of the Word of God? Some critics of the Reformer believe that Luther's conception of the Word of God underwent considerable change, a change from a spiritual, almost mystical, view of the Bible to an emphasis on the written Word of God.[53] According to this view, Luther stressed at first the inner Word of God and his subjective experience of salvation, and interpreted Scripture according to God's voice within his heart. The written Word of God was thus subservient to the inner Word, that is, to a subjective, highly individualistic, interpretation of Scripture.[54] When he encountered, however, radicals who like him interpreted the Bible according to their understanding, often in opposition to what he believed, and identified their dreams with the Word of God, often contrary to what Scripture clearly taught, Luther saw the danger of such individualism and thus began to stress the written Word of God. It is no doubt possible to interpret Luther's view of God's Word and the Bible in this way. There are statements in Luther's early writings which stress the individual experience and the Word of God in the heart of man. In fact, for Luther the Word of God and individual faith could not be separated; faith for Luther was the Word of God in the human heart.[55] But this does not mean that Luther was a subjectivist in his approach to Scripture, nor did he revise his view of the Word of God as time went on. He was merely compelled to define and clarify his position with regard to Scripture as he encountered those who placed themselves above the Word of God.

In his exposition of the Magnificat (Luke 1:46-55) in 1520, Luther stated that only the Holy Spirit can properly interpret the Word of God and inscribe it in the heart of man: "No one can correctly understand God or his Word unless he has received such understanding directly from the Holy Spirit. But no one can receive it from the Holy Spirit without experiencing, proving and feeling it. In such experience the Holy Spirit instructs us as in his own school, outside which nothing is learned but empty words and prattle."[56] Luther stresses here the individual experience of Mary, to be sure, but this experience is tied to God, his Word, and the Spirit who is the mediator between the individual and God. This being so, we must, according to Luther, approach the study of God's Word with due modesty and without preconceived notions of our own. In his exposition of Jeremiah 23:5-8 (1526), Luther warns against heretics who bend Scripture according to their notions. Instead, we should hear the Word of God with fear and study it with humility; we should not pounce upon it with our own ideas of what is right or wrong. It would be better to fall into all sins than into self-conceit, so dangerous and damaging it is to read one's own notions into the Word. The Word of God insists that it be honoured and observed.[57] According to Luther, it is characteristic of all false prophets that they are absolutely sure of their mission and their understanding of God's Word, when in effect they place themselves and not God in the centre of things.[58] In a sermon in 1534 Luther insisted that the Word be heeded implicitly. The sacramentarians and the enthusiasts, according to Luther, do not accept the Word for what it states. They thus judge the Word according to their reason. For example, concerning the sacrament they find it difficult to accept the words of Christ "This is my body" and "This is my blood." With regard to God's Word we do not ask questions, but simply obey and follow. If God's Word were obeyed, neither sects nor heretics would arise, but all churches would remain in accord and sound in doctrine.[59]

In his exposition of John 6:63 in 1531, Luther stated that the Holy Spirit and the Word of God are always in agreement. If someone boasts that he has something by inspiration and from the Holy Spirit, but is without God's Word, it is from the devil. God has ordained it so that his Holy Spirit comes in an orderly fashion through Scriptures. We must test all human notions against Holy Scriptures. No matter how good a certain idea might be, if it is not grounded and commanded in Holy Scripture, it means nothing.[60] All subjectivism is thus excluded. In his open letter to two pastors about

Anabaptism (1528), Luther stated that we must rely on the Word of God and look at nothing else, not even at our faith. God's Word is greater and more important than faith. The Word of God is not based and built on faith, but faith is built on the Word of God. Faith may waver and change, but the Word remains forever.[61] In 1533 Luther stated that only the Word of God made him sure that he was right. Without the Word a man must fall into despair, for he lacks divine assurance for what he is called upon to do and is borne onward merely by the egotism of his heart.[62] In a sermon of 1528 Luther spoke of the manner in which God reveals himself. According to the enthusiasts, Luther stated, the internal Word comes before the external Word. But God, according to the Reformer, does not reveal himself in the heart except through the external Word of God. This is why the external Word must be the beginning of our consideration and enlightenment. Otherwise human notions replace what God has spoken.[63] Similarly in a sermon preached in 1527 Luther insisted that God speaks to the heart through the external Word. According to Luther there is great comfort in the knowledge that God speaks to the hearts of men through human preaching; the preacher preaches the Word and God instructs the hearts of men. But this teaching in the hearts comes about through the external Word which God has ordained to serve as a means and as a hollow reed through which divine truths are conveyed to men.[64]

For Luther the Word of God was alive, not dead. The enthusiasts, according to Luther, regarded Scripture as a dead letter. For Luther Scripture was the means through which come faith and external life. The Word for Luther meant the spoken or written Word, not merely the inner Word. The Word, Luther taught, should be heard and read above all else; the Word is the vehicle of the Holy Spirit; when the Word is heard or read, the Holy Spirit is present.[65] In his exposition of 1 Corinthians 15 in 1532, Luther again exalted the written Word. The letter does not in and of itself give life, yet it must be there, it must be heard and received, and the Holy Spirit must work through it in the human heart, and in and through the Word the heart must keep itself in faith against the devil and all temptations. For if the heart were to let the Word go, it would soon entirely lose Christ and the Spirit of God. We should not boast about the Holy Spirit if we do not have the visible, external Word. The Holy Spirit has embodied his wisdom and counsel and all mysteries in the Word and has revealed them in Scripture.[66] And again, the Holy Spirit does not come to anyone without the external Word.[67] Any supposed revelation apart from the written Word of God is a devilish suggestion. It is the Word which touches and changes the hearts of men; revelations puff people up and make them arrogant.

God speaks to people through Scripture and through the men who preach and teach the Word. Men ought to flee from special revelations concerning the faith, for they are satanic impostures.[68]

In opposition to Luther, Schwenckfeld believed that "the inner word of the spirit must be differentiated from the external word spoken by the preacher; that the living Word of God is not the Scriptures, but Christ; that the Scriptures must be interpreted spiritually; that external ceremonies, services and ministers are of value, but must be distinguished from the power and service of Christ, the living Word."[69] Selina Schultz points out the difference between Luther and Schwenckfeld in this regard as follows:

> Luther not only called the literal, external, printed word the Gospel, but also emphatically stated that the preached word from the pulpit was the genuine, inspired Gospel. Schwenckfeld maintained that the preached word about the Gospel was no more the true Gospel than the preached word about Christ was the genuine Christ. He denied that Luther's preached gospel, accepted through faith, had any saving power, and that ministerial services are indispensable in the fostering of faith and the Holy Spirit.[70]

Schultz's differentiation between the two views is valid in so far as one keeps in mind that for Luther, as we have seen, the Holy Spirit uses the written Word and the proclaimed gospel to touch the hearts of the hearers or readers and thus brings them to a saving knowledge of Christ. For Schwenckfeld and other Spiritualists preaching and the reading of the written Word were merely useful functions, but not essential for salvation, which depended on the inner Word and the spiritual Christ in the hearts of men.

Schwenckfeld's opposition to physical things and externals went so far that he not only spiritualized the sacraments and Scriptures but also aroused suspicion about his view concerning the nature of Christ. Schwenckfeld stressed the oneness of Christ, believing that Christ's human nature was divine, entirely different from sinful carnality. Charged by Luther as a Eutychian, Schwenckfeld replied in his *Answer to Luther's Malediction* that he had been misunderstood:

> I recognize nothing of creation or creatureliness in Christ but rather a new divine birth and natural Sonship (*kindtschafft*) of God. Wherefore I cannot consider the Man Christ with his body and blood to be a creation or a creature. Rather, I believe and confess with Scripture that he is wholly God's only-begotten Son and that Christ, the Son of God, his Heavenly Father, the whole Person indivisibly (*unzertailig*) God and Man, was born in time of the Virgin Mary; also that he suffered and died for us upon the cross in personal unity and wholeness, and as such rose again and ascended into heaven, that he sits at the right hand of God and rules also in his human nature wholly with God his father in divine glory, unity, and essence.[71]

Sinful man derives his nature from Adam; the spiritual man in Christ derives his divine nature from Christ, the new Adam who was without sin. Interpreting Schwenckfeld's theology on this point, George Williams correctly observes:

> Man was entirely corrupt after the fall of Adam, but now the pure and holy man, the new Adam, can nourish those reborn in him to a new life. Since the human nature of Christ is uncreaturely, the believer, in receiving this celestial or mystical flesh, is enabled to progress toward deification. Christ, not partaking of Adam's sinful flesh, was born of woman to become the founder of a new order of being.[72]

Believing himself in essential agreement with Luther's view on the nature of Christ, Schwenckfeld in 1543 sent Luther some of his pamphlets on the doctrine of Christ and a letter, in the hope that a friendly understanding between the two men would be brought about. Luther's answer was most disheartening for the Silesian reformer. On december 6, 1543, Luther wrote a letter, addressing it not to Schwenckfeld personally, but to his messenger Hermann Riegel who had delivered the letter and tracts.[73] Luther accuses Schwenckfeld of preaching and teaching when no one had called or sent him.[74] "And the mad fool," Luther continues, "possessed of the devil, does not understand anything; does not know what he is babbling. But if he will not cease, so let him leave me unmolested with his booklets which the devil excretes and spews out of him."[75] Luther concludes the short letter by pronouncing a final verdict on this Spiritualist: "The Lord punish Satan in you, and your spirit which has called you, and your course which you are following."[76]

Schwenckfeld replied to this abusive letter, which even Luther's wife found to be coarse,[77] with his *An Answer to Luther's Malediction*,[78] in which the nobleman attempts to clear himself of the charges against him, particularly with regard to his views concerning the Lord's supper and the humanity of Christ. Schwenckfeld advances in the *Answer* no new arguments in favour of his position; he simply reiterates that the divine mysteries, including the sacraments, the nature of Christ, and Scripture must be viewed and experienced spiritually, not materially or physically. The language of the pamphlet as well as Schwenckfeld's attitude towards Luther speak well for the nobleman, who expresses genuine sorrow for his opponent and whom he had come to love and admire.

Why did Luther react so violently against the Spiritualists and men like Denck and Schwenckfeld? Selina Schultz writes in her biography of Schwenckfeld:

> In the Reformation century, Schwenckfeld was without doubt the

> pre-eminent exponent of the spirit, and the greatest champion of religious liberty. His contemporaries, like Pharisees, could not and would not understand him. They were engrossed in building great churches of external things through preaching, baptism, and the Sacraments, saying: Lo! here is Christ. Lo! there. Schwenckfeld answered: Believe it not, for the kingdom of God is within you; Christ is the Word of God; external ceremonies, sacraments, services, ministers, and preaching, although of great value to the carnal man, have no divine or saving power, and must therefore be distinguished from the power and service of Christ, the living Word. The preachers of his time were almost unanimously of the opinion that by this doctrine he was destroying their prestige. This was the cause of their relentless bitterness toward him to the end of his life.[79]

While it is true that Schwenckfeld was "the pre-eminent exponent of the spirit," Schultz oversimplifies the reasons for the Reformer's opposition to men such as Schwenckfeld. Luther understood the Spiritualists all too well; he knew that the difference between himself and them was not merely a different understanding of some minor doctrinal points. Both Luther and Schwenckfeld appealed to the Word of God for what they believed, but in their basic orientation they stood worlds apart, as has become evident from the evidence presented. It is not true that Luther was concerned with building churches, preaching the external Word, and capturing Christ physically in certain elements or locations. He, too, emphasized time and again that the Kingdom of God is in the hearts of men and that the sacraments must be appropriated in faith and experienced in the heart. As we have seen, Luther also believed that only the Holy Spirit can open the Word of God to individuals, thus bringing them to repentance, faith, and holy living. But he also realized that the emphasis of the Spiritualists on the inner Word and the spirit would destroy the concept of the New Testament church, that is, a local congregation of believers where the Word of God is preached and the sacraments are administered. Moreover, Luther saw that once the real presence of Christ in the sacrament was denied and the written Word undermined, there was nothing objective left to cling to, but all depended on subjective experiences. "What a precious and noble thing it is," he wrote in 1533, "to have the Word of God on our side! For such a person can be safe and happy, however much he may be tried."[80] Again he wrote: "God has always worked with something physical. . . . Whenever he wanted to do something with us, he did it through the Word and matters physical."[81] To minimize the external channels through which God has chosen to work, and to rely instead on the inner Word, subjective experiences, and revelations, was for Luther to put man and not God in the centre. This is why Luther hesitated to stress holiness, perfection, and divinity in man, for he saw that it was so easy for man to boast of his achievements and thus minimize his complete dependence on the grace of God. These were some of the real issues that separated Luther and the Spiritualists. This is why he reacted so vehemently against individuals and doctrines that threatened to destroy what he believed was the gospel of Christ.

Luther and the Antinomians

The Antinomians pushed Luther's doctrine of justification by faith alone to what they thought was its logical conclusion, asserting that as good works do not promote salvation, so neither do evil works hinder it. Since all Christians are necessarily sanctified by their very vocation and profession, the Antinomians argued, justified Christians are incapable of losing their spiritual holiness, justification, and final salvation by any violation of the law of God. The Antinomians preached freedom from God's law, emphasized the gospel over the commandments of the Old Testament, and rejected any moral coercion or discipline as part of the Christian life. In all this the Antinomians at first appealed to Luther who, according to them, had freed them from all legalism.

Luther encountered a certain kind of Antinomianism as easly as 1525. Eloy Pruystinck, a slater of Antwerp, came in the middle of March of that year to Wittenberg to see what the Reformer would make of his Antinomian views, hoping that he would get Luther's authority for his doctrine.[82] A disputation took place in Luther's house between Luther's followers and Eloy, with the result that the heretic's views were exposed for what they were. In a letter addressed to the Lutherans at Antwerp (April, 1525), Luther warns his adherents against the dangerous heresies of the "poltergeists" and the "new prophets" from Antwerp.[83] According to Luther's letter, the Loists held the following views: All men have the Holy Spirit; the Holy Spirit is none other than man's reason; everyone believes; there is no hell or damnation except for the flesh; all souls will have eternal life; nature teaches that one must wish for one's neighbour what one wishes for oneself. This good-will toward one's neighbour is faith; God's law is not broken so long as one does not intend to sin; whoever does not have the Holy Spirit has no sin, for he is without reason. Luther concludes his letter by stating that he cannot explain the mystery of sin and its relation to God, but he knows from Scriptures that God is against sin and that those who wilfully sin break the law of God.

Eloy, "adopting what looks like an Averroist view ... of the universal Intellect (*spiritus*), held that man's intellectual nature is a spiritual substance and that everyone that is reborn possesses the Holy Spirit."[84] "Since man's flesh and spirit are thoroughly independent, and with no influence upon each other," Eloy argued, the renewed spirit of man "incurs no responsibility for the weakness of the flesh. His spirit, as such, is sinless. The final goal of man is to vanish into the divine being."[85]

Luther's letter found a practical response in Antwerp. On his return, Eloy and several of his followers were, on February 26, 1526, subjected to an examination by the Inquisition. They recanted their heresy publicly, but Eloy continued to circulate libertine works and in 1544 he was condemned and burned alive. In 1545 three leading Loists were executed and the sect came thus to an end in the Netherlands, although some Loists fled to England. George H. Williams believes that the execution of the last Loists in Antwerp may have contributed to Calvin's decision in 1545 to write a major treatise against all the libertines.[86]

The leader of the Antinomian party in Luther's camp was John Agricola, a one-time teacher in Eisleben. In the autumn of 1536 Luther approached Agricola about a possible position as university professor at Wittenberg. Agricola left Eisleben immediately with his wife and nine children, was received in Luther's house, and substituted that year for Luther both at the university and in the pulpit. Before long, in March and June, 1537, Agricola offended orthodox people by using a "new vocabulary" in his sermons and particularly by stating that the preaching of law should be banned from the churches.[87] Luther in a sermon in July preached against "our Antinomians" without mentioning Agricola's name, stating that some people conclude from Romans 2:4 that repentance comes from preaching the gospel and not the law, and that first of all the grace of God should be preached and only later should people hear about the wrath of God. Agricola published a series of theses in which he advocated the abolition of the law. According to Agricola and his followers, the gospel was to be preached in all its sweetness, without any reference to the Decalog, and the godless should be admonished in private and not criticized from the pulpits.

Between 1538 and 1540 Luther held five disputations against the Antinomians without mentioning the names of his adversaries, although he was at times angry when Agricola did not even appear at the proceedings.[88] In the disputation of September 13, 1538, Luther admitted that in his earlier years he had emphasized the gospel of Christ; but at that time the Christians were weak and in need of comfort, whereas now they need the strong hand of the law. It was thus a matter of emphasis, not a basic belief that the law was superfluous for Christians. The abolition of the Decalog from all preaching, Luther stated, would discredit the gospel, ruin all governments and church life, do away with all repentance and salvation, and result in Müntzerism and complete anarchy.[89] Even Christians need to observe the law; although they are made holy through grace, they nevertheless live in a sinful body. And because of this remaining sin, they must be admonished, rebuked, and terrified by the law of God.[90] Luther advised the magistrates to take action against the Antinomians, accused Agricola of hypocrisy and destroying all moral discipline and order, and finally demanded that his adversary revoke his heretical views.[91] It came to several reconciliations between Luther and Agricola, but in the end the Reformer felt compelled to write a pamphlet *Against the Antinomians* (1539).[92]

Against the Antinomians is addressed to Luther's "good friend in Christ," Caspar Guttel, preacher at Eisleben. Luther begins by lamenting over the fact that his opponents appeal to his writing in support of their heretical views, thus making him their patron. Luther finds it ironic and surprising to hear that he should have abolished the ten commandments when throughout his life he taught the law, preached on the necessity of it, included it in the *Catechism*, and repeated it daily like a child. He did of course teach that sinners should be brought to repentance through sermons and contemplation on Christ's suffering, but this must be done to show the wrath of God against sin which necessitated the death of Christ. How can one know sin without the law? And how can one learn of Christ and grace without the law of God? The law must be preached so that man's conscience is terrified and thus driven to the grace of God.

In this pamphlet Luther expresses the thought that when he sees what his adversaries are doing with his writings, he comes close to the despair of Job. At times he had wished he had not written anything. In his struggles he has come to the conclusion that the devil is lord of this world. From the very beginning of the Christian church the devil sought to extinguish the Word of God in the world. He, Luther, alone, not to mention the many men of God before him, has had to endure more than twenty storms from the devil. There were first his difficulties with the papacy; as soon as he was no longer afraid of the pope, the devil broke into his house with Müntzer and the rebels, which nearly extinguished the light; then came the struggles with Carlstadt; after that came the Anabaptists, breaking in the door and the windows in the hope of destroying the gospel; now it is the Antinomians through whom the devil seeks to extinguish the candle of the gospel. Luther, however, is confident that the church will stand forever, for Christ, not a human leader, is the lord of the church. The sorry end to which Müntzer and the Anabaptists of

Münster came should be a warning to all that the devil is at work and a reminder that human works come to no good.

Agricola retracted his heresy and in 1540 he was appointed court preacher in Berlin by Joachim II of Brandenburg, after which he again fell out of Luther's grace. When Agricola several years later sought another reconciliation with his former friend and co-worker, Luther refused to receive him. With tears in her eyes Agricola's wife pleaded with Luther to give in somewhat, and the Elector of Brandenburg also spoke for Agricola, but the rift between the two men had become too wide for healing.[93] A gifted teacher, preacher, theologian, and administrator, Agricola's character was marred, as Luther observed, by vanity, contentiousness, and moral weakness.[94]

Throughout his long ministry Luther never failed on the one hand to differentiate between the functions of the law and the gospel and on the other to stress the necessity of teaching both. According to Luther, to distinguish correctly between the law and the gospel requires Christian maturity. By "law" the Reformer understood the Word of God and the commandments which demand the obedience and service of man. The "gospel," on the other hand, is the Word of God which does not demand human works but bids man simply to receive the offered grace of forgiveness and eternal salvation as a gift.[95] The gospel is the message about the incarnate Son of God. It is the word of salvation, grace, joy, and peace. The law is the word of perdition, wrath, sadness, pain, unrest, and malediction. The law is the ministry of wrath; the gospel is the ministry of grace. The law is the letter; the gospel is the spirit. The preaching of the law is not only necessary; it is the first thing a sinner must hear. Once the sinner has been convicted of his sinfulness by the law, he must hear the gospel in order to find pardon for his sins.[96] A penitent sinner should no longer be terrified with the law, but hear the gracious words of the gospel. Moreover, when the subject of preaching is righteousness, life in Christ, and eternal salvation, the law must be put out of sight as if it had never existed.[97] And yet, while the law and the gospel are far apart, they are nonetheless most intimately joined together in the heart. Nothing is linked more closely together than fear and confidence, sin and grace, law and gospel.[98] In his exposition of Galatians 1:16 in 1531 Luther stated: "Oh, for the man who can distinguish well here and does not look for law in the gospel but keeps the two as far apart as heaven is distant from the earth! This difference is easy, certain, and plain by itself; but for us it is difficult, in fact, almost incomprehensible."[99]

Luther at no time questioned the validity of the law. In his exposition of the first twenty-two Psalms in 1519, he insisted that as human beings we must not tamper with the law of God but keep it *God's* law, pure and unadulterated.[100] In his *Small Catechism*

(1529) he explained the ten commandments and their importance in the life of Christians, urging that they be committed to memory. In a sermon of 1537 on Matthew 22:34-46, he taught that in Christ there is freedom from sin and the demands of the Old Testament law, but this does not mean that a Christian is free to sin or disobey the law. It is God's will that the commandments are kept, and Christ enables the Christian to keep the law of God.[101] The freedom in Christ is not license: "We, too, who are now made holy through grace, nevertheless live in a sinful body. And because of this remaining sin, we must permit ourselves to be rebuked, terrified, slain, and sanctified by the Law until we are lowered into the grave."[102] Human nature, according to Luther, is always the same. The church of the Old Testament needed the law, and the church of the New Testament must likewise keep it. The Antinomians who hold that the teaching of the law is to be thrown out of the churches are not to be tolerated, for they advocate license and thus pervert the liberty in Christ.[103]

Luther and the Antitrinitarians

Luther also had to contend with those who denied the Trinity. Earl M. Wilbur states that even the more conservative leaders of the Reformation inquired into the scriptural foundation of this traditional doctrine:

> Thus Luther disliked the term *homoousios* as being a human invention, not found in Scripture, and he preferred to say "oneness." Trinity, he said, has a cold sound, and it would be far better to say God than Trinity. He therefore omitted these terms from his Catechism, and the invocation of the Trinity from his Litany. Hence Catholic writers did not hesitate to call him an Arian.[104]

Wilbur goes on to assert that Melanchton, Calvin, and other leaders of the Reformation at first doubted the scripturalness of the doctrine, but since the Protestant cause depended "upon the sympathy and support of the German Protestant Princes as against the Catholic Emperor, it could not afford to do anything to alienate the former, nor to furnish the latter with gratuitous grounds of attack."[105] Thus Luther, according to Wilbur, was at first less than orthodox about the Trinity, but dared not to deviate from the Nicene and Athanasian Creeds on this point for fear of doing damage to his cause.

Without overstating the point, it is fair to say that few theologians of the Reformation era have stressed the doctrine of the

Trinity more strongly than Luther. True, in many statements on the subject he referred to the problem of adequate expression. Luther was not quite satisfied with the designation "persons" in the Trinity, but concluded that there was no better term to express the thought that there were indeed three distinct persons but only one God or a single Godhead.[106] Concerning human terms employed to designate the Trinity he wrote in 1537: "To be sure, it is not very good German and does not sound well to designate God by the word *Dreifaltigkeit* (threefoldness). Even the Latin *Trinitas* does not sound very well. But since we have nothing better, we must speak as we can."[107] In a sermon of 1538 on Luke 9:19-36, he stated:

> We should stay with the true, ancient belief that there are three distinct Persons—Father, Son, and Holy Ghost—in the eternal Godhead. This is the most sublime and the first article of Christian faith.... But to say that God is threefold is very poor language, for in the Godhead the highest Oneness exists.... Augustine, too, complains that he has no fitting word for the mmystery.... To be sure, a threeness does exist in the Godhead, but this threeness exists in the Persons of the one Godhead.... I cannot give this Being a fitting name.[108]

If Wilbur refers to passages such as these, he may indeed find Luther's dissatisfaction with the terms describing the divine mystery, but these references do not in any way cast doubt on the Reformer's orthodoxy concerning the Trinity. Not only did Luther see the Trinity revealed in the New Testament, but he also stated that it was dimly discerned in Old Testament times and believed, although not emphasized, by the prophets.[109] In fact, Scripture, according to Luther, opens with the revelation of a triune God, the Father who creates the universe through his Son, the Word, and the Holy Spirit who broods over all things.[110]

It is not known when Luther first came in touch with Antitrinitarianism. Wilbur states that this heresy appeared in Protestant circles in Nürnberg as early as 1524. When asked by the council of the city as to what to do with people who deny the doctrine, Luther, according to Wilbur, ascribed this heresy to the influence of Carlstadt and Müntzer and counselled to regard the persons involved as Turks and apostates.[111] Martin Cellarius may have been the first Protestant to express Antitrinitarian views in writing. After a heated quarrel with Luther he left in 1525 for East Prussia where he defended Anabaptism and was imprisoned for his radical views. His numerous statements concerning God and Christ were adopted by the early Unitarians, thus making Cellarius one of their own.[112]

Luther's real encounter with Antitrinitarianism came in the

person of Johannes Campanus from Belgium, who in 1528 had enrolled as a student in Wittenberg. Campanus questioned the Trinity, denied the personality of the Holy Spirit, attacked Luther's doctrine of justification and the sacraments, and believed he had rediscovered the truth which was lost since the time of the apostles. In 1532 he wrote a book entitled *Against the Whole World since the Apostles*, which was followed in print by an abridged version under the title *Restitution*. The booklet covers Campanus' system of theology and is distinctly anti-Lutheran. Excluding the Holy Spirit as a person from the Godhead, Campanus postulates an eternal binity of persons, God the Father and Christ the Son in one essence and nature, just as husband and wife are two persons but one flesh. According to Campanus, the passage of Genesis 1:26-27 explains the mystery of relationship between God and Christ. The words "Let us make man in our image, after our likeness ... male and female he created them" point out the two persons in the Godhead and the relationship between the two. Just as Eve was subject to Adam, so Christ is subject to his Father. The Holy Spirit is not a person but the common bond between the Father and the Son. Campanus believed that when the church lost this biblical understanding of God and man, it fell and is thus now in need of restitution.[113]

Melanchton suggested that Campanus be hanged on the highest tree, but Luther counselled that no attention be paid to this blasphemer, lest he become puffed up over his own importance.[114] In his pamphlet *Against the Antinomians* Luther mentions Servetus and Campanus as persons who had stormed against "the old teachers, the pope, and Luther."[115] Since Luther names Campanus together with Servetus, he no doubt considered Antitrinitarianism as a storm which threatened to extinguish the light of the gospel.

In 1531 Michael Servetus (1511-1553) published in Strassburg his *On the Errors of the Trinity*, a work consisting of seven books. In the first book Servetus propounds his "conception of Christ as the natural Son of God, begotten, not eternally, but in a mysterious way through the operation of the Holy Spirit."[116] The Holy Spirit is here thought of as the seed of God through which Mary conceived and not as a distinct person of the Trinity. Christ, in Servetus' view, remains the great saviour of the world to whom God gave all power in heaven and earth. Christ can thus legitimately be called divine. The remaining six books develop the Antitrinitarian theme and attack Luther's justification by faith in strong language, stating that the Reformer's emphasis weakened the importance of sanctification in the life of believers. Moreover, Servetus believed in baptismal regeneration or deification of adults, in eucharistic nutriment which comes from eating the celestial body of Christ, and in the complete unity of God. "It was for this God, thus visible in the countenance of the historic Jesus, audible in Scripture preached, and palpable in the breaking of the Eucharistic body, that Servetus was prepared to die a martyr."[117] Having escaped from the Catholics, Servetus came in 1553 into the clutches of Calvin who charged him with Anabaptism, Antitrinitarianism, pantheism, and psychopannychism (the soul's sleep in death). The court found him guilty of Antitrinitarianism and Anabaptism, and following the old Justinian law against these "crimes," he was condemned to be burned at the stake. Servetus remained steadfast to the end, his last words being, "O Jesus, Son of the eternal God, have pity on me!"

Servetus did not occupy a prominent place in Luther's life and thinking. His *Table Talks* deal at length with Carlstadt, Müntzer, the Anabaptists, the sacramentarians, Zwingli, Agricola, Erasmus, and Campanus, but Servetus is not mentioned by name. It is not known whether Luther had read *On the Errors of the Trinity* (1531), but he knew of Servetus and his Antitrinitarianism. In his *Against the Antinomians* Luther referred to Servetus as one who had attacked both the pope and him, and in a disputation of 1544, which dealt primarily with the doctrine of the Trinity, the Reformer again referred to Campanus and Servetus. In this disputation Luther emphasized again that human reason is inadequate to deal with the mystery of the Trinity, in fact, it is a dangerous undertaking to reason about it, and that we must avoid assuming any distinction between the three persons because each person is the very God and God in his entirety.[118] For Luther this article of faith was a matter of either believing it or of being lost.[119] As early as 1529 he had explained: "We could never attain to a knowledge of the Father's favour and grace except through the Lord Christ, who is a mirror of His Father's heart. Outside Christ we see in God nothing but a wrathful and terrible Judge. But about Christ we could know nothing if the Holy Spirit had not revealed it to us."[120]

The two heresies punished by death in the Codex Justinianus were the denial of the Trinity and the repetition of baptism. This legislation directed against the ancient Arians and Donatists was revived in the sixteenth century and applied to both the Antitrinitarians and the Anabaptists. Even Luther, who at one time had pleaded for tolerance and religious liberty on behalf of himself and his cause, later appealed to this imperial law against the dissenters. From the preceding chapters it is not difficult to understand the reasons for Luther's changed attitude; the purpose of the next chapter is to trace this change in Luther's attitude and to consider the question of tolerance among the radicals who opposed the Reformer.

CHAPTER VII

LUTHER AND THE RADICALS ON TOLERANCE AND RELIGIOUS LIBERTY

Luther and Religious Liberty

Critics of Luther are almost unanimous in believing that the Reformer was tolerant toward religious dissenters when he himself was in danger of death but that he changed to being intolerant when Protestantism became the established religion of the realm.[1] The argument is as follows: In his early works Luther advocated religious liberty, that is, patience and fairness toward those whose religious opinions and practices differed from the accepted dogma of the church. However, his early language on behalf of religious liberty was dictated by his constant fear of persecution, assassination, poisoning, or murder.[2] Only later, when he had passed from the status of a fugitive to that of a builder of a church, did he express his true views on the question of personal beliefs and outward coercion. When Luther, then, at the beginning of his reformation work pleaded for clemency toward heretics, it must be accepted that he spoke and wrote primarily in his own behalf and that of his cause.

Luther no doubt changed in his views toward heretics and persecution. He was certainly not a consistent champion of religious liberty. His later pronouncements on the subject are as much an embarrassment to his followers as are his harsh words against the peasants in 1525. It is, however, simplistic to state that the Reformer later changed his views on tolerance merely because he now found himself in a position of power. As we shall see, the reasons for Luther's changed views on religious liberty must be clearly understood, and it may well be found that he was more consistent in this question than is commonly believed.

In the Ninety-five Theses (1517) Luther stated that the burning of heretics is contrary to the will of the Holy Spirit. A little later he went so far as to state that there has never been a heresy that had not expressed some truth. In 1520 he wrote in his *To the Christian Nobility* that one should overcome heretics with the Word of God and not with fire. "If it were scholarly to conquer heretics with fire, then the henchmen would be the most learned doctors on earth."[3] In the same year he wrote in his *Babylonian Captivity:*

> I say, then, neither pope nor bishop, nor any man whatever has the right of making one syllable binding on a Christian man, unless it be done with his consent. Whatever is done otherwise is done in the

> spirit of tyranny.... I cry aloud on behalf of liberty of conscience, and I proclaim with confidence that no kind of law can with any justice be imposed on Christians, whether by men or by angels, except so far as they themselves will; for we are free from all.[4]

In a Pentecost sermon in 1522, Luther taught that the sword has no power over the hearts of men and that heresy cannot be fought with carnal weapons. Secular rulers ought not to meddle in purely spiritual things; the ministers of the Word of God must capture the love and delight of the human heart and thus win men for the truth. Princes and bishops are foolish when they use force in an effort to press and compel people to believe.[5] Faith is personal and free; all outward compulsion in matters of faith must be excluded. As Luther wrote in his treatise on *Secular Authority* (1523), in matters of faith we are dealing with free actions towards which no person can be forced. Faith is a divine action in the Spirit of God, and it is therefore out of the question that an external power can obtain it by force. One neither can nor should compel anyone to believe.[6] Similarly heresy is something spiritual. One cannot strike it with iron, burn it with fire, or drown it in water. Only the Word of God can overcome it.[7]

As late as 1525, during the height of Luther's struggle with the revolutionary radicals, the Reformer was still against the use of force in religious matters. Commenting on the parable of the tares in a homily in 1525, Luther stated:

> As to heretics and false doctors, we must not pluck them out or destroy them. Christ tells us plainly to allow them to grow. The Word of God is our only resource, for in this field whoever is bad today may become good tomorrow. Who knows whether his heart will not be touched by the Word of God? But if he is burnt or eliminated, his conversion has been made impossible. He is cut off from the Word of God, and he who otherwise might have been saved is of necessity lost. That is why the Lord said that the good grain might be uprooted with the tares. This is abominable in the eyes of God and absolutely indefensible.[8]

Even Carlstadt and Müntzer, Luther wrote in 1524 to the princes of Saxony, should be allowed to preach as much as they wish; the Word of God must go to battle; let the spirits combat with one another; some will no doubt be led astray, for that is what happens in the real course of war; where there is strife and battle, there some must fall.[9] When in 1525 some Anabaptists in Switzerland were drowned in mockery of adult baptism, Luther did not approve of such cruel measures.[10] Writing in 1528 to two pastors concerning the Anabaptists, Luther expressed uneasiness about putting these people to death. It is not right, he wrote, and he was deeply troubled that the Anabaptists were so cruelly put to death. Let every one believe what he likes, for if he is wrong he will have punishment enough in hell. Unless there is sedition and outright rebellion on the part of the fanatics, one should oppose them with the Word of God only.[11] In a letter to W. Link, a friend of his, Luther wrote on July 14, 1528:

> You ask whether the magistrates may kill false prophets. I am slow in a judgment of blood even when it is deserved. In this matter I am terrified by the example of the papists and the Jews before Christ, for when there was a statute for the killing of false prophets and heretics, in time it came about that only the most saintly and innocent were killed. ... I cannot admit that false teachers are to be put to death. It is enough to banish.[12]

It seems that by 1528 a new element had entered Luther's thinking with regard to the punishment of heretics, namely that heretics should be banished whereas rebels against the governments should be put to death. There is here no inconsistency between what Luther believed and practised earlier and now. Both Müntzer and Carlstadt became fugitives in the early 1520's, and in 1525 Luther advocated the death penalty for the rebellious peasants. In 1528 Luther still believed that heretics should be allowed to believe whatever they wished, provided they did not undermine the constituted secular authorities. As to the question of banishing dissenters from the official religious belief, it is obvious that Luther at no time had advocated liberty of worship. Dissenting individuals and groups could believe what they wished, but they were not necessarily allowed to express or practise their beliefs, especially if that expression or practice was detrimental or dangerous to what was commonly believed to be the true faith. It is in this light that we must understand Luther's pronouncements of intolerance towards the Anabaptists and heretics.

It has been pointed out that Luther's "ecclesiastical visitations," initiated in 1527, registered the Reformer's increasing impatience with religious dissenters.[13] There are, to be sure, many statements in this connection which could be interpreted as expressions of Luther's changed views on liberty of conscience. In 1529 Luther wrote to Joseph Lewin Metzsch, who took part in the visitation of the parishes, that even if people do not believe they should be compelled to hear sermons in order to learn at least the outward works of obedience.[14] And writing to Thomas Lösscher, a parish priest of Milau, Luther insisted that people should go to hear sermons, so that they may learn political obedience and social duties, whether they believe in the gospel or not.[15] In 1533 Luther described in a letter to a parish priest of Zwickau the practice of visitations prevailing in

Wittenberg:

> By the authority and in the name of the Most Serene Prince we usually frighten and threaten with punishment and exile those who are negligent in religion and do not come to the sermons. This is the first step. If they do not improve, we instruct the priests in charge to set them a time-limit, one month or more, that they may listen to reason. After that, if they remain obstinate, they are excluded from the community and all contact with them ceases, as if they were pagans.[16]

The letter is "remarkable," as Joseph Lecler observes,[17] foreshadowing the principle of *cujus regio, ejus religio* of the Peace of Augsburg (1555). Moreover, the above statements from the various letters seem to portray Luther as a bigot, intolerant of religious views other than his own. In a lengthy exposition of Psalm 82 (1530) Luther explains his position in detail.[18] He first of all makes it clear that no person should be forced to believe this or that; an individual's belief or unbelief is his private matter. However, when it comes to teaching falsehoods or to blaspheming, the secular authorities should step in. A blasphemer should go to where there are unbelievers and not be allowed to disturb the peace in Christian lands. To preserve the peace, each region should have but one religion. The papists and the Lutherans should not be allowed to carry on their religious activities in the same region. If the Lutherans are not wanted in a certain location, they should leave voluntarily, for the Word of God should not be forced upon people. If on the other hand both the Catholics and Lutherans insist that they will carry on their activities in a certain region, the magistrates should arrange a hearing between the two, listen to the arguments of both sides, and then decide between the one or the other on the basis of which side has the better scriptural arguments. It is not advisable to tolerate two types of preaching, as this causes suspicion, hatred, and the formation of sects.[19] The "corner preachers," as Luther called the Anabaptists, Spiritualists, and radicals who preached secretly, should not be tolerated to preach or teach. They should be reported to the parish minister, for tolerance toward them could lead to disturbances of the peace. Had Müntzer and Carlstadt been restrained in time, the misfortunes which resulted from their activities would not have happened. Only the duly elected and ordained ministers should be allowed to preach. Luther would gladly discontinue his own ministry, but since he is a doctor of theology and God's minister, he must preach and teach, however difficult it might be at times.[20] Luther concludes the first major point of his exposition by stating that he is in no way strengthening the hands of the magistrates against the believers and spiritual matters. According to

Luther, Christian magistrates will not punish anyone, except those who disturb the peace and blaspheme God.

The exposition of Psalm 82 is significant as a document clarifying Luther's distinction between liberty of conscience and liberty of worship. On the question of personal beliefs Luther had not changed from his former position expressed in his earlier works. The individual was free to believe or to disbelieve. However, when it came to proclaiming a certain creed or to expressing certain beliefs publicly, the outward consequences had to be taken into account. In an age of religious fanaticism, different religious opinions often led to public disorders and social disturbances. The breaking of images here and there in the sixteenth century is only one example of this religious zeal. Add to this the political implications of certain emphases in preaching and religious instruction, as exemplified in Müntzer and the Münster fanatics, and it is not difficult to understand the Reformer's apprehensions with regard to what he believed were anti-Christian preachers and notions.

In 1531 the theologians of Wittenberg, headed by Melanchton, prepared a document on the question of whether Anabaptists should be punished by the sword and sent it to Johann Frederick, Elector of Saxony. Melanchton clearly demanded capital punishment for heretics, including Anabaptists, who were found guilty of blasphemy and sedition. The Wittenberg reformers defined blasphemy to mean the teaching of certain doctrines that were contrary to Scripture, rejection of an article in the Apostolic Creed, rejection of infant baptism, and denial of hereditary sin. For all practical purposes this meant that people who did not believe or practise the accepted creed were liable to prosecution by the secular authorities. Sedition was defined as refusal to participate in war or to serve as a magistrate, the belief in community of goods, and any act that undermined or threatened the constituted governments.[21] Blasphemy and sedition were to be dealt with by the state, while the church was to deal with purely doctrinal matters according to Christ's directives in Matthew 18:16ff. Applying the Justinian Code to sixteenth-century heretics, the 1531 document read in part: "We may therefore conclude that my gracious Lord is entitled to apply to them in good conscience the penalties laid down by the Code, law II (L. I. tit. 5)."[22] Luther signed his name to the document but added the following significant note: "Although it is cruel to admit that they be punished by the sword, it is more cruel still on their part that they wish to condemn preaching, propagate dangerous doctrines, suppress orthodox teaching and seek the overthrow of the kingdoms of this world."[23] Luther must have been fully convinced that the document he signed was directed against religious fanatics who were religiously and politically dangerous people. It is also to his credit that he remained sensitive to the suffering of those whom he considered enemies of the established order.

The erection of the Anabaptist kingdom in Münster confirmed Luther in his thinking about the danger of tolerating the teaching of heretical views. He seems to have fully concurred with the action of the Catholics and Lutherans against the Anabaptists following their defeat in Westphalia. But not all secular princes were certain that all Anabaptists deserved death. The Landgrave Philip of Hesse, for example, asked the theologians of Wittenberg what he should do with some Anabaptists who had just been arrested in his domain. In answer to this question the Wittenberg theologians released in 1536 a document which bore the title: *Are Christian Princes Bound to Repress the Anabaptist Sect by Corporal Punishment and by the Sword?*[24] This document is a clear statement of what the reformers in Wittenberg understood by sedition and blasphemy and the reason for their severity against the Anabaptists.

The 1536 document first of all makes it clear that only the secular authorities, not the ministers and servants of the gospel, are responsible for the social and political well-being of their subjects. When ministers of God meddle in worldly government, as Müntzer and the Münsterites had done, they become guilty of rebellion. It is the duty of governments to punish those who seek the destruction of worldly states. The document then proceeds to differentiate between sedition among the Anabaptists and blasphemy. The following beliefs and practices among the Anabaptists are considered seditious: Christians should not serve in government; Christians should not swear; Christians should not own property; Christians may leave their wives if they do not wish to become Anabaptists. These articles are considered seditious because they undermine the social and political structure and thus lead to chaos as happened at Münster. Governments thus do not punish the Anabaptists for what they privately believe but for what their beliefs lead to. Then there are doctrinal articles advocated by the Anabaptists which are blatant blasphemy: the rejection of infant baptism; the denial of original sin; illumination by the Holy Spirit outside of God's Word, and other heretical views. These beliefs and practices are both blasphemous and dangerous, for they are contrary to the clear teaching of Scripture and they destroy, as sedition does, not only the social structure but also the church. Some may object, the document states, that the civil authorities have nothing to do with spiritual matters. It is true that church and state have two distinct functions, but both must work to the glory of God.

> Princes must not only protect the goods and material existence of their subjects, but their most essential function is to promote the honour of God, and to repress blasphemy and idolatry. That is why in the Old Testament the kings, and not only the Jewish kings, but also kings converted from paganism, had the false prophets, together with the idolaters, put to death. Such examples apply to the function of princes, as St Paul also teaches: 'The law is good, for the chastisement of the blasphemers.'[25]

The parable concerning the tares, which may be an argument in favour of tolerance, is now interpreted as follows: The Word that both the tares and the good grain should grow together does not apply to the secular authorities, but to the ministers of God who should not exert any physical compulsion. The document points out confidently: "From all this it is clear that the secular authority is bound to repress blasphemy, false doctrine and heresy, and to inflict corporal punishment on those that support such things."[26] The document concludes by stating that the heretics should be banished or put to death only after all attempts at converting the misguided people have failed. It also warns that those who have erroneous views concerning governments may be "pregnant with the Münster spirit."

The 1536 document was signed by Luther, Bugenhagen, Creutziger, and Melanchton. Before Luther signed he added the following postscript: "This is the general rule of how to deal with the Anabaptists, but may our gracious lord at all times let mercy exist besides punishment, according to circumstances and cases."[27]

It is a sad fact that Luther's early pronouncements in favour of religious liberty had later given way to supporting the princes in their suppression of beliefs and practices which seemed to undermine the social and political institutions of the time. "From the point of religious freedom," J. Lecler writes, "the situation created in Luther's Reformation in Germany represented no appreciable progress. There was liberty of conscience in the evangelical States, if you like, but freedom of worship did not exist. But can one really speak of freedom of conscience if one is not allowed to give expression to one's belief or to show it in outward acts of worship?"[28] Luther no doubt knew that he had changed from his earlier views on tolerance to sanctioning persecution, but throughout he remained most uneasy about this and in his later life he came back to his former statements, namely, that banishment and imprisonment were sufficient penalties.[29] Circumstances and his encounter with fanatics led Luther to intolerance. Carlstadt, Müntzer and the peasants in 1525 left Luther "in a state of distraught nerves," as Bainton puts it,[30] and ready, for the future, to suppress all elements which misapplied the gospel he preached. The Anabaptists did not agree with Müntzer's revolutionary views, but they insisted on the separation of church and state, thus in effect advocating the principle of a holy community separated from the world, and the secularization of the state. Luther viewed such separation with grave misgivings. According to him it was not only impossible to reach perfection on earth by thus separating from the world, but such separation was also undesirable because it led to human pride on the one hand and to a withdrawal of the Christian influence from governmental institutions on the other. For Luther, as well as for the other leading reformers, both the church and the state existed under God, and Christian magistrates were not only responsible for the maintenance of law and order in society, but as Christians they also shared the spiritual concerns of the church. The Anabaptists' separation of church and state, their rejection of infant baptism, which in Luther's view withdrew the grace of God from a large section of society, their refusal to participate actively in matters of state, their rather unorthodox views and practices with regard to private property—all this made Luther fearful as to what the consequences of tolerating the Anabaptists might be. In 1534 a little group of fanatics revived Thomas Müntzer's programme, forcibly seizing the city of Münster in Westphalia. Luther should have differentiated between these fanatics and the majority of the evangelical Anabaptists who believed themselves to be disciples of Christ and who took their Christian life as seriously as Luther did. However, in an age of strong religious convictions, doctrinal differences, and political and social turmoil and even violence left little room for objectivity, forbearance and Christian understanding. When it is remembered that the humanists Zwingli and Melanchton were most severe in their condemnation of the Anabaptists, Luther's relative moderation with regard to the treatment of heretics is remarkable.

The anti-Anabaptist writings of the Wittenberg theologians had their dreadful effect not only in electorial Saxony but also in other areas of the empire. In justification of the execution of Anabaptists and other sectarians, the rulers often appealed to the teaching of the leading reformers on the subject. Philip of Hesse was one of the few princes who did not resort to harsh measures against the radical reformers. Philip did not see in the Anabaptists rebels and blasphemers, but only poor people who erred concerning their faith. As late as 1545 Philip was unable to persuade himself to inflict the death penalty on the radicals, "since over night a man may be instructed and turn from his error. If we should condemn such a one so summarily to death we fear greatly that we should not be innocent of his blood."[31] In his last will this prince distinguished between the peaceful and rebellious Anabaptists—something the mainline reformers seldom did—and advised the educated to win the dissenters back to the true doctrine, for to "kill anybody because he's of false belief, this we have never done and wish also to warn our sons against it."[32] Philip's measures paid off well—in his territory many Anabaptists were won back to the Lutheran fold, and many more contributed to the economy of the land through good farming. While Philip of Hesse cannot be hailed as a champion of religious liberty, among the Lutherans he was one of the few individuals who at least questioned the wisdom and justice of persecuting those of other religious persuasion. It is disappointing to note that the leader of the Reformation in Germany had to betray his early views on tolerance and move with severity, although reluctantly, against the dissident spiritual children. It now remains to be seen whether the radical reformers, against whom the darts of persecution were hurled, were true champions of religious liberty.

The Radicals and Tolerance

Most Protestant and Catholic theologians and historians do not believe that there was any religious group in the sixteenth century that was genuinely tolerant towards creeds other than their own. Some go as far as to state that it was over two hundred years later that the German poet and critic Gotthold Ephraim Lessing (1729-1781) fought for complete tolerance toward non-Christian and other confessions of faith.[33] Others see the institution of freedom and religious liberty coinciding with the inauguration of the American constitution in the eighteenth century.[34] There are, however, writers who see the birth of religious liberty in some of the radical reformers of the sixteenth century. R. J. Smithson, for example, feels that "an unprejudicial examination of the work and teaching of the Anabaptists reveals them as outstanding pioneers in the struggle for religious liberty."[35] E. H. Harbison states that the Anabaptists first caught the vision of religious freedom.[36] C. H. Smith makes Anabaptism "the essence of individualism," for these radical reformers believed that "the greatest degree of liberty must be granted the individual conscience in spiritual matters."[37] Franklin Littell looks upon the Anabaptists as people who consistently championed religious liberty in the modern sense.[38] And Harold Bender goes so far as to say:

> There can be no question but that the great principles of freedom of conscience, separation of church and state, and voluntarism in religion, so basic to American Protestantism, and so essential to democracy, ultimately are derived from the Anabaptists of the Reformation period, who for the first time clearly enunciated them, and challenged the Christian world to follow them in practice.[39]

In considering the question of religious liberty among the radicals, it must be stated at the outset that certain individuals and groups within the radical reformation knew nothing of tolerance. Müntzer and the Anabaptists of Münster advocated the use of the sword against the "godless." The Münsterites compelled people against their will to be baptized and to accept their religious views and practices. It was these revolutionaries, as we have seen, who made the entire Anabaptist movement suspect in the eyes of the leading reformers. The question remains whether the evangelical Anabaptists and certain Spiritualists were truly tolerant toward persons and groups who did not share their beliefs. By tolerance in this connection is not meant indifference or neutrality in religious matters, but a willingness to let others believe and practise their creeds as they see fit, and not to interfere with those beliefs and practices by any force whatsoever.

There is no question that the evangelical Anabaptists were in principle against any physical compulsion in religious matters. We have seen from the letter of Conrad Grebel to Müntzer that the Swiss Brethren repudiated all forms of physical violence, believing in excommunication as the only weapon against spiritual offenders in the church. During the period that Balthasar Hubmaier was persecuted as an evangelical preacher, he wrote a pamphlet entitled *Concerning Heretics and those who Burn Them* (1524).[40] The tract is one of the earliest pleas for complete toleration of all dissenters. Menno Simons also wrote against the persecution of heretics; he even went so far as to challenge the moral basis of capital punishment.[41] Hans Mueller of Medikon stated before the Zürich authorities: "Do not lay a burden on my conscience, for faith is a free gift given freely by God, and is not common property. The mystery of God lies hidden, like the treasure in the field, which no one can find but he to whom the spirit shows it. So I beg you, ye servants of God, let my faith stand free."[42] According to Heinrich Bullinger, an avowed enemy of the Anabaptists, the Swiss Brethren taught that one cannot and should not use force to compel anyone to accept the faith; that it is wrong to put to death anyone for the sake of his erring faith; that the secular kingdom should be separated from the church; that no temporal ruler should exercise any authority in the church; that the Lord has commanded simply to preach the gospel, not to compel anyone by force to accept it; that the true church of Christ has the characteristics that it suffers and endures persecution, but does not inflict persecution on others.[43] Pilgram Marbeck, another Anabaptist, when accused of refusing to recognize other religious groups as scriptural, defended himself as follows: "It is not true that we refuse to count as Christians those who disagree with our baptism and reckon them as misguided spirits and deniers of Christ. It is not ours either to judge or condemn him who is not baptized according to the command of Christ."[44]

While testimonies such as these appear to be genuine pleas for religious liberty, in reading them one cannot help but suspect that they are isolated expressions of individuals under duress, and not characteristic of the Anabaptist movement. According to the records, Anabaptist tolerance did not extend to those who remained true to the state churches, whether Catholic or Protestant. An anonymous Anabaptist writer, for example, in a tract entitled *Christian Baptism*, condemns vigorously the churchmen of his day, regarding them as instruments of the devil because they uphold an unscriptural state church.[45] Another anonymous pamphlet, *Concerning Evil Overseers*, warns its readers against ministers such as Hans Denck, who regard infant baptism as an insignificant point, not worth causing strife on account of it.[46] In yet another pamphlet, *The Hearing of False Prophets or Antichrist*, the writer warns against listening to Luther and other state church ministers, for it is like drinking poison and true Christians must guard against it.[47] Even Menno Simons found it difficult to tolerate certain individuals and groups within the Anabaptist movement, and his criticism of the state churches was at times most severe. In reviewing the doctrines of the Catholics, Lutherans, and Zwinglians, Menno comes to the conclusion that these three groups must rightly be considered as sects, for their teachings and lives are contrary to the Word of God.[48] Pleading for tolerance on behalf of his persecuted followers, Menno tells the state churchmen that their "office and service are not of God and His Word but issue from the bottomless pit."[49]

In answer to passages such as these, it could be argued that the Anabaptists and Mennonites did not understand liberty of conscience to mean a general tolerance of all creeds, but took "liberty of conscience to imply the separation of church and state and the rejection of all persecution."[50] It must be remembered, however, that while the Anabaptists and early Mennonites taught that Christians should not take part in governmental affairs, the point "was purely a theoretical conclusion because in those days no Mennonite could have become a magistrate even if he had wanted to do so."[51] Heretics were automatically excluded from all governmental offices and privileges; they were not even considered full citizens of the state. When religious liberty was granted in Holland, Switzerland, and Prussia, the Mennonites in Europe began to participate freely in state affairs; some of them even became generals in the army.[52] As for the use of force in matters of faith among the Anabaptists, the sixteenth century provides some drastic examples. Hans Hut, a somewhat overly zealous Anabaptist, who in his enthusiasm almost literally baptized people on the run, was for a time imprisoned by a fellow Anabaptist, Leonard von Liechtenstein.[53] Balthasar Hubmaier, who earlier had written in favour of religious tolerance, approved of the action, setting forth his views in a pamphlet entitled *On the Sword*. Hubmaier argued in support of the actions of the magistrates in matters of religion.[54] One is thus almost forced to conclude that intolerance and some degree of persecution were present in all religions, churches, and sects which had the power, while on the other hand all persecuted religions and parties advocated tolerance and religious liberty. Luther had the misfortune of turning from a persecuted heretic to a powerful leader of a dominant church. His early pleas for tolerance and his later views with regard to religious liberty thus stand out in sharp contrasting focus. The Anabaptists of the sixteenth century remained for a long time a persecuted sect. Their pleas for tolerance were a matter of survival. They had no more patience for people who held views other than their own than their enemies who persecuted them.

Among the Spiritualists there seem to have been at least two or three individuals who advocated and practised genuine tolerance. Hans Denck, for example, believed in extreme non-resistance and the separation of church and state, yet this did not prevent him from co-operating and having fellowship with Balthasar Hubmaier who did not share his views concerning the sword and the state. Denck testified that he could not associate with godless men and pronounced heretics, but admitted that he might be in error concerning some article of faith and that other believers who did not share his views could be right in certain points.[55] The humility and tolerance of this Christian humanist were most exceptional in an age of bigotry and fanaticism. His patient love included not only his friends but also his persecutors, against whom he did not vituperate as Menno Simons and some of the other Anabaptists did, but stated that nothing could separate his heart from them.[56] Denck believed that Christians should not quarrel over such rites as baptism and the Lord's supper, but practise Christian love toward each other and all men. Before he died he went so far as to express sorrow for having caused strife and divisions by his zeal for what he had believed to be true. After all, Denck stated, the adversaries worship the same God he worships and honour the same redeemer in Christ. Denck's expression of tolerance rings true.

Sebastian Franck (1499-1542), another Spiritualist, at first followed Luther's teaching but soon turned against Lutheranism and all organized denominations. The following factors seem to have contributed to Franck's decision to follow an independent course. In Luther's quarrel with Erasmus on free will, Franck sided with the humanist; the horrors of the Peasants' War and Luther's siding with the princes and the Reformer's later persecution of the Anabaptists affected him deeply; the many divisions provoked by the Reformation, with each group claiming to possess the absolute truth, made him cautious with regard to religious claims and protestations; and the weakness of the Reformation on the ethical level caused Franck to question the scripturalness of Luther's *sola fide* principle.[57] Franck distinguished between four Protestant groups in the sixteenth century: the Lutherans, the Zwinglians, the Anabaptists, and a fourth group. The fourth group, according to Franck, would discard as unnecessary all such outward things as preaching, ceremonies, sacraments, and pastoral functions; it would seek to form a spiritual church, "gathered from among the nations by the unity of the Spirit and the faith, ruled without exterior means by the invisible and eternal word of God."[58] In 1531 Franck published his *Chronica* or *Bible of History* in which the author seeks to prove that throughout the ages many devout men had been persecuted as heretics. According to the *Chronica*, persecution is an unmistakable sign of heresy. Both Protestants and Catholics thought themselves implicated by this work, and as a result Franck himself was forced to flee.

Rejecting all outward authority, including that of the Bible, Franck championed the complete freedom of the believer. According to this Spiritualist, God wants men to be free to such an extent that they do nothing by compulsion. Whatever is done under pressure of any kind is not from faith. Franck praised God for giving him the love and understanding for all men and religious groups, including those who did not agree with him on certain theological points. "I reject no heretic," he wrote in his *Chronica,* "at the risk of throwing out the grain with the rest, that is, the truth with the falsehood, but I do separate the gold from the mud. For there is hardly a pagan, a philosopher or a heretic who did not have a glimpse of something good."[59] For Franck the truth was truth, whoever proclaimed it, be it heretics or orthodox Christians, and he prayed to God that he would either "forgive their errors, or to reveal these errors to them so that they may see and abandon them."[60] In 1539 Franck wrote:

> To me, anyone who wishes my good and can bear with me by his side, is a good brother, whether Papist, Lutheran, Zwinglian, Anabaptist, or even Turk, even though we do not feel the same way, until God gathers us in his own school and unites us in the same faith.... Let no one try to be master of my faith and to force me to follow his belief.... I reject no one who does not reject me.... I do

> not stand apart from any sect, knowing full well that God's community cannot be pointed out like a sect of which it can be said that it is here or there, but I believe in a holy Christian Church, a communion of saints; I love and consider as my brother and neighbor every man, especially those who, among all sects, beliefs and peoples, belong to Christ.[61]

Joseph Lecler points out: "In the history of the freedom of conscience, Sebastian Franck occupies a radical position. It is surprising that such a definite religious individualism could develop already in the beginning of the sixteenth century."[62] It is the more remarkable when it is considered that Franck's individualism was not that of a pure humanist, sceptic, or rationalist, but that of a deeply spiritual man. Franck's tolerance was the result of mystic spirituality and a sense of realism, as paradoxical as that may seem to be. All men were dear to him in so far as they lived sincerely for God. He did not ask anyone what he believed, but how he lived. And he confessed: "I am so accustomed to errors and mistakes in all men that, because of these, I do not hate anyone on earth, but I deplore, admit and see in them my own misery and condition."[63] There seems to be no doubt as to the sincerity of Franck's tolerance.

Like Sebastian Franck, Caspar Schwenckfeld insisted, as we have seen from his clash with Luther, on the invisible character of religion. According to him, the Word of God was completely free and not attached to such visible things as the sacraments and an outward ministry.[64] Consequently, in matters of faith there was to be complete freedom. While Schwenckfeld established small groups for prayer, instructions, and the practice of charity, he always maintained, contrary to Luther, that the church was invisible. He refused to become a leader of a specific sect, and he was opposed both to the Anabaptists who organized into groups independently of the civil governments and the Lutherans who set up their state churches. He frequently wrote against the practice of civil authorities interfering in religious matters. In a letter of 1533 he argued that if the Christian religion was to consist of outward worship, justice, and prescriptions, the civil authorities might have the power to command and punish with weapons in religious things. Since, however, Christianity is based on inward justice, faith, devotion and freedom of conscience, the state has no power to order or prohibit in such matters at all.[65]

Both Schwenckfeld and Luther made use of the expression "freedom of conscience," but the concept was understood differently. Luther believed that while the Christian conscience was set free from human regulations, especially those of "papism," it was the more strongly bound to the Word of God.[66] And a conscience bound to the Word of God would submit to scriptural teaching on matters of church and state, including obedience to the powers that be. Schwenckfeld, on the other hand, did not have the same respect for the "letter" of the Bible. For him freedom of conscience was primarily concerned with the use of outward things. Since faith is a highly individual matter, the outward expression of that faith must be left up to the individual Christian. Christians have individual needs, hence there are various manifestations of religious practice. No outward force may interfere in the practice of one's faith.[67]

Although Schwenckfeld had some strong theological convictions, in his writings and personal conduct he seems to have stuck to his principle of religious liberty. He did not want to organize a religious denomination because he believed in the freedom of the spirit and individual faith; he was criticized, attacked, and sometimes persecuted, but he never resorted to revenge or violence; he was sad when the Lutherans and other mainline reformers persecuted the Anabaptists; and he wanted to be tolerant towards people of different creeds as long as he could practise his own religion. In 1534 he wrote to Philip of Hesse: "I only ask to be a brother and a friend to anyone who has the zeal of God, loves Christ with all his heart, clings to the truth and is devoted to piety."[68] The Anabaptists, according to Schwenckfeld, were not to be persecuted but persuaded by gentleness. And even if they refused to change their mind, they should not be forced or punished by the stake but simply separated from devout people by excommunication.[69] Because of his tolerance and leniency, Schwenckfeld frequently had to clear himself of the charge of belonging to the Anabaptists. Nevertheless, he visited Anabaptists in prison, and to the end insisted that the magistrates had no right to interfere in spiritual affairs.

In conclusion, then, while Luther advocated religious liberty in his earlier writings, he was forced to modify his views on tolerance when he realized that radicalism might threaten the Reformation and the social and political order. In this Luther was no exception. There had been advocates of tolerance and liberty of conscience since the beginning of Christianity. For example, such church fathers as Tertullian and St. Augustine had spoken in favour of religious toleration when the Christian church was in the minority and oppressed; when the church became accepted in society, these very men counselled coercion and even physical punishment, for according to them the salvation of souls was at stake.[70] The Anabaptists, who remained minority groups in the sixteenth century, cannot be considered as genuine champions of religious tolerance because their sectarianism was often too exclusive and sometimes even fanatical. Nevertheless, they laid the foundation of religious liberty by separating church and state, by baptizing believers only, by rejecting violence for Christians, and by holding the view that the individual is primarily responsible to God and not to human authority. Moreover, through suffering persecution the Anabaptists eventually contributed to the realization among the persecutors that most coercion is useless as a method for achieving desired objectives.[71] The Spiritualists were perhaps the only true advocates of liberty of conscience, for they conceded freedom of belief and practice to all those who dissented from the status quo. The Spiritualists not only wrote against all coercion in religious matters, but also admitted that others who differed from them might have as much, if not more, light on certain doctrinal points as they had. Such humility and understanding may well be the touchstones of sincerity. There seems to be no doubt that our modern concept of religious liberty owes much to the Spiritualists of the sixteenth century.

CHAPTER VIII

CONCLUSION

As a result of the mainline reformers' hostile attitude toward them, the dissident sects not only had to endure persecution in the sixteenth century but also had to bear suspicion, ridicule, and reproach for almost four hundred years. Especially Lutheran Protestantism, to which the radicals had constantly appealed, has sinned against them most, for it failed to appreciate that they simply endeavoured to follow Luther's early reformation principles to their logical conclusion and live in accordance with the precepts of the gospel as they understood them. As late as the nineteenth and twentieth centuries, the descendants of the radical reformers were compelled to leave their soil, country, home and property, only in order to be able to live their lives according to the dictates of their conscience. The general attitude towards them, however, was bound to change in their favour. In 1905 the Baptist historian Henry Vedder wrote: "The time is rapidly approaching when the Anabaptists will be as abundantly honoured as, in the past four centuries, they have been unjustly condemned."[1] Since that time the radical reformers have been vindicated.

The Catholic scholar C. A. Cornelius, as has been mentioned, was one of the first in the middle of the nineteenth century to speak an effective word in mitigation of judgment upon the radicals and declared that their real history was yet to be written. There were others who soon followed Cornelius to the Anabaptist sources—which had been largely neglected until then—and found what Sebastian Castellio (1515-1563), humanist scholar of Savoy, had found already in the sixteenth century. In a manuscript addressed to Theodore Beza (1519-1605), French Protestant theologian and heir of John Calvin in Geneva, Castellio writes:

> With regard to the Anabaptists I would like to know how you know that they condemn legitimate marriage and the magistracy and condone murders. Certainly it is not in their books and much less in their words. You have heard it from their enemies. . . . I do not believe what you say about the Anabaptists . . . . Neither should people be held responsible for a position which they have themselves repudiated, any more than you, Beza, should be reproached for the amatory verses of your youth.[2]

All groups and persons against whom Luther was compelled to fight have been defended and in many instances rehabilitated by historians and theologians. Herman Barge has demonstrated that the Wittenberg radicals, especially Carlstadt, were not mere misguided people whose sole ambition was to destroy what Luther had carefully built up, but sincere individuals who believed they put into practice what Luther had preached. Such revolutionary radicals as Thomas Müntzer have been shown, although somewhat unconvincingly, as complimenting Luther in his reform efforts. Walter Nigg, for example, states that Müntzer rightly stood up for the socially and politically oppressed peasants, whose suffering he sought to alleviate in accordance with Scripture.[3] The Spiritualists and mystical Anabaptists, notably Schwenckfeld and Denck, have been vindicated in numerous works.[4] The Antitrinitarians, or Unitarians, as they are known today, have also found their defenders among reputable scholars. Wilbur's *History of Unitarianism* and Bainton's *Hunted Heretic*, which tells the tragic story of Protestant persecution, have left their mark in favour of these "stepchildren of the Reformation." And the Mennonite historians and theologians have not failed to do their part in clearing the evangelical Anabaptists of the charges against them and portraying them as advocates of a truly biblical Christianity. The *Mennonite Quarterly Review*, Goshen, Indiana, continues to publish the fruit of excellent research into the life and faith of the radical reformers. Today the estranged children of the mainline reformers enjoy a greater reputation than they ever have; both Catholic and Protestant scholars and leaders acknowledge their important contribution to western civilization. Only a few excerpts from their writings and statements shall be cited here.

E. A. Payne, a leader of the Baptist Union of Great Britain and Ireland, states concerning the Anabaptists:

> The doctrine of the church as a fellowship of believers, free from the control of the state . . . ; emphasis on the spirit of man as the candle of the Lord; the claim for toleration and freedom of conscience; the recognition of the obligations resting on all Christians to charity, community and evangelism; these ideas, with varying degrees of emphasis, have become influential in all parts of the world.[5]

Roland H. Bainton, although feeling that the radical reformers may have advocated tolerance because they were persecuted, nevertheless observes: "The Anabaptists anticipated all other religious bodies in the proclamation and exemplification of three principles which are on the North American continent among those truths which we hold to be self-evident: the voluntary church, the separation of church and state, and religious liberty."[6] Concerning the radicals of the sixteenth century in general, Philip Hughes, Catholic historian, writes:

> They were the means of preserving what, in the nature of things, would seem to be the aim and the first justification of Luther,

> Calvin, and of all the other successful Reformers who were their deadliest foes: the principle, that is to say, that men have the right to form their own religious groups, to join a group or not to join, to leave it when they choose; that these groups are equal in their rights and subject to no authority but what they themselves choose; that the groups are free to choose the way they shall worship; that every individual is free to choose what he shall believe. Whatever the theologians may need to say ... about the value of these principles, they have had a great history (thanks, first, to the Anabaptists) in the last three hundred years, nor is that history at an end.[7]

Hans George Fischer, a Lutheran Protestant, confesses: "Only too often have we reviled the alleged works-righteousness of the Anabaptists while we ourselves have been all too forgetful and negligent concerning the divine commandment of brotherly love. Over all the joy and satisfaction of justification by faith alone, we have forgotten the call for sanctification of our lives."[8] Even the question of infant versus adult baptism did not die with the radicals of the sixteenth century. Reformed theologians such as Karl Barth and Emil Brunner, as Payne points out, have raised several questions with regard to this subject, and what they have said has caused some anxious debate in various circles.[9] And Dom Gregory Dix and Kenneth Kirk, both of the Anglican church, "have come to feel that the rites of baptism and confirmation must be brought more closely together again."[10]

There is, however, as we have seen, another side to the story. Leonard Verduin writes in his most sympathetic account of the evangelical Anabaptists: "One can speak very well of them indeed before he becomes guilty of a bias as pronounced as that of those who have so long spoken evil of them; one can let these Stepchildren play the rôle of the hero and he will be at least as near to historic truth as is the tradition that has so long assigned to them the rôle of the rogue."[11] Verduin's approach to Anabaptism, as expressed here, is representative of Anabaptist scholarship in the last thirty or forty years. Inasmuch as the radicals have been abused and misunderstood in the past, Mennonite historiography in our century has gone in the other extreme by heaping all the praise on the dissidents and most of the blame on the mainline reformers. Scholars such as Henry Vedder, John Horsch, Harold Bender, and John S. Oyer have in their writings presented the case of Anabaptism very well, but often at the expense of the Reformer's side of the story. In their treatment of the struggle between Luther and the radicals, the Reformer does not come off too well. He is either shown as a heartless enemy of all those who opposed him, or else his reasons for attacking the radicals are oversimplified. The following quotation from Verduin's *The*

Reformers and their Stepchildren is a good example of this oversimplification:

> In his haste to establish the doctrine of justification by faith rather than by works Luther down-graded good works; the only place he had left for good works was at the very end, as a sort of postscript or appendage, something that needed attention after salvation was an accomplished fact. We meet in Luther, to put it theologically, a very heavy emphasis on the forensic aspect of salvation and a correspondingly light emphasis on the moral aspect. Luther was primarily interested in pardon, rather than in renewal. His theology was a theology that addresses itself to the problem of guilt, rather than to the problem of pollution. There is an imbalance in this theology between what God does *for man* and what He does *in man*.[12]

Our study of Luther's struggle with the dissenters has demonstrated that Luther did not establish his doctrine of justification by faith in haste, that he did not downgrade good works, and that the question of salvation was for him not of a forensic nature but a matter of spiritual life or death. In our study we have tried to understand both the Reformer and the sects, particularly the reasons for the clash between them. We have seen that Luther's attitude towards the radicals did not spring from his capriciousness or jealousy, or because of a mere difference of opinion concerning the principle of justification by faith. The heart of the problem with regard to Luther's difficulties with the radicals lay in the Reformer's agonizing conversion experience and his theology which resulted from this experience and his understanding of the gospel. Not to realize this is to fail to understand fully the life and death conflict which Luther waged with his enemies.[13] For Luther the doctrine of justification by faith alone was of such importance that not to accept it was to blaspheme God and to repudiate the Christian religion. In view of this justification by faith, to which Luther had come through much agony of soul, the radicals' emphasis on outward piety, the freedom of the spirit, the separation of church and state, and social reform, was, in the opinion of Luther, missing the very heart of the Christian faith.[14] Luther was mainly concerned with establishing a right relationship with God, although he believed, and stressed, that once a right relationship between a believer and God was established, good works would or should follow.

As a result of his salvation experience and study of the Bible, Luther at first loudly proclaimed the reformation principles of *sola fide* and *sola scriptura* and advocated complete religious liberty. When he realized, however, what men such as Carlstadt and Müntzer did with these principles, misapplying and perverting the

Conclusion

newly-discovered freedom in Christ, as far as Luther was concerned, the Reformer felt that he had no choice but to attack his former followers, co-workers, and friends. When these men, particularly Müntzer, became associated with the Peasants' War, Luther was certain that his attitude and action against them were justified. As we have seen, Luther at first even sympathized with the peasants who believed that the time had come to alleviate their difficult feudal existence. Again, the peasants appealed to the Reformer's teaching regarding love, freedom, equality in Christ, and the laymen's duty and responsibility within the Christian church. Luther's emphasis on the spiritual side of Christianity was applied by the peasants to the social conditions, and, what is more, translated into concrete, violent actions against the oppressors. It cannot be held against Luther that he did not try to pacify the justly enraged peasants. Pleading with them not to resort to violence, he explained to them the real meaning of freedom and justice in Christ. When according to Luther the peasants abused the gospel of Christ by using it as a cover for their purely social, economic, and in some cases, political goals, he felt he had to separate himself from them and their cause lest the inevitable conflict would undo the work of the Reformation. Luther's violent and un-Christian attitude and language cannot be excused, however sympathetic one might feel toward the Reformer and his cause. When one realizes, however, that Luther saw in the destructiveness of the peasants not only a threat to the Reformation but also a threat to all institutions of society, it should be at least possible to understand the fury with which he moved against the insurgents. Any doubts that Luther may have had about his harshness toward the revolutionary radicals and the peasants were definitely dispelled when the fanatical Anabaptists established their kingdom in Münster. Luther was thus confirmed in his thinking that all dissenters were enthusiasts and fanatics and many of them rebels against constituted governments. As far as Luther was concerned, unscriptural theological views with regard to the Christian mysteries, such as the Lord's supper and baptism, went hand in hand with civil disobedience.

Luther's attitude toward all the Anabaptists received its initial hue from his encounters with the Wittenberg radicals, Müntzer, the Zwickau prophets, and the rebellious peasants. Some have suggested that had the Reformer first met such peaceful Anabaptists as the Swiss Brethren, he would perhaps have been more lenient and tolerant toward the whole "left wing" of the Reformation.[15] This is no doubt debatable, but Payne observes correctly when he states that the revolt of the Anabaptists in Münster was the "main cause of Anabaptism's passing under a cloud of obloquy and shame, thus preventing any honest facing of the basic issues raised by the Swiss Brethren and their more responsible followers."[16] It must also be remembered that in the sixteenth century the distinction between the various groups of the dissident sects was not as obviously clear to Luther and other mainline reformers as to most twentieth-century historians of the Anabaptist movement. As we have seen, there were several points of contact between the various individuals and groups within the radical reformation.

For Luther, as our study has demonstrated, the views of the radicals with regard to the sacraments, Scripture, church-state relations, and the place of the law in the preaching of the gospel were not mere opinions with no or little spiritual consequences but weighty matters which concerned the salvation of people who held them. When Luther insisted on the real presence in the eucharist, he was in effect fighting to maintain the certainty of his salvation; in the real body and blood of Christ in communion he partook of the real Redeemer. Similarly in the baptismal water Luther saw a tangible manifestation of God's grace which the infant experienced without any action on his part. The Anabaptists' practice of adult baptism, with their insistence that the baptismal candidate first believe and profess his faith, was for Luther a denial, at least a weakening, of the doctrine of justification through grace alone.

The Spiritualists' emphasis on the inner Word was in Luther's view another attempt to negate the tangible written Word in which God had revealed himself to man. To give in to the Spiritualists was not only to fall prey to subjectivism but also to elevate human reason and the mere opinions of men above Scripture.

While Luther believed that the state had no business in purely religious matters, the radicals' attempt to separate church and state was for Luther both unscriptural and dangerous. In his co-operation with the princes Luther was no doubt led by the reality of circumstances in which he found himself. He believed, however, that the principle of the priesthood of all believers applied also to the Christian magistrates who had a share in the building of the church in their realms. Moreover, the removal of the state from the church would, according to Luther, bring about a complete secularization of many human institutions, a fear which later proved well founded.

Luther's struggle with the Antinomians within his own camp is a clear indication that the Reformer was not apathetic to the practice of "good works" among believers. It will be remembered that in connection with the Antinomians and those who denied the Trinity Luther expressed his greatest agony, saying that it might have been better had he never written anything than to endure the onslaught of the devil in this respect.

Conclusion 157

Luther's fear of and struggle against those who at one time had appealed to him can only be understood when it is considered that the dissident groups were radicals in the true sense of the word, proposing to turn the long-established order and institutions upside down. Commenting on the persecution of the Anabaptists, Philip Hughes states: "Let it once be believed in any society that a particular group is really threatening to overthrow the distribution of property, to introduce a new conception of right and wrong, to prohibit and to crush all ways of life but its own, and the society will react savagely."[17] To this may be added that the radicals' idea of a free church and their opposition to official Christendom were so clearly in opposition to the still dominant mediaeval idea of a social order as expressed in the concept of the church and the empire, that most men could see in the Anabaptist movement "nothing less than the destruction of the very basis of society itself."[18] The documents seem to indicate "a real possibility that Anabaptism, if unimpeded by the sword of the magistrate, might have become the prevailing form of the church in Germany."[19] Had Anabaptism triumphed in the sixteenth century, it is difficult to say what would have happened to the states, the principles of non-resistance and religious liberty, the idea of a free church. The fact seems to be that persecution contributed in no small measure to what the radical reformers later became, and many of the positive traits which we today find praiseworthy in the Anabaptist movement are the result of past hardships and hostilities towards it.

In the nineteenth century the German poet Heinrich Heine stated: "Luther was wrong and Müntzer right."[20] In the twentieth century the same view has been expressed in connection with most radicals of the sixteenth century. Verduin states that in his book he has given the radicals of the Reformation a sympathetic treatment because "history has to a large extent demonstrated that they were in a large way right."[21] He then goes on to say that Protestantism has come to endorse the emphases for which the radicals pioneered: "The free Church, the Church by voluntary association, the missionary Church, and a host of other features for which the Stepchildren agonized, have become part and parcel of the Protestant vision—so much so that men are often surprised to learn that it was not always thus."[22]

While history may have to a large extent vindicated the radicals, it is not the purpose of this study to assign guilt to any individual or group or to absolve from guilt, but to see the struggle between Luther and the dissidents in its historical and theological perspectives and to remind scholars of Anabaptism that in their zeal to correct the image of the radical reformers they sometimes become one-sided and less than charitable toward the mainline reformers who in good faith could not tolerate what they considered alien views. If, however, we want to speak of right and wrong in connection with Luther and the radicals, it may be suggested that we have here a case of two rights and two wrongs. The radicals, notably Carlstadt, Müntzer, the peasants, and the Münsterites, were, according to Luther, wrong in what he thought was misapplying the gospel to their religious, social and political views and in perverting the intentions of his writings; Luther, according to the radicals, was wrong and certainly un-Christian in moving with fury and violence against the peasants and the Anabaptists. The radicals, particularly some of the Spiritualists and the evangelical Anabaptists thought they were right in believing that each individual should have the freedom to live his faith according to his conscience; Luther believed he was right in insisting that the freedom of a Christian did not include the right to undermine or destroy social structures and political institutions. Moreover, while the theological differences between Luther and the dissidents were at times of a fundamental nature, as in the sacramental controversy, it was often a matter of emphasis that separated the two sides. For example, both Luther and the evangelical Anabaptists believed in salvation through the grace of God. Luther, however, stressed justification by faith alone, believing that good works would follow, whereas the Anabaptists emphasized the Christian life. In the heat of battle the different emphases often assumed the appearance of insurmountable doctrinal differences. And compromise, tolerance, and understanding were largely unknown in the intense religiosity of the sixteenth century.

In their approaches to the sacraments and the divine mysteries the radicals and Luther revealed their basic views of man, God, and life in general. Luther, generally pessimistic about human nature and mediaeval in many of his views, approached God as a helpless sinner in need of forgiveness and healing. He believed implicitly in the sacramental value of the eucharist and baptism, experiencing in the sacraments tangible expressions of God's grace and love for the sinner. The radicals, on the other hand, were radical in the true sense of the word, intent on severing all connections with mediaeval Christianity. Their rational explanations of the sacraments and such concepts as the Trinity and the incarnation, and their stress on practical living rather than on dogma, seemed to reveal them as Christian humanists, although most of them would have repudiated the term. Paradoxically, however, Luther the pessimist considered all reality and life as given by God and thus worthy of acceptance and enjoyment; most radicals either turned away from the secular world, or sought to destroy it, and emphasized the inward reality of the spirit.

It is hoped that the religious fanaticism and intolerance of the sixteenth century are things of the past. In an age of increasing religious indifference and scepticism it may indeed appear incredible that the struggle between Luther and the radical reformers was fought with such seriousness on both sides. And yet, it may have been because of this profound seriousness that throughout history both the Lutheran and the radical tradition have contributed significantly to the development of Protestant religious thought.

ABBREVIATIONS

CS   *Corpus Schwenckfeldianorum.* 19 vols. Leipzig and Pennsburg, Pennsylvania, 1907-1961.

EA   *Martin Luthers Sämmtliche Werke.* 65 vols. Erlangen and Frankfurt a.M., 1826-1855.

LW   *Luther's Works.* Published by Concordia Publishing House and Fortress Press, 1956ff. (References to the American Edition of *Luther's Works* are given in parentheses, following the notes to the German editions. Only references to the most frequently used works by Luther in English translation are given.)

MQR   *Mennonite Quarterly Review.* Goshen, Indiana.

SLA   *Martin Luthers Sämmtliche Schriften.* 23 vols. St. Louis, Missouri, 1880-1910.

WA   *Martin Luthers Werke. Kritische Gesammtausgabe.* Weimar, 1883-1948.

WA, Br. *Martin Luthers Werke. Briefwechsel.* Weimar, 1930-1948.

WA, DB *Martin Luthers Werke. Die Deutsche Bibel.* Weimar, 1906-1961.

WA, Tr. *Martin Luthers Werke. Tischreden.* Weimar, 1912-1921.

NOTES

Chapter I

[1] Heinrich Boehmer, *Martin Luther: Road to Reformation*, trans. by J. W. Doberstein and J. G. Tappert (Living Age Books; New York, 1957), p. 87.

[2] *WA*, 40, 1, p. 137.

[3] *WA*, 47, p. 275.

[4] J. T. Mueller, "A Survey of Luther's Theology," *Bibliotheca Sacra*, CXIII (1956), 156-157.

[5] *WA*, 43, p. 461.

[6] *WA*, 10, 2, p. 262.

[7] *WA, Br.* 3, p. 643.

[8] *WA, Br.* 5, p. 531.

[9] *WA, Tr.* 5, p. 544.

[10] Walter Zeeden, *The Legacy of Luther*, trans. from the German by Ruth M. Bethell (Westminster, Maryland, 1954), p. 5.

[11] H. H. Kramm, *The Theology of Martin Luther* (London, 1947), p. 121.

[12] *WA*, 25, p. 375.

[13] *WA*, 40, 1, p. 48.

[14] *WA, DB,* 6, p. 10.

[15] *WA, DB,* 7, pp. 385-387 (*LW*, 35, pp. 395-397).

[16] *WA*, 1, pp. 527-529.

[17] *WA*, 6, pp. 404-469 (*LW*, 44, pp. 115-217).

[18] *WA*, 6, pp. 497-573 (*LW*, 36, pp. 3-126).

[19] *WA*, 7, pp. 12-38 (*LW*, 31, pp. 329-377).

[20] One of the best studies of the radical reformation to date is George H. Williams, *The Radical Reformation* (Philadelphia, 1962).

[21] In B. Bax, *Rise and Fall of the Anabaptists* (London, 1903), p. 51.

[22] L. Keller, *Ein Apostel der Wiedertäufer* (Leipzig, 1882), p. 5.

[23] A. H. Newman, *A Manual of Church History* (2 vols.; Philadelphia, 1931), II, 156-200.

[24] Keller, *Ein Apostel*, pp. 3-4.

[25] R. A. Knox, *Enthusiasm: A Chapter in the History of Religion* (New York, 1950), pp. 126-127.

[26] Ricarda Huch, *Das Zeitalter der Glaubensspaltungen* (Berlin/Zürich, 1937), pp. 240-241.

[27] Robert Stupperich, *Das Münsterische Täufertum* (Münster, 1958), p. 14.

[28] A. J. F. Zieglschmid (ed.), *Die älteste Chronik der Hutterischen Brüder. Ein Sprachdenkmal aus frühneuhochdeutscher Zeit* (Ithaca, New York, 1943), pp. 39-40.

[29] Thomas M. Lindsay, *A History of the Reformation* (2 vols.; Edinburgh, 1907), II, 441.

[30] R. Kreider, "Anabaptism and Humanism: An Inquiry into the Relationship of Humanism to the Evangelical Anabaptists," *MQR*, XXVI (April, 1952), 123-141.

[31] Ernst Troeltsch, *The Social Teaching of the Christian Churches*, trans. by Olive Wyon (2 vols.; London, 1931), II, 699. Cf. G. Zschäbitz, *Zur Mitteldeutschen Wiedertäuferbewegung nach dem grossen Bauernkrieg* (Berlin, 1958), pp. 122-140.

[32] F. Littell, *The Anabaptist View of the Church. A Study in the Origins of Sectarian Protestantism* (2nd ed., revised and enlarged; Boston, 1958), p. 4.

[33] In H. S. Bender, "The Anabaptist Vision," *MQR*, XVIII (April, 1944), 76.

[34] Menno Simons, *Complete Writings*, trans. from the Dutch by L. Verduin and ed. by J. C. Wenger (Scottdale, Pennsylvania, 1956), p. 334.

[35] *Ibid.*, p. 712.

[36] H. J. Hillerbrand (ed.), "An Early Anabaptist Treatise on the Christian and the State," *MQR*, XXXII (January, 1958), 30 and 38.

[37] Zieglschmid, *Die älteste Chronik*, pp. 42-44. This is obviously an oversimplification and a misrepresentation of Lutheran teaching concerning the Christian life. Luther taught that good works do not make a person good. "The opposite is true: a person must be good before he can do good works. Hence, where justification is concerned, works are altogether out of place. There faith alone reigns. . . . According to Luther, Christian ethics has two basic marks. First, it finds its norm in the will of God expressed in the structure of life and in Scripture. . . . Second, no compulsive action can please the unconditional demand of the divine will. Instead, the right love must spring freely and joyfully from the heart. Luther's ethics is an

ethics of love [and an ethics of freedom]." Otto W. Heick, *A History of Christian Thought* (2 vols.; Philadelphia, 1965-1966), I, 339.

³⁸For example, the Swiss Anabaptists protested against tithes and other standing economic institutions, a fact which some Mennonite historians do not wish to emphasize in their attempt to stress the spiritual nature of the Anabaptists' conflict with Zwingli. See E. Crous, *et al.*, *Gedenkschrift zum 400-jährigen Jubiläum der Mennoniten oder Taufgesinnten, 1525-1925* (Ludwigshaven a.RH., 1925), pp. 42-44.

Chapter II

[1] The best sympathetic study of Carlstadt is still Hermann Barge's *Andreas Bodenstein von Karlstadt* (2 vols.; Leipzig, 1905). See also: Gordon Rupp, "Andrew Karlstadt and Reformation Puritanism," *The Journal of Theological Studies*, New Series, X (1959), 308-326; Hans J. Hillerbrand, "Andreas Bodenstein of Carlstadt, Prodigal Reformer," *Church History*, XXXV, No. 4 (December, 1966), 379-398; Gordon Rupp, *Patterns of Reformation* (London, 1969).

[2] Barge, *Andreas Bodenstein*, I, 196-200.

[3] R. H. Bainton, W. A. Quanbeck, and E. G. Rupp, *Luther Today* (Decorah, Iowa, 1957), pp. 110-111.

[4] R. H. Bainton, *Here I Stand: A Life of Martin Luther* (A Mentor Book; New York, 1950), pp. 157-158.

[5] "Vom Missbrauch der Messe," *WA*, 8, pp. 477ff. (*LW*, 36, pp. 127-230).

[6] *WA, Br.* 2, p. 409.

[7] In Luther, *The Letters*, selected and trans. by M. A. Currie (London, 1908), pp. 91-93.

[8] "Eine treue Vermahnung zu allen Christen, sich zu hüten vor Aufruhr," *WA*, 8, pp. 676-687 (*LW*, 36, pp. 51-74).

[9] Henry C. Vedder, *The Reformation in Germany* (New York, 1914), p. 194.

[10] In Bainton, *Here I Stand*, p. 155.

[11] In Vedder, *The Reformation in Germany*, p. 183.

[12] *EA*, 61, pp. 1-2.

[13] Bainton, *Luther Today*, p. 118.

[14] In Bainton, *Here I Stand*, p. 161.

[15] *Ibid.*, pp. 161-162.

[16] *EA*, 28, pp. 202-284 (*LW*, 51, pp. 67-100).

[17] "Von beider Gestalt des Sacraments zu nehmen," *WA*, 10, 2, pp. 11-41 (*LW*, 36, pp. 233-267).

[18] *The Catholic Encyclopedia*, ed. by Charles G. Herbermann, *et al.* (15 vols.; New York, 1907-1912), IX, 449.

[19] See Vedder, *The Reformation in Germany*, p. 191, and Littell, *The Anabaptist View of the Church*, p. 7.

[20] *EA*, 61, p. 4.

[21] Walter Nigg, *The Heretics*, ed. and trans. by Richard and Clara Winston (New York, 1962), p. 305.

[22] *WA, Br.* 2, pp. 462-465.

[23] Luther, *The Letters*, p. 105.

[24] *WA, Br.* 2, pp. 472-473.

[25] In Vedder, *The Reformation in Germany*, p. 191.

[26] Luther, *The Letters*, pp. 119-120.

[27] For the dramatic episode in Jena see *EA*, 64, pp. 384-395.

[28] For Luther's meeting with the Orlamünders, see *EA*, 64, pp. 398-404.

[29] *WA, Br.* 3, p. 353.

[30] Quoted by Luther, *WA, Br.* 3, p. 361.

[31] *WA, Br.* 3, p. 361.

[32] J. A. Jungmann, *The Mass of the Roman Rite. Its Origins and Development*, trans. by F. A. Brunner (new revised and abridged ed. in one vol.; New York, 1959), pp. 129-130.

[33] In Gregory Dix, *The Shape of the Liturgy* (Westminster, 1945), p. 115.

[34] In Jungmann, *The Mass of the Roman Rite*, p. 140.

[35] In N. O'Rafferty, *Instructions on Christian Doctrine—The Sacraments* (New York, 1939), p. 94.

[36] See Kramm, *The Theology of Martin Luther*, p. 53.

[37] *EA*, 29, pp. 265-266.

[38] *EA*, 30, pp. 108-110.

[39] *EA*, 30, pp. 144-145.

[40] H. Bornkamm, *Luther's World of Thought*, trans. by M. H. Bertram (St. Louis, 1958), p. 112.

[41] *Ibid.*

[42] Ernst Ludwig Enders (ed.), *Dr. Martin Luthers Briefwechsel* (10 vols.; Calw and Stuttgart, 1884-1903), VI, 339-353.

[43] *WA*, 18, pp. 197ff. (*LW*, 40, pp. 73-223).

[44] Letter to Christians at Strassburg, December 15, 1524, *EA*, 53, p. 274 (*LW*, 40, p. 68).

[45] Luther, *The Letters*, p. 169.

⁴⁶*Ibid.*, p. 133.

⁴⁷Enders, *Briefwechsel*, V, 193-194.

⁴⁸"Schrift D.M.L. an alle Christen, D. Karlstadts Büchlein belangend, darin er sich des Aufruhrs entschuldigt," *EA*, 64, pp. 404-408. Both Carlstadt and his congregation at Orlamünde repudiated Müntzer's recourse to arms and violence. They rejected the Allstedt League and pointed out that they would depend wholly on God and not on the might of men. Eric W. Gritsch, *Reformer Without a Church. The Life and Thought of Thomas Muentzer 1488 [?] - 1525* (Philadelphia, 1967), p. 109.

⁴⁹"Luthers Vorrede zu Karlstadts Erklärung," *EA*, 64, pp. 408-410.

⁵⁰Barge, *Andreas Bodenstein*, II, 505.

Chapter III

[1] E. B. Bax, *The Peasants' War in Germany 1525-1526* (London, 1899), pp. 27-28.

[2] *WA*, 6, p. 259. Cf. *WA*, 37, p. 597, and 47, p. 284.

[3] *WA, Br.* 2, p. 167.

[4] See Gerhard Ritter, *Luther. Gestalt und Tat* (München, 1959), pp. 136-137.

[5] *WA, Br.* 2, p. 305.

[6] "Von weltlicher Oberkeit, wie weit man ihr Gehorsam schuldig sei," *WA*, 11, pp. 229-281 (*LW*, 45, pp. 77-129).

[7] *Ibid.*, p. 277.

[8] *Ibid.*, pp. 277-278.

[9] "Dass eine christliche Versammlung oder Gemeine Recht und Macht habe, alle Lehre zu urtheilen und Lehrer zu berufen, ein und abzusetzen, Grund und Ursach aus der Schrift," *WA*, 11, pp. 401-416 (*LW*, 39, pp. 301-314).

[10] Rudolf Thiel, *Luther* (Wien, 1935), p. 445.

[11] In Gritsch, *Reformer Without a Church*, p. 56.

[12] *Ibid.*, p. 57.

[13] *Ibid.*, p. 58.

[14] *Ibid.*

[15] There may have been as many as four versions, two in German, one in Latin, and one in Czechoslovakian. See Rupp, *Patterns of Reformation*, pp. 174-181.

[16] Gritsch, *Reformer Without a Church*, p. 59.

[17] Rupp, *Patterns of Reformation*, pp. 181-182.

[18] *Ibid.*, p. 186. On Müntzer's mysticism and on how he applied his mysticism to political and social circumstances, see H.-J. Goertz, *Innere und äussere Ordnung in der Theologie Thomas Müntzers* (Leiden, 1967), p. 149.

[19] Gritsch, *Reformer Without a Church*, p. 79.

[20] Hayo Gerdes, *Luthers Streit mit den Schwärmern um das rechte Verständnis des Gesetzes Mose* (Göttingen, 1955), p. 89.

[21] Alfred Meusel, *Thomas Müntzer und seine Zeit. Mit einer Auswahl der Dokumente des grossen deutschen Bauernkrieges* (Berlin, 1952), p. 285.

[22] *Ibid.*

[23] *EA*, 61, p. 64.

[24] Thiel, *Luther*, p. 445.

[25] Luther, *The Letters*, p. 117.

[26] We follow the German version of the *Fürstenpredigt* as printed in Meusel, *Thomas Müntzer*, pp. 278-293. A good analysis of the sermon is that of Carl Hinrichs, *Luther und Müntzer. Ihre Auseinandersetzung über Obrigkeit und Widerstandsrecht* (Berlin, 1962), pp. 41-65.

[27] "Man sieht jetzt hübsch, wie sich die Aale und Schlangen zusammen verunkeuschen auf einem Haufen. Die Pfaffen und alle bösen Geistlichen sind Schlangen, . . . und die weltlichen Herren und Regenten sind Aale." Meusel, *Thomas Müntzer*, pp. 288-289.

[28] Hinrichs, *Luther und Müntzer*, pp. 43-44.

[29] "Ein Brief an die Fürsten zu Sachsen von dem aufrührerischen Geist" (1524), *WA*, 15, pp. 199-221 (*LW*, 40, pp. 45-59).

[30] Meusel, *Thomas Müntzer*, pp. 152-153.

[31] "Thomas Müntzers hoch verursachte Schutzrede und Antwort wider das geistlose, sanftlebende Fleisch zu Wittenberg, welches mit verkehrter Weise durch den Diebstahl der Heiligen Schrift die erbärmliche Christenheit also ganz jämmerlich besudelt hat." Meusel, *Thomas Müntzer*, pp. 294-308.

[32] *EA*, 53, pp. 253-255.

[33] Robert Friedmann, "Thomas Müntzer's Relation to Anabaptism," *MQR*, XXXI (April, 1957), 78.

[34] Bax, *The Peasants' War*, pp. 33-34.

[35] Otto Schiff, "Thomas Müntzer und die Bauernbewegung am Oberrhein," *Historische Zeitschrift*, Band 110 (München/Berlin, 1913), pp. 89-90.

[36] "Thomas Müntzers Manifest an die Mansfeldischen Bergknappen," Meusel, *Thomas Müntzer*, pp. 273-274.

[37] For the text see Meusel, *Thomas Müntzer*, pp. 275-276.

[38] "Eine schreckliche Geschicht und Gericht Gottes über Thomas Müntzer, von Dr. Luther herausgegeben" (1525), *WA*, 18, pp. 362-374.

[39] Luther, *The Letters*, p. 139.

[40] *EA*, 61, pp. 14-15. In his *Table Talks* Luther is reported as telling a story about how Müntzer went to a young girl and asked her

to sleep with him so that he could better teach the Word of God. *Ibid.*, p. 56.

[41] Bax, *The Peasants' War*, p. 30. See also A. C. McGriffin, *Martin Luther. The Man and His Work* (New York, 1914), p. 250.

[42] In Franz-Funk Brentano, *Luther*, trans. from the French by E. F. Buckley (London, 1936), p. 197.

[43] In Vedder, *The Reformation in Germany*, p. 253.

[44] In Brentano, *Luther*, p. 197.

[45] A. H. Newman, *A History of Anti-Pedobaptism* (Philadelphia, 1897), p. 84. Torsten Bergsten, *Balthasar Hubmaier* (Kassel, 1961), pp. 282-284, doubts very much that Hubmaier was the author of the articles. Bergsten shows, however, that Hubmaier was in agreement with them.

[46] Newman, *A History of Anti-Pedobaptism*, p. 84. See also Bax, *The Peasants' War*, pp. 34-35.

[47] "Ermahnung zum Frieden auf die zwölf Artikel der Bauernschaft in Schwaben" (1525), *WA*, 18, pp. 279-334 (*LW*, 46, pp. 3-43)

[48] *WA, Br.* 3, pp. 479-482.

[49] *WA, Br.* 3, p. 508.

[50] "Wider die räuberischen und mörderischen Rotten der Bauern" (1525), *WA*, 18, pp. 344-361 (*LW*, 46, pp. 49-55).

[51] R. J. Smithson, *The Anabaptists. Their Contribution to our Protestant Heritage* (London, 1935), pp. 177-178.

[52] *WA*, 18, pp. 360-361.

[53] "Ein Sendbrief von dem harten Büchlein wider die Bauern" (1525), *WA*, 18, pp. 375-401 (*LW*, 46, pp. 59-85).

[54] *WA, Br.* 3, p. 507.

[55] *WA, Br.* 3, p. 515.

[56] In Bax, *The Peasants' War*, pp. 352-353.

[57] "Ob Kriegsleute auch in seligem Stande sein können" (1526), *WA*, 19, p. 625 (*LW*, 46, 89-137).

[58] Ekkehard Krajewski, *Leben und Sterben des Züricher Täuferführers Felix Manz* (Kassel, 1957), p. 156.

Chapter IV

[1] Harold S. Bender, "Die Zwickauer Propheten, Thomas Müntzer und die Täufer," *Theologische Zeitschrift*, Heft 4 (1952), 262ff.

[2] Harold S. Bender, *Conrad Grebel c. 1498-1526. The Founder of the Swiss Brethren, Sometimes Called Anabaptists* (Scottdale, Pennsylvania, 1950), p. 173.

[3] Paul Peachey, *Die soziale Herkunft der Schweizer Täufer in der Reformationszeit* (Karlsruhe, 1954), pp. 91-94. This also applies to the south-German Anabaptists. Balthasar Hubmaier had been a professor at the University of Ingolstadt and Hans Denck was a humanist scholar.

[4] Fritz Blanke, "Zollikon 1525. Die Entstehung der ältesten Täufergemeinde," *Theologische Zeitschrift*, Heft 4 (1952), 262.

[5] Cf. Zieglschmid, *Die älteste Chronik*, pp. 46-47.

[6] Zschäbitz, *Zur Mitteldeutschen Wiedertäuferbewegung*, pp. 49-50.

[7] *WA*, 12, p. 288.

[8] *WA*, 28, pp. 24-25.

[9] In Bender, "The Anabaptist Vision," p. 69.

[10] Cf. Jan J. Kiwiet, *Pilgram Marbeck. Ein Führer in der Täuferbewegung der Reformationszeit* (Kassel, 1957), p. 148. It is still not clear whether the Swiss-south-German Anabaptists had a direct influence on the rise of Anabaptism in the Netherlands. Some believe that while the similarities between the southern and northern Anabaptists were great, the direct influence was negligible. See Guy F. Hershberger (ed.), *The Recovery of the Anabaptist Vision* (Scottdale, Pennsylvania, 1957), p. 71.

[11] "Von der Wiedertaufe an zwei Pfarrherrn," *WA*, 26, pp. 137-174 (*LW*, 40, pp. 229-262).

[12] See Bender, *Conrad Grebel*, p. 119.

[13] See Barge, *Andreas Bodenstein*, II, 207-208.

[14] G. H. Williams (ed.), *Spiritual and Anabaptist Writers* (London, 1957), p. 83. See also Bender, *Conrad Grebel*, pp. 119-120.

[15] Bender, *Conrad Grebel*, p. 119.

[16] *WA, Br.* 3, p. 464.

[17] In Alfred Coutts, *Hans Denck 1495-1527 Humanist and Heretic* (Edinburgh, 1927), p. 114.

[18] "Das diese Wort Christi 'Das ist mein Leib' noch fest stehen, wider die Schwärmgeister," *WA*, 23, pp. 38-320 (*LW*, 37, pp. 3-150).

[19] *WA*, 26, pp. 145-146.

[20] See Bender, "Die Zwickauer Propheten," pp. 262ff.

[21] Blanke, "Zollikon 1525," pp. 249-251. On excesses among the Anabaptists, see also Lowell H. Zuck, "Anabaptism: Abortive Counter-Revolt Within the Reformation," *Church History*, XXVI (September, 1957), 211-226.

[22] Barge, *Andreas Bodenstein*, II, 205.

[23] Charles Garside, "Ludwig Haetzer's Pamphlet Against Images: A Critical Study," *MQR*, XXXIV (January, 1960), 20-36. It has also been shown that Carlstadt's influence on Zwingli's views concerning the Lord's supper was more substantial than has been commonly assumed. Hillerbrand, "Andreas Bodenstein of Carlstadt," p. 393.

[24] Bender, *Conrad Grebel*, pp. 109-110. It may be pointed out that some of Carlstadt's writings against Luther were taken to Basel where, according to Gordon Rupp, they were "printed with the aid of the future Anabaptist leader, Felix Manz." Rupp, "Andrew Karlstadt and Reformation Puritanism," p. 321.

[25] For a detailed analysis of Bullinger's statements concerning possible personal contacts between Müntzer and Grebel, see Bender, *Conrad Grebel*, pp. 110-116.

[26] For an English translation of the letter, see Williams, *Spiritual and Anabaptist Writers*, pp. 73ff.

[27] Bender, *Conrad Grebel*, p. 116.

[28] *Ibid.*, pp. 116-117. Italics are mine.

[29] *Ibid.*, p. 172. Italics are mine.

[30] *Ibid.*, p. 117.

[31] Williams, *Spiritual and Anabaptist Writers*, p. 73. The quotations from Grebel's letter to Müntzer that follow are from this source.

[32] In Bender, *Conrad Grebel*, p. 286.

[33] See Zschäbitz, *Zur Mitteldeutschen Wiedertäuferbewegung*, p. 29.

[34] Zuck, "Anabaptism," p. 225.

[35] Newman, *A History of Anti-Pedobaptism*, pp. 3-5; Johannes Warns, *Baptism. Studies in the Original Christian Baptism, Its History and Conflicts, Its Relation to a State or National Church and Its Significance for the Present Time*, trans. from the German by G. H.

Lang (London, 1957), pp. 75-77.

[36] William A. Be Vier, "Modes of Water Baptism in the Ancient Church," *Bibliotheca Sacra*, CXVI (July-September, 1959), 232-234.

[37] In Warns, *Baptism*, p. 79.

[38] Simons, *Complete Writings*, p. 236. Cf. Zieglschmid, *Die älteste Chronik*, pp. 270-276.

[39] Simons, *Complete Writings*, pp. 229-287.

[40] In Williams, *Spiritual and Anabaptist Writers*, p. 80.

[41] *Ibid.*, p. 81.

[42] *Ibid.*

[43] *WA*, 37, pp. 640-641.

[44] *WA*, 10, 3, p. 142.

[45] *Ibid.*

[46] *WA*, 11, p. 300.

[47] *WA*, 2, p. 727. The Anabaptists baptized by affusion as well as by immersion. See B. J. Kidd (ed.), *Documents Illustrative of the Continental Reformation* (Oxford, 1911), p. 455.

[48] See A. W. Dieckhoff, *Luthers Lehre von der kirchlichen Gewalt historisch dargestellt* (Berlin, 1865), pp. 87-90.

[49] In Mueller, "A Survey of Luther's Theology," p. 230.

[50] *WA*, 30, 1, p. 310.

[51] *Ibid.*, pp. 310-312.

[52] *WA*, 26, pp. 148-149.

[53] "Es ist ja billicher, das Gottes wort einen andern glawben mache ... denn das der glaube ander weit das wort mache, Weil sie denn bekennen mussen, das ynn der ersten tauffe nicht an Gottes wort, sondern am glawben mangele, und nicht ein ander wort, sondern ein ander glawbe not sey. Warumb handeln sie denn nicht viel mehr, das em ander glawbe werde und lassen das wort unverendert?" *WA*, 26, p. 172.

[54] *Ibid.*, p. 170.

[55] On the arguments of some of the Anabaptists against Luther's position on infant baptism, see Simons, *Complete Writings*, pp. 126ff.

[56] *Ibid.*, p. 126.

[57] *EA*, 23, pp. 163-165.

[58] *EA*, 19, pp. 108-113.

[59] *WA, Br.* 7, p. 129.

[60] *WA*, 2, p. 190.

[61] *WA*, 6, pp. 301-302.

[62] See Bender, "The Anabaptist Vision," pp. 76-77. It is of interest to note that the idea of a congregation within the main church came in part from the Silesian nobleman Caspar Schwenckfeld, who was at first drawn to the Reformer but later became estranged from him, as we shall see in a subsequent chapter.

[63] See John Horsch, *Mennonites in Europe* (2nd ed., slightly revised; Scottdale, Pennsylvania, 1950), p. 28.

[64] *WA*, 46, p. 734.

[65] See Dieckhoff, *Luthers Lehre*, pp. 182-183.

[66] Cf. Simons, *Complete Writings*, pp. 739-742. See also Erland Waltner, "The Anabaptist Conception of the Church," *MQR*, XXV (January, 1951), 5-16; Littell, *The Anabaptist View of the Church*, pp. 82-108. The Swiss Brethren, the Mennonites, and the Hutterites also included non-resistance in the list, but the south-German Anabaptists, led by Balthasar Hubmaier, believed in taking up arms for the government.

[67] Hillerbrand, "An Early Anabaptist Treatise on the Christian and the State," p. 31.

[68] Samuel Geiser, "An Ancient Anabaptist Witness for Nonresistance," *MQR*, XXV (January, 1951), 67.

[69] *EA*, 62, p. 191.

[70] In Coutts, *Hans Denck*, p. 184.

[71] *SLA*, 12, pp. 1234-1237.

[72] *EA*, 39, p. 136.

[73] *WA*, 47, p. 110.

[74] *EA*, 16, pp.255-256.

[75] *WA*, 7, pp. 278-279.

[76] *EA*, 53, p. 265.

[77] *WA*, 33, p. 371.

[78] Edward Langton, *History of the Moravian Church. The Story of the First International Protestant Church* (London, 1956), pp. 41-43.

[79] In Coutts, *Hans Denck*, p. 244.

[80] Horsch, *Mennonites in Europe*, p. 28.

[81] *EA*, 23, pp. 166-167.

[82] See Luther's letter to Philip of Hesse, *EA*, 55, pp. 258-264.

[83] Enders, *Briefwechsel*, V, 228-229.

[84] Philip Schaff, *History of the Christian Church* (reproduction of the 2nd ed., revised; Grand Rapids, Michigan, 1953), VII, 667.

[85] Simons, *Complete Writings*, p. 333.

[86] Coutts, *Hans Denck*, p. 81.

[87] *EA*, 53, pp. 263-265.

[88] *SLA*, 13a, p. 799.

[89] *SLA*, 13b, p. 2441.

[90] In Coutts, *Hans Denck*, p. 256.

[91] In Smithson, *The Anabaptists*, p. 118.

[92] *Ibid.*, pp. 117-118.

[93] John Horsch, "The Character of the Evangelical Anabaptists as Reported by Contemporary Reformation Writers," *MQR*, VIII (July, 1934), 129.

Chapter V

[1] Cornelius' writings on the subject include *Geschichte des Münsterischen Aufruhrs* (1855) and *Historische Arbeiten vornehmlich zur Reformationszeit* (1899). Ludwig Keller and others followed Cornelius in introducing an objective, scholarly method of research on the Anabaptists in general. See *The Mennonite Encyclopedia*, ed. by H. S. Bender, et al. (4 vols.: Scottdale, Pennsylvania, 1957), III, 780-782.

[2] *WA, Br.* 6, pp. 398-401.

[3] The Melchiorites were followers of Melchior Hofmann, a former associate of Luther in Wittenberg. Hofmann is known for his apocalyptic visions and his views on the speedy return of Christ. As early as 1525, when he was still a follower of the Reformer, Hofmann expressed his visionary views in letters. (See, for example, his letter to the church of Dorpat, Latvia, in which he warns against "enthusiasts" in religious matters! Enders, *Briefwechsel*, V, 213-217.) Hofmann became quite active in northern Germany and in the Rhine regions, preaching and baptizing with great success. However, he never advocated the use of violence, and while in prison in Strassburg, he warned against the spirit of Münsterites and counselled moderation. Cf. Wilhelm Wiswedel, *Bilder und Führergestalten aus dem Täufertum* (Kassel, 1952), III, 60ff.

[4] *Ibid.*, p. 202.

[5] Walter G. Tillmanns, *The World and Men Around Luther* (Minneapolis, 1959), p. 280.

[6] *WA, Br.* 6, pp. 398-401.

[7] Tillmanns, *The World and Men*, p. 280.

[8] *WA, Br.* 6, pp. 401-403.

[9] "Vorrede zu Urban Regii Widerlegung der Münsterischen neuen Valentinianer und Donatisten Bekenntnis," *EA*, 63, pp. 332-336.

[10] "Vorrede zur Neuen Zeitung von den Wiedertäufern zu Münster" (1535), *WA*, 38, pp. 347-350.

[11] As will be seen in a subsequent chapter, a year later Luther was more severe against rebellious Anabaptists, advising the secular authorities that for sedition and blasphemy, the radicals should be banished, imprisoned, and even executed. *WA*, 50, pp. 6-15.

[12] Melchior Hofmann had widely disseminated this view throughout northern Germany and the Rhine regions. Even such men

as Menno Simons were influenced by this doctrine. On Menno's point of view, see C. Krahn, *Menno Simons (1496-1561) Ein Beitrag zur Geschichte und Theologie der Taufgesinnten* (Karlsruhe, 1936), pp. 155-158.

[13] *WA*, 47, pp. 561-562.

[14] Ethelbert Stauffer, "The Anabaptist Theology of Martyrdom," *MQR*, XIX (July, 1945), 197.

[15] *WA, Br.* 2, p. 167.

[16] *WA*, 7, p. 774.

[17] *WA*, 8, p. 554.

[18] *WA*, 8, p. 185.

[19] See John Horsch, "An Inquiry into the Truth of Accusations of Fanaticism and Crime Against the Early Swiss Brethren," *MQR*, VIII (April, 1934), 83-84.

[20] John Horsch, "The Rise and Fall of the Anabaptists of Münster," *MQR*, IX (July, 1935), 138-139.

[21] See Zschäbitz, *Zur Mitteldeutschen Wiedertäuferbewegung*, pp. 119-121. Ludwig Hätzer was charged with sexual immorality, and it is difficult to clear him of these charges. See Gerhard J. F. Goeters, *Ludwig Hätzer (ca. 1500-1529) Spiritualist und Antitrinitarier. Eine Randfigur der frühen Täuferbewegung* (Gütersloh, 1957), pp. 147-148.

[22] Horsch, "The Rise and Fall," p. 139.

[23] Knox, *Enthusiasm*, p. 132.

[24] C. Henry Smith, *The Story of the Mennonites* (3rd ed. revised and enlarged; Newton, 1950), pp. 76-77.

[25] *Ibid.*, p. 77.

[26] Zschäbitz, *Zur Mitteldeutschen Wiedertäuferbewegung*, pp. 53-54. See also Luther's reference to the greed and political ambition of the Münsterites. *WA*, 38, pp. 347-350.

[27] Horsch, "The Rise and Fall," p. 134.

[28] Krahn lists the titles of Luther's works read by Menno Simons. *Menno Simons*, pp. 43-44.

[29] *Ibid.*, pp. 42-43.

[30] Lindsay, *A History of the Reformation*, II, 496. Tillmanns states: "The disaster of the Heavenly Kingdom led Menno to his ... great doctrine: His teaching of non-resistance." *The World*

and Men, p. 281. This is obviously incorrect. Menno believed in non-resistance before the Münster tragedy.

[31] Simons, *Complete Writings*, p. 34.

[32] *Ibid.*, p. 37.

[33] *Ibid.*, p. 44.

[34] *Ibid.*, p. 49. The fact that Menno does not mention the immorality and polygamy of the Münsterites strikes one as somewhat strange. Krahn explains, with good reason, that Menno may not have had time to elaborate on these excesses. *Menno Simons*, pp. 31-32.

[35] Simons, *Complete Writings*, p. 284.

[36] G. R. Elton (ed.), *The New Cambridge Modern History* (Cambridge, 1958), II, 129.

[37] Tillmanns, *The World and Men*, p. 282.

[38] See John Horsch, "Menno Simons' Attitude Toward the Anabaptists of Münster," *MQR*, X (January, 1936), 67.

[39] In *ibid.*, p. 68.

[40] F. H. Littell, *The Free Church* (Boston, 1957), p. 27.

[41] Horsch, *Mennonites in Europe*, p. 226.

Chapter VI

[1] Coutts, *Hans Denck*, p. 102.

[2] *Ibid.*, pp. 103-104.

[3] See, for example, Luther's Exposition of the Magnificat in 1520, *WA*, 7, p. 746, where the Reformer states that no one can understand God or his Word unless he has received such understanding directly from the Holy Spirit, and no one can receive it from the Holy Spirit without experiencing, proving and feeling it.

[4] Aarne Siirala, *Gottes Gebot bei Martin Luther* (Helsinki, 1956), pp. 122, 126-128.

[5] Coutts, *Hans Denck*, p. 20, states that Denck made the acquaintance of Müntzer at Nürnberg. Walter Fellmann, however, doubts that Denck ever made personal contact with the revolutionist. *Hans Denck Schriften: Religiöse Schriften* (Gütersloh, 1956), II, 10.

[6] *Ibid.*, p. 108. Not even Menno Simons, the acknowledged leader of Dutch Anabaptism, took his peace principle as far as this; his writings against the Catholics, Lutherans, and those Anabaptists with whom he did not agree theologically often betray an impatience and a severity which ill becomes one who had abjured all recourse to violence. For Simons' intolerance toward others, see *Complete Writings*, pp. 207, 332-355.

[7] "Bekenntnis für den Rat zu Nürnberg," Fellmann, *Hans Denck Schriften*, II, 20-26.

[8] "... wirt durch die liebe Gottes gantz vergottet und Gott in im vermenscht." *Ibid.*, p. 25.

[9] "Was geredet sei," *ibid.*, pp. 27-47.

[10] *Ibid.*, p. 32.

[11] *Ibid.*, p. 36.

[12] *Ibid.*, p. 38.

[13] *Ibid.*, p. 43.

[14] *Ibid.*, p. 44.

[15] *Ibid.*, pp. 104-110.

[16] "do eyn rechter funck götlichs eifers ist." *Ibid.*, p. 106.

[17] Rufus M. Jones, *Spiritual Reformers in the 16th and 17th Centuries* (Boston, 1959), p. 27.

[18] *Ibid.*, p. 30.

[19] *WA*, *Br.* 3, p. 433.

[20] *WA, Br.* 3, pp. 432-433.

[21] In Jones, *Spiritual Reformers*, p. 66. See also *CS*, 1, pp. 44-45.

[22] In *CS*, 2, p. 281.

[23] *CS*, 2, pp. 129-130.

[24] *CS*, 2, p. 130.

[25] *CS*, 2, p. 130.

[26] *CS*, 2, p. 131.

[27] *CS*, 2, pp. 129-140.

[28] *CS*, 2, p. 133.

[29] *CS*, 2, p. 133.

[30] *CS*, 2, p. 136.

[31] *CS*, 2, p. 138. Schwenckfeld thus clearly differentiated between the ordinary bread in the Lord's supper and the spiritual bread which is Christ himself. The words of institution, "This is," refer, according to Schwenckfeld, to the spiritual body and blood of Christ. *CS*, 2, pp. 271-274.

[32] Selina G. Schultz, *Caspar Schwenckfeld von Ossig (1498-1561), Spiritual Interpreter of Christianity, Apostle of the Middle Way, Pioneer in Modern Religious Thought* (Norristown, Pennsylvania, 1946), p. 73.

[33] When Schwenckfeld reminded Luther of the twelve questions, Luther, according to Schwenckfeld's diary (December 1-4, 1525), interrupted the nobleman with the words: "Yes, Zwingli!" *CS*, 2, p. 241. This seems to confirm the point that Luther had read Schwenckfeld's letter and arguments but had not studied them well enough so as to differentiate between Schwenckfeld's and Zwingli's views on the Lord's supper.

[34] The interview is recorded by Schwenckfeld, *CS*, 2, pp. 240-282. There is an English translation in Schultz, *Caspar Schwenckfeld*, pp. 75-96. All quotations are from this translated version of the interview.

[35] Schultz, *Caspar Schwenckfeld*, p. 75.

[36] *Ibid.*, p. 36.

[37] *Ibid.*, p. 37.

[38] *Ibid.*

[39] Crautwald's letter is included in *CS*, 2, Doc. XV.

[40] Schultz, *Caspar Schwenckfeld*, p. 78. German version in *CS*, 2, pp. 247-248.

[41] Schultz, *Caspar Schwenckfeld*, p. 79.

[42] *Ibid.*, pp. 92-93.

[43] Toward the end of the interview between Luther and Schwenckfeld, there is the following entry: "Martin asked: How can you be so sure of your opinion? Schwenckfeld: I will not withhold this from you. I am positive of what I wrote in my article: That Christ did not leave his flesh and blood, etc. (i.e., in the bread and wine), and that the former interpretation is not right. But concerning the words, you will keep in mind that I cannot feel so sure, not being well versed in languages. . . . I am confirmed in our view more and more and know it can be understood in no other way." Schultz, *Caspar Schwenckfeld*, p. 95.

[44] The *Stillstand* was proposed in a public letter written by Schwenckfeld, Valentine Crautwald, and the Liegnitz pastors, April 21, 1526. *CS*, 1, pp. 325-333.

[45] On Luther's later harshness toward Schwenckfeld, see *CS*, 14, p. 1030; 9, pp. 29-30; *WA, Tr.* 5, pp. 300-301.

[46] Editor in *CS*, 2, p. 238.

[47] Paul L. Maier, *Caspar Schwenckfeld on the Person and Work of Christ. A Study of Schwenckfeldian Theology at Its Core* (Assen, The Netherlands, 1959), p. 26. On Schwenckfeld's differentiation between the inner and outer Word, see *CS*, 2, p. 485; 3, p. 354; 9, p. 457; 12, p. 510; 13, p. 308.

[48] Maier, *Caspar Schwenckfeld*, p. 26. See *CS*, 2, pp. 40-41; 2, pp. 454, 485, 569. The influence of St. Augustine and Tauler is in evidence here. See also *CS*, 11, p. 385; 14, p. 349.

[49] For some references on the function of the Word, see *CS*, 9, pp. 461-468.

[50] *CS*, 5, p. 126.

[51] *CS*, 4, p. 183; 8, p. 463; 3, pp. 902-904.

[52] In Schultz, *Caspar Schwenckfeld*, p. 96.

[53] See Coutts, *Hans Denck*, pp. 101-104; Jones, *Spiritual Reformers*, pp. 12-13. Heick, *A History*, I, 346-347, points out that Luther's theology was a theology of the Word and then proceeds to show that the Reformer uses the term "Word of God" in several ways: Christ is the Word of God; creation is a Word of God; the redemptive deeds of God in history are a Word of God; preaching is the Word of God; and the Bible is the Word of God. Heick is correct

in his analysis of Luther's uses of the term "Word of God." The failure to understand the Reformer's uses of the term has led to the erroneous view that Luther's conception of the Word underwent considerable change.

[54] Catholic scholarship has frequently stressed Luther's subjectivism in his approach to the Scriptures. See, for example, Joseph Lortz, *Die Reformation in Deutschland* (2 vols., 3rd ed.; Freiburg, 1940), I, 213, 223-225, 396-405.

[55] Siirala, *Gottes Gebot*, p. 132. "Der Ausdruck 'Die Schrift' ist für Luther nicht ohne weiteres identisch mit der Bibel in der Bedeutung der kanonischen Schriften des Alten und Neuen Testaments. Wenn Luther betont, dass die Schrift klar sei, dann will er damit vor allem herausstellen, dass Gott wirklich sein Wort zu den Menschen gesprochen hat. In und durch 'Schriften' und durch 'die Schrift' hat Gott ein bestimmtes Wort in die Herzen der Menschen geschrieben. Wenn man dieses Wort verliert, so verliert man auch Gott." *Ibid.*, p. 134. See *WA*, 18, p. 626, and *WA*, 8, p. 82.

[56] *WA*, 7, p. 546.

[57] *WA*, 20, p. 571.

[58] *WA*, 27, pp. 285-286.

[59] *WA*, 52, pp. 400-401.

[60] *WA*, 33, pp. 273-275.

[61] *WA*, 26, p. 172.

[62] *WA, Tr.* 1, p. 248.

[63] *WA*, 27, pp. 75-76.

[64] *WA*, 23, p. 686.

[65] *WA*, 20, pp. 789-790.

[66] *WA*, 36, pp. 500-501.

[67] *WA*, 43, p. 505.

[68] *WA*, 25, p. 120.

[69] In Schultz, *Caspar Schwenckfeld*, p. 330.

[70] *Ibid.*, p. 330.

[71] Williams, *Spiritual and Anabaptist Writers*, pp. 180-181.

[72] Williams, *The Radical Reformation*, p. 335.

[73] Luther's message to Schwenckfeld is printed in *WA, Tr.* 5, pp. 300-301.

[74] According to Schwenckfeld, Luther had approved, probably

in 1522, of the nobleman's preaching in Silesia: "I am glad to hear that you have become a preacher. May you continue in God's name, and may He grant you His grace and blessing." In Schultz, *Caspar Schwenckfeld*, p. 15. Similarly Bugenhagen wrote in 1525: "It is well that you are preaching, insofar as you seek the honor of God; and I consider that your calling is good." *Ibid.*

[75] In Williams, *Spiritual and Anabaptist Writers*, p. 163.

[76] *Ibid.*

[77] Luther replied to his wife that the fanatics teach him to be coarse and that the devil does not deserve a better answer. *WA, Tr.* 5, p. 300. See also *LW*, 54, pp. 186, 469-471.

[78] An English version of Points I to III is found in Williams, *Spiritual and Anabaptist Writers*, pp. 163-181.

[79] Schultz, *Caspar Schwenckfeld*, pp. 334-335.

[80] *WA, Tr.* 1, p. 248.

[81] *WA*, 27, p. 60

[82] *WA*, 18, p. 544.

[83] *WA*, 18, pp. 541-550.

[84] Williams, *The Radical Reformation*, p. 352.

[85] *Ibid.*

[86] *Ibid.*, p. 354. Calvin's refutation of the libertines: *Conte la secte phantastique et furieuse des Libertins qui se nomment Spirituels* (Geneva, 1545).

[87] *WA*, 50, p. 461.

[88] *WA*, 50, p. 464.

[89] *EA*, 61, pp. 28-36.

[90] *WA*, 51, p. 440.

[91] *WA*, 50, p. 465.

[92] "Wider die Antinomer," *WA*, 50, pp. 468-477 (*LW*, 47, pp. 101-119).

[93] *EA*, 61, pp. 123-124.

[94] *WA*, 50, p. 474.

[95] *WA*, 36, pp. 30-31. For a good analysis of Luther's conception of the law and gospel, see Heinrich Bornkamm, *Luther and the Old Testament*, trans. Eric W. and Ruth C. Gritsch, ed. by Victor I. Gruhn (Philadelphia, 1969).

[96] *WA*, 22, p. 188.

[97] *WA*, 4, 1, p. 490.

[98] *WA*, 40, 1, p. 527.

[99] *WA*, 40, 1, p. 141.

[100] *WA*, 5, p. 32.

[101] *WA*, 45, p. 149.

[102] *WA*, 51, p. 440.

[103] *WA*, 39, 1, p. 356.

[104] Earl M. Wilbur, *A History of Unitarianism. Socinianism and Its Antecedents* (2 vols.; Cambridge, Mass., 1945), I, 15.

[105] *Ibid.*, p. 17.

[106] *WA*, 46, p. 550.

[107] *WA*, 21, p. 508.

[108] *WA*, 46, p. 436. Translated in Ewalt M. Plass (ed.), *What Luther Says: An Anthology* (3 vols.; Saint Louis, 1959), III, 1382.

[109] *WA*, 46, p. 443; *WA*, 50, p. 278.

[110] *WA*, 42, p. 8.

[111] Wilbur, *A History of Unitarianism*, pp. 23-24. Wilbur no doubt has Hans Denck in mind, who lived in Nürnberg at this time and who, upon Luther's counsel, was treated as a heretic. *Ibid.*, pp. 25-29. There is, however, no substantial evidence from Denck's writings that this humanist held Antitrinitarian views, although he associated with such Antitrinitarians as Ludwig Hätzer.

[112] *Ibid.*, pp. 24-25.

[113] See Williams, *The Radical Reformation*, p. 324. For Sebastian Franck's positive appraisal of Campanus, see Williams, *Spiritual and Anabaptist Writers*, p. 158.

[114] "Diesen verfluchten Unflath und Buben, Campanum, soll man nur verachten und sobald nicht wider ihn schreiben; denn da man wider ihn schriebe, so würde er deste kühner, stölzer und muthiger. Man verachte ihn nur, damit wird er am besten gedämpft." *EA*, 61, p. 5.

[115] *WA*, 50, p. 475.

[116] Williams, *The Radical Reformation*, p. 269. For a concise and sympathetic biography of Michael Servetus, see Roland H. Bainton, *Hunted Heretic. The Life and Death of Michael Servetus 1511-1553* (Boston, 1953).

[117] Williams, *The Radical Reformation*, p. 612.

[118] *WA*, 39, 2, p. 253.

[119] *WA*, 50, p. 278.

[120] *WA*, 30, 1, p. 192. Translated in Plass, *What Luther Says*, III, 1389.

Chapter VII

[1] On the question of religious liberty during the time of the Reformation, see the following studies: J. Kühn, *Toleranz und Offenbarung* (Leipzig, 1923), pp. 72-139; K. Holl, *Luther* (Tübingen, 1932), pp. 288-380; K. Völker, *Toleranz und Intoleranz im Zeitalter der Reformation* (Leipzig, 1912); R. H. Bainton, *Hunted Heretic* and *The Travail of Religious Liberty. Nine Biographical Studies* (Philadelphia, 1951); Joseph Lecler, *Toleration and the Reformation* (2 vols.; New York, 1960).

[2] J. E. E. Acton, *Essays on Freedom and Power* (Glencoe, Ill., 1948), p. 93.

[3] *WA*, 6, p. 455.

[4] In Luther, *First Principles of the Reformation*, trans. and ed. by H. Wace and C. A. Buchheim (London, 1883), p. 196.

[5] *WA*, 10, 3, p. 156.

[6] *WA*, 11, p. 264.

[7] *WA*, 11, p. 268.

[8] *WA*, 17, 2, p. 125. Translated in Lecler, *Toleration*, I, 152.

[9] *WA*, 15, pp. 218-219.

[10] Bainton, *Travail*, p. 61.

[11] *WA*, 26, pp. 145-147.

[12] *WA, Br.* 4, pp. 495-500. Translated in John S. Oyer, "The Writings of Luther Against the Anabaptists," *MQR*, XXVII (April, 1953), 107.

[13] Lecler, *Toleration*, I, 158-160.

[14] *WA, Br.* 5, pp. 136-137.

[15] *WA, Br.* 5, p. 137.

[16] *WA, Br.* 6, p. 564. Translated in Lecler, *Toleration*, I, 159-160.

[17] Lecler, *Toleration*, I, 160.

[18] *WA*, 31, 1, pp. 189-218 (*LW*, 13, pp. 42-72).

[19] *WA*, 31, 1, pp. 208-209.

[20] *WA*, 31, 1, p. 212.

[21] *WA*, 50, pp. 10-13. On the question of sedition and blasphemy, see Horst W. Schraepler, *Die rechtliche Behandlung der Täufer in der Deutschen Schweiz, Südwestdeutschland und Hessen,*

1525-1618 (Tübingen, 1957), pp. 24-29.

[22] In Lecler, *Toleration*, I, 162.

[23] *Ibid.*

[24] "Dass weltliche Oberkeit den Wiedertäufern mit leiblicher Strafe zu wehren schuldig sei, Etlicher Bedenken zu Wittenberg" (1536), *WA*, 50, pp. 6-15.

[25] *WA*, 50, p. 13. Translated in Lecler, *Toleration*, I, 163.

[26] *WA*, 50, p. 13.

[27] "Dis ist die gemeine Regel, doch mag unser gn. herr, allezeit, gnade neben der straffe gehen lassen, nach gelegenheit der zufelle." *WA*, 50, p. 15.

[28] Lecler, *Toleration*, I, 164.

[29] Bainton, *Travail*, p. 64.

[30] *Ibid.*, p. 63.

[31] Bainton, "The Parable of the Tares as the Proof Text for Religious Liberty to the End of the Sixteenth Century," *Church History*, I (June, 1932), 87. On Philip's success in reconverting the Anabaptists in his realm, see F. H. Littell, *The Origins of Sectarian Protestantism. A Study of the Anabaptist View of the Church* (Macmillan Paperback ed.; New York/London, 1964), pp. 35-36.

[32] Littell, *The Anabaptist View of the Church*, p. 33.

[33] Kramm, *The Theology of Martin Luther*, p. 149.

[34] Leo Pfeffer, *Church, State and Freedom* (Boston, 1953), p. ix.

[35] Smithson, *The Anabaptists*, p. 17.

[36] E. Harris Harbison, *The Age of Reformation* (Ithaca, 1955), p. 65.

[37] Smith, *The Story of the Mennonites*, p. 21.

[38] Littell, *The Anabaptist View of the Church*, p. 66.

[39] Bender, "The Anabaptist Vision," p. 68.

[40] For complete text in English translation see Henry C. Vedder, *Balthasar Hübmaier the Leader of the Anabaptists* (New York, 1905).

[41] Harold S. Bender, "The Anabaptists and Religious Liberty in the 16th Century," *MQR*, XXIX (1955), 94.

[42] In Lindsay, *A History of the Reformation*, II, 441-442.

[43] For an analysis of Bullinger's statements, see Bender, "The Anabaptist Vision," pp. 68-69.

[44] In Smithson, *The Anabaptists*, p. 127.

[45] J. C. Wenger (trans. and ed.), "Three Swiss Brethren Tracts," *MQR*, XXI (October, 1947), 282-284.

[46] *Ibid.*, pp. 280-281.

[47] *Ibid.*, pp. 276-278.

[48] Simons, *Complete Writings*, pp. 332-355.

[49] *Ibid.*, p. 207.

[50] Horsch, *Mennonites in Europe*, p. 323.

[51] Bender, "Church and State in Mennonite History," p. 89.

[52] *Ibid.*, pp. 89-90.

[53] Smith, *The Story of the Mennonites*, p. 41.

[54] Elton, *The New Cambridge Modern History*, II, 123. It may be pointed out that the Mennonites do not regard Hubmaier as a true Anabaptist because he believed in bearing arms for the government. But the history of the Mennonite people is not wholly free of violence and even persecution. It is well known that when the Mennonite Brethren church was organized in Russia in 1860, there were threats, arrests, and actual punishment levelled against them by their fellow Mennonites until the Russian government recognized the dissenting body as a legal religious denomination. See Horsch, *Mennonites in Europe*, p. 279.

[55] Fellmann, *Hans Denck Schriften*, II, 108.

[56] *Ibid.*

[57] Lecler, *Toleration*, I, 166-167.

[58] *Ibid.*, p. 167.

[59] *Ibid.*, p. 175.

[60] *Ibid.*

[61] *Ibid.*

[62] *Ibid.*, p. 176.

[63] *Ibid.*, p. 175.

[64] *CS*, 2, p. 596.

[65] *CS*, 4, pp, 752-753.

[66] *WA, Br.* 4, p. 28.

[67] *CS*, 3, pp. 440-469.

[68] *CS*, 5, p. 100. Translated in Lecler, *Toleration*, I, 184.

[69] *CS*, 3, p. 79.

[70] See A. F. Carrillo de Albornoz, *Roman Catholicism and Religious Liberty* (Geneva, 1959), p. 67.

[71] It was believed, as Bainton points out, that persecution would bring about the salvation of the heretic's soul, vindicate the honour of God (Calvinism), and bring about orthodoxy and unity within the church. As time went on, persecution proved ineffective in achieving these desired ends, and the Enlightenment undermined some of the principles underlying the theory of persecution. See Bainton, *Travail*, pp. 17 ff.

Chapter VIII

[1] Vedder, *Balthasar Hübmaier*, p. 21. For the changing reputation of the Anabaptists, see Littell, *The Anabaptist View of the Church*, pp. 138-161.

[2] In Hershberger, *The Recovery*, p. 319.

[3] "Luther and Müntzer no longer appear to be mutually exclusive. Müntzer must be understood as a corrective of Luther. For Müntzer stood for another and highly important aspect of Protestantism: he carried the Protestant protest into the social area." Nigg, *The Heretics*, p. 316. Cf. Zschäbitz, *Zur Mitteldeutschen Wiedertäuferbewegung*.

[4] Jones, *Spiritual Reformers*; Keller, *Ein Apostel der Wiedertäufer*; Coutts, *Hans Denck*; Schultz, *Caspar Schwenckfeld*.

[5] In Hershberger, *The Recovery*, p. 315.

[6] *Ibid.*, p. 317.

[7] Philip Hughes, *A Popular History of the Reformation* (Image Books: Garden City, New York, 1957), p. 143.

[8] H. G. Fischer, "Lutheranism and the Vindication of the Anabaptist Way," *MQR*, XXVIII (1954), p. 38.

[9] See particularly Karl Barth, *The Teaching of the Church Regarding Baptism*, trans. by E. A. Payne (London, [1948]).

[10] Hershberger, *The Recovery*, p. 315. In this connection Payne cites G. Dix, *The Theology of Confirmation in Relation to Baptism* (London, 1946), and K. Kirk, *Oxford Diocesan Magazine* (1946).

[11] L. Verduin, *The Reformers and their Stepchildren* (Grand Rapids, Michigan, 1964), p. 276.

[12] *Ibid.*, p. 12.

[13] Cf. Zeeden, *The Legacy of Luther*, pp. 8-9.

[14] Cf. Ernst Troeltsch, *The Social Teaching of the Christian Churches*, trans. by Olive Wyon (2 vols.; London, 1931), II, 756.

[15] Samuel Geiser, *et al.*, *Die Taufgesinnten Gemeinden* (Karlsruhe, 1931), pp. 279-280.

[16] In Hershberger, *The Recovery*, p. 307.

[17] Hughes, *A Popular History*, p. 140.

[18] Troeltsch, *The Social Teaching*, II, 704.

[19] Hershberger, *The Recovery*, p. 321.

[20] In Nigg, *The Heretics*, p. 315.
[21] Verduin, *The Reformers*, p. 276.
[22] *Ibid.*, p. 277.

BIBLIOGRAPHY

Source Material

Corpus Schwenckfeldianorum. 19 vols. Published under the auspices of the Schwenckfelder Church, Pennsylvania. Leipzig and Pennsburg, Pennsylvania, 1907-1961.

Enders, Ernst Ludwig (ed.). *Dr. Martin Luthers Briefwechsel.* 10 vols. Calw/Stuttgart, 1884-1903.

Fellmann, Walter (ed.). *Hans Denck Schriften: Religiöse Schriften.* Vol. II. (Quellen und Forschungen zur Reformationsgeschichte, XXIV.) Gütersloh, 1956.

Hillerbrand, Hans J. (ed.). "An Early Anabaptist Treatise on the Christian and the State," *MQR*, XXXII (January, 1958), 28-47.

Kidd, B. J. (ed.). *Documents Illustrative of the Continental Reformation.* Oxford, 1911.

Loserth, J. (ed.). *Quellen und Forschungen zur Geschichte der oberdeutschen Taufgesinnten im 16. Jahrhundert. Pilgram Marbecks Antwort auf Kaspar Schwenckfelds Beurteilung des Buches der Bundesbezeugung.* Wien, 1929.

Luther, Martin. *First Principles of the Reformation or the Ninety-five Theses and the Three Primary Works.* Translated and edited by Henry Wace and C. A. Buchheim. London, 1883.

―――――. *The Letters.* Selected and translated by Margaret A. Currie. London, 1908.

―――――. *Reformation Writings.* Translated by Bertram Lee Woolf. 2 vols. London, 1952.

―――――. *Sämmtliche Schriften.* Herausgegeben von Dr. Joh. Georg Walsch. Neue revidirte Stereotypausgabe. 23 vols. St. Louis, Missouri, 1880-1910.

―――――. *Sämmtliche Werke.* 65 vols. Erlangen and Frankfurt a.M., 1826-1855.

—————. *Werke. Kritische Gesammtausgabe.* Weimar, 1883-1948.

—————. *Werke. Kritische Gesammtausgabe. Briefwechsel.* Weimar, 1930-1948.

—————. *Werke. Kritische Gesammtausgabe. Die Deutsche Bibel.* Weimar, 1906-1961.

—————. *Werke. Kritische Gesammtausgabe. Tischreden.* Weimar, 1912-1921.

—————. *Luther's Works.* Published by Concordia Publishing House and Fortress Press, 1956ff.

Plass, Ewald M. (ed.). *What Luther Says: An Anthology.* 3 vols. Saint Louis, 1959.

Simons, Menno. *The Complete Writings.* Translated from the Dutch by Leonard Verduin and edited by John Christian Wenger, with a biography by H. S. Bender. Scottdale, Pennsylvania, 1956.

Wenger, John C. (trans. and ed.). "The Schleitheim Confession of Faith." *MQR*, XIX (October, 1945), 244-253.

————— (trans. and ed.). "Three Swiss Brethren Tracts." *MQR*, XXI (October, 1947), 276-285.

Williams, G. H. (ed.). *Spiritual and Anabaptist Writers.* The Library of Christian Classics, Vol. XXV. London, 1957.

Zieglschmid, A. J. F. (ed.). *Die älteste Chronik der Hutterischen Brüder. Ein Sprachdenkmal aus frühneuhochdeutscher Zeit.* Ithaca, New York, 1943.

Books and Articles

Acton, J. E. E. *Essays on Freedom and Power.* Selected with an introduction by Gertrude Himmelfarb. Glencoe, Illinois, 1948.

Albornoz, A. F. Carillo de. *Roman Catholicism and Religious Liberty.* Geneva, 1959.

Althaus, Paul. *Luthers Haltung im Bauernkrieg.* Darmstadt, 1952.

Bibliography

Arnold, Gottfried. *Unparteiische Kirchen- und Ketzerhistorie vom Anfang des Neuen Testaments bis auf das Jahr Christi 1688.* 2 vols. (Reprographischer Nachdruck der Ausgabe Frankfurt a.M. 1729.) Hildesheim, 1967.

Bainton, Roland H. *The Age of the Reformation.* An Anvil Original. Princeton, New Jersey, 1956.

——————. *Here I Stand. A Life of Martin Luther.* A Mentor Book. New York, 1950.

——————. *Hunted Heretic. The Life and Death of Michael Servetus 1511-1553.* Boston, 1953.

——————. "Interpretations of the Reformation." *The American Historical Review,* LXVI (October, 1960), 74-84.

——————. "The Left Wing of the Reformation." *The Journal of Religion,* XXI (April, 1941), 124-134.

——————. "The Parable of the Tares as the Proof Text for Religious Liberty to the End of the Sixteenth Century." *Church History,* I (June, 1932), 67-87.

——————; Quanbeck, Warren A.; and Rupp, E. Gordon. *Luther Today.* Martin Luther Lectures, Vol. I. Decorah, Iowa, 1957.

——————. *The Reformation of the Sixteenth Century.* Boston, 1952.

——————. *The Travail of Religious Liberty. Nine Biographical Studies.* Philadelphia, 1951.

Barge, Hermann. *Andreas Bodenstein von Karlstadt.* 2 vols. Leipzig, 1905.

Bauman, Clarence. *Gewaltlosigkeit im Täufertum. Eine Untersuchung zur theologischen Ethik des oberdeutschen Täufertums der Reformationszeit.* Leiden, 1968.

Bax, E. Belford. *The Peasants' War in Germany 1525-1526.* London, 1899.

——————. *The Rise and Fall of the Anabaptists.* London, 1903.

Bender, Harold S. "The Anabaptist Theology of Discipleship." *MQR*, XXIV (January, 1950), 25-32.

——————. "The Anabaptist Vision." *MQR*, XVIII (April, 1944), 67-88.

——————. "The Anabaptists and Religious Liberty in the 16th Century." *MQR*, XXIX (1955), 83-100.

——————. *Conrad Grebel c. 1498-1526 The Founder of the Swiss Brethren, Sometimes Called Anabaptists.* Scottdale, Pennsylvania, 1950.

——————. "Church and State in Mennonite History." *MQR*, XIII (April, 1939), 83-103.

——————. "Die Zwickauer Propheten, Thomas Müntzer und die Täufer." *Theologische Zeitschrift*, Heft 4 (1952), 262ff.

Bergsten, Torsten. *Balthasar Hubmaier. Seine Stellung zu Reformation und Täufertum, 1521-1528.* Kassel, 1961.

Be Vier, William A. "Modes of Water Baptism in the Ancient Church." *Bibliotheca Sacra*, CXVI (July-September, 1959), 230-240.

——————. "Summary and Conclusions Concerning Water Baptism in the Ancient Church." *Bibliotheca Sacra*, CXVI (October-December, 1959), 317-321.

——————. "Water Baptism in the Ancient Church." *Bibliotheca Sacra*, CXVI (April-June, 1959), 136-144.

Blanke, Fritz. "Täuferforschung: Ort und Zeit der ersten Wiedertaufe." *Theologische Zeitschrift*, Heft 1 (January-February, 1952), 74-76.

——————. "Zollikon 1525. Die Entstehung der ältesten Täufergemeinde." *Theologische Zeitschrift*, Heft 4 (1952), 241ff.

Bloch, Ernst. *Thomas Müntzer als Theologe der Revolution.* Berlin, 1962.

Boehmer, Heinrich. *Martin Luther. Road to Reformation.* Translated from the German by J. W. Doberstein and T. G. Tappert. Living Age Books. New York, 1957.

Bornkamm, Heinrich. *Luther and the Old Testament.* Translated by Eric W. and Ruth C. Gritsch; edited by V. I. Gruhn. Philadelphia, 1969.

————. *Luther's World of Thought.* Translated by M. H. Bertram. St. Louis, 1958.

Brentano, Franz-Funk. *Luther.* Translated from the French by E. F. Buckley. London, 1936.

Brons, A. *Ursprung, Entwickelung und Schicksale der altevangelischen Taufgesinnten oder Mennoniten.* Dritte Auflage, neu bearbeitet. Amsterdam, 1912.

The Catholic Encyclopedia. Edited by Charles G. Herbermann, et al. 15 vols. New York, 1907-1912.

Cooper, J. C. "Some Radical Elements in Luther's Theology." *Lutheran Quarterly* (May, 1968), pp. 194-201.

Coutts, Alfred. *Hans Denck 1495-1527 Humanist and Heretic.* Edinburgh, 1927.

Crous, E., et al. *Gedenkschrift zum 400-jährigen Jubiläum der Mennoniten oder Taufgesinnten 1525-1925.* Ludwigshaven A.RH., 1925.

Dallmann, William. *Martin Luther. His Life and His Labor.* St. Louis, 1951.

Dieckhoff, A. W. *Luthers Lehre von der kirchlichen Gewalt historisch dargestellt.* Berlin, 1865.

Dix, Gregory. *The Shape of the Liturgy.* 2nd ed. Westminster, 1945.

Dollar, George W. "The Lord's Supper in the Second Century." *Bibliotheca Sacra,* CXVII (April, 1960), 144-154.

Elton, G. R. (ed.). *The New Cambridge Modern History.* Vol. II. Cambridge, 1958.

Fast, Heinold. "The Dependence of the First Anabaptists on Luther, Erasmus and Zwingli." *MQR*, XXX (1956), 104ff.

——————, and Yoder, John H. "How to Deal with Anabaptists: An Unpublished Letter of Heinrich Bullinger." *MQR*, XXXIII (April, 1959), 83-95.

Fife, Robert Herndon. *The Revolt of Martin Luther*. New York, 1957.

Fischer, H. G. "Lutheranism and the Vindication of the Anabaptist Way." *MQR*, XXVIII (1954), 27-38.

Fretz, J. Winfield. "Mennonites and Their Economic Problems." *MQR*, XIV (October, 1940), 195-213.

Friedmann, Robert. "Anabaptism and Protestantism." *MQR*, XXIV (January, 1950), 12-24.

——————. "The Encounter of Anabaptists and Mennonites with Anti-Trinitarians." *MQR*, XXII (July, 1948), 139-162.

——————. "An Example of the Spirit of Early Anabaptism." *MQR*, XXX (1956), 289ff.

——————. "The Schleitheim Confession (1527) and Other Doctrinal Writings of the Swiss Brethren in a Hitherto Unknown Edition." *MQR*, XVI (April, 1942), 82-98.

——————. "Thomas Müntzer's Relation to Anabaptism." *MQR*, XXXI (April, 1957), 75-87.

Friesen, Abraham. "Thomas Müntzer in Marxist Thought." *Church History*, XXXIV (1965), 306-327.

——————. "Thomas Müntzer and the Old Testament." *MQR*, XLVII (January, 1973), 5-19.

Furcha, Edward J. *Schwenckfeld's Concept of the New Man. A Study in the Anthropology of Caspar Schwenckfeld as Set Forth in His Major Theological Writings*. Pennsburg, Pennsylvania, 1970.

Gane, E. R. "Luther's View of Church and State." *Andrews University Seminary Studies* (July, 1970), pp. 120-143.

Garret, James Leo. "The Nature of the Church According to the Radical Continental Reformation." *MQR*, XXXII (April, 1958), 111-127.

Garside, Charles. "Ludwig Haetzer's Pamphlet Against Images: A Critical Study." *MQR*, XXXIV (January, 1960), 20-36.

Geiser, Samuel. "An Ancient Anabaptist Witness for Nonresistance." *MQR*, XXV (January, 1951), 66-69, 72.

——————, et al. *Die Taufgesinnten Gemeinden*. Karlsruhe, 1931.

Gerdes, Hayo. *Luthers Streit mit den Schwärmern um das rechte Verständnis des Gesetzes Mose*. Göttingen, 1955.

Gerdtell, Ludwig von. *Die Revolutionierung der Kirchen*. Schöneiche bei Berlin Friedrichshagen, 1924.

Goertz, H.-J. *Innere und äussere Ordnung in der Theologie Thomas Müntzers*. Leiden, 1967.

Goeters, Gerhard J. F. *Ludwig Haetzer (ca. 1500-1529) Spiritualist und Antitrinitarier. Eine Randfigur der frühen Täuferbewegung*. Quellen und Forschungen zur Reformationsgeschichte, XXV. Gütersloh, 1957.

Grisar, Hartmann S. J. *Martin Luther: His Life and Work*. Westminster, Maryland, 1930.

Gritsch, Eric W. *Reformer Without a Church. The Life and Thought of Thomas Muentzer 1488[?]-1525*. Philadelphia, 1967.

——————. "Thomas Müntzer and the Origins of Protestant Spiritualism." *MQR*, XXXVII (1963), 172-194.

Harbison, E. Harris. *The Age of Reformation*. Ithaca, 1955.

Heick, Otto W. *A History of Christian Thought*. 2 vols. Philadelphia, 1965-1966.

Hershberger, Guy F. "Christian Nonresistance: Its Foundation and Its Outreach." *MQR*, XXIV (April, 1950), 156-162.

—————— (ed.). *The Recovery of the Anabaptist Vision*. Scottdale, Pennsylvania, 1957.

Hillerbrand, Hans J. "Andreas Bodenstein of Carlstadt, Prodigal Reformer." *Church History*, XXXV (December, 1966), 379-398.

───────. "Anabaptism and the Reformation: Another Look." *Church History*, XXIX (December, 1960), 404-423.

───────. "Luther's Deserting Disciples: An Anniversary Reflection on the Anabaptists of the 16th Century." *McCormick Quarterly* (November, 1967), pp. 105-113.

───────. *Die politische Ethik des oberdeutschen Täufertums. Eine Untersuchung zur Religions- und Geistesgeschichte des Reformationszeitalters.* Leiden/Köln, 1962.

───────. "Thomas Müntzer's Last Tract Against Luther." *MQR*, XXXVIII (1964), 20-36.

Hinrichs, Carl. *Luther und Müntzer. Ihre Auseinandersetzung über Obrigkeit und Widerstandsrecht.* Berlin, 1962.

Horsch, John. "The Character of the Evangelical Anabaptists as Reported by Contemporary Reformation Writers." *MQR*, VIII (July, 1934), 123-135.

───────. *The Hutterian Brethren 1528-1931: A Story of Martyrdom and Loyalty.* Goshen, Indiana, 1931.

───────. "An Inquiry into the Truth of Accusations of Fanaticism and Crime Against the Early Swiss Brethren." *MQR*, VIII (January, 1934), 18-31; (April, 1934), 73-89.

───────. *Mennonites in Europe.* 2nd ed. Scottdale, Pennsylvania, 1950.

───────. "Menno Simons' Attitude Toward the Anabaptists of Münster." *MQR*, X (January, 1936), 55-72.

───────. "Persecution of the Evangelical Anabaptists." *MQR*, XII (January, 1938), 3-26.

───────. "The Rise and Fall of the Anabaptists of Münster." *MQR*, IX (April, 1935), 92-103; (July, 1935), 129-143.

Huch, Ricarda. *Das Zeitalter der Glaubensspaltungen.* Berlin/Zürich, 1937.

Hughes, Philip. *A Popular History of the Reformation.* Image Book Edition. Garden City, New York, 1960.

Hyma, Albert. *The Brethren of the Common Life.* Grand Rapids, Michigan, 1950.

Iserloh, Erwin, et al. *Reformation, Katholische Reform und Gegenreform.* Freiburg, Basel, Wien, 1967.

Jones, Rufus M. *Spiritual Reformers in the 16th and 17th Centuries.* Boston, 1959.

Jordan, W. K. *The Development of Religious Toleration in England.* Cambridge, 1932.

Jungmann, Joseph A. *The Mass of the Roman Rite. Its Origins and Development.* Translated by F. A. Brunner; revised by Charles K. Riepe. New revised and abridged edition in one volume. New York, 1959.

Kamen, Henry. *The Rise of Toleration.* New York, Toronto, 1967.

Kaufman, Gordon D. "Some Theological Emphases of the Early Swiss Anabaptists." *MQR*, XXV (April, 1951), 75-99.

Keller, Ludwig. *Die Anfänge der Reformation und die Ketzerschulen.* Berlin, 1897.

—————. *Ein Apostel der Wiedertäufer.* Leipzig, 1882.

Kiwiet, Jan J. *Pilgram Marbeck. Ein Führer in der Täuferbewegung der Reformationszeit.* Kassel, 1957.

Klaassen, W. "Anabaptism and the Reformation." *Canadian Journal of Theology* (January, 1962), pp. 34-42.

—————. "Hans Hut and Thomas Müntzer." *The Baptist Quarterly*, XIX (1962), 209-227.

—————. "Spiritualization in the Reformation." *MQR*, XXXVII (1963), 67-77.

Knox, R. A. *Enthusiasm. A Chapter in the History of Religion.* New York, 1950.

Koestlin, Julius. *Martin Luther. Sein Leben und Seine Schriften.* 3rd ed. 2 vols. Erberfeld, 1883.

Kolde, Theodor. "Hans Denck und die gottlosen Maler in Nürnberg." *Beiträge zur Bayerischen Kirchengeschichte,* VIII (1902), 1ff.

Krahn, Cornelius. *Dutch Anabaptism. Origin, Spread, Life and Thought (1450-1600).* The Hague, 1968.

——————. *Menno Simons (1496-1561) Ein Beitrag zur Geschichte und Theologie der Taufgesinnten.* Karlsruhe, 1936.

Krajewski, Ekkehard. *Leben und Sterben des Züricher Täuferführers Felix Manz.* Kassel, 1957.

Kramm, H. H. *The Theology of Martin Luther.* London, 1947.

Kreider, Robert. "Anabaptism and Humanism. An Inquiry into the Relationship of Humanism to the Evangelical Anabaptists." *MQR,* XXVI (April, 1952), 123-141.

Langton, Edward. *History of the Moravian Church. The Story of the First International Protestant Church.* London, 1956.

Lecler, Joseph. *Toleration and the Reformation.* Translated by T. L. Westow. 2 vols. New York, 1960.

Lilje, Hanns. *Luther Now.* Translated by Carl J. Schindler. Philadelphia, 1952.

Lindsay, Thomas M. *A History of the Reformation.* 2 vols. Edinburgh, 1907.

Littell, Franklin H. "The Anabaptist Doctrine of the Restitution of the True Church." *MQR,* XXIV (January, 1950), 33-52.

——————. *The Anabaptist View of the Church. A Study in the Origins of Sectarian Protestantism.* 2nd ed., revised and enlarged. Boston, 1958.

——————. *The Free Church.* Boston, 1957.

Lohse, Bernhard. "Die Stellung der 'Schwärmer' und Täufer in der Reformationsgeschichte." *Archiv für Reformationsgeschichte,* Jahrgang 60, Heft 1 (1969), 5-26.

Lortz, Joseph. *Die Reformation in Deutschland.* 2 vols. 3rd ed. Freiburg, 1940.

McGriffin, A. C. *Martin Luther. The Man and His Work.* New York, 1914.

MacKensen, H. "Historical Interpretation and Luther's Role in the Peasants' Revolt." *Concordia Theological Monthly* (April, 1964), pp. 197-209.

Mackinnon, James. *A History of Modern Liberty.* Vol. II. London, 1906.

───────. *Luther and the Reformation.* Vol. III. Toronto, 1929.

Maier, Paul L. *Caspar Schwenckfeld on the Person and Work of Christ. A Study of Schwenckfeldian Theology at Its Core.* Assen, The Netherlands, 1959.

Meihuizen, H. W. "Spiritualistic Tendencies and Movements Among the Dutch Mennonites of the 16th and 17th Centuries." *MQR*, XXVII (October, 1953), 259-304.

The Mennonite Encyclopedia. Edited by H. S. Bender, *et al.* 4 vols. Scottdale, Pennsylvania, 1957.

Meusel, Alfred. *Thomas Müntzer und seine Zeit. Mit einer Auswahl der Dokumente des grossen deutschen Bauernkrieges.* Berlin, 1952.

Moyers, Elgin S. *Great Leaders of the Christian Church.* Chicago, 1951.

Mueller, John Theodore. "A Survey of Luther's Theology." *Bibliotheca Sacra,* CXIII (April, 1956), 153-161; (July, 1956), 227-238.

Murray, John. *Christian Baptism.* Philadelphia, 1952.

Newman, Albert Henry. *A History of Anti-Pedobaptism.* Philadelphia, 1897.

───────. *A Manual of Church History.* Revised and enlarged. 2 vols. Philadelphia, 1931.

Nigg, Walter. *Das Buch der Ketzer*. Zürich, 1949. English edition: *The Heretics*. Edited and translated by Richard and Clara Winston. New York, 1962.

O'Rafferty, Nicholas. *Instructions on Christian Doctrine—The Sacraments*. New York, 1939.

Oyer, John S. *Lutheran Reformers Against Anabaptists*. The Hague, 1964.

——————. "The Writings of Luther Against the Anabaptists." *MQR*, XXVII (April, 1953), 100-110.

Peachey, Paul. *Die soziale Herkunft der Schweizer Täufer in der Reformationszeit*. Karlsruhe, 1954.

Pelikan, Jaroslav. *Spirit Versus Structure. Luther and the Institutions of the Church*. New York, 1968.

Pfeffer, Leo. *Church, State and Freedom*. Boston, 1953.

Pinomaa, Lennard. "Die Heilung bei Luther." *Theologische Zeitschrift*, Heft 1 (Januar-Februar, 1954), 30-50.

Ritter, Gerhard. *Luther. Gestalt und Tat*. 6. Auflage. München, 1959.

Rupp, Gordon. "Andrew Karlstadt and Reformation Puritanism." *The Journal of Theological Studies*, New Series, X (1959), 308-326.

——————. *Patterns of Reformation*. London, 1969.

Schaber, Will (ed.). *Weinberg der Freiheit. Der Kampf um ein demokratisches Deutschland von Thomas Müntzer bis Thomas Mann*. New York, 1945.

Schaff, Harold H. "The Anabaptists, the Reformers, and the Civil Government." *Church History*, I (March, 1932), 27-46.

Schaff, Philip. *History of the Christian Church*. Vols. VII and VIII. Reproduction of the 2nd ed., revised. Grand Rapids, 1953.

Schiff, Otto. "Thomas Müntzer und die Bauernbewegung am

Oberrhein." *Historische Zeitschrift.* Band 110. München/Berlin, 1913.

Schraepler, Horst W. *Die rechtliche Behandlung der Täufer in der deutschen Schweiz, Südwestdeutschland und Hessen, 1525-1618.* Tübingen, 1957.

Schultz, Selina G. *Caspar Schwenckfeld von Ossig (1498-1561). Spiritual Interpreter of Christianity, Apostle of the Middle Way, Pioneer in Modern Religious Thought.* Norristown, Pennsylvania, 1946.

Schwiebert, E. G. *Luther and His Times.* Saint Louis, Missouri, 1950.

Seyppel, Joachim H. *Schwenckfeld Knight of Faith. A Study in the History of Religion.* Pennsburg, Pennsylvania, 1961.

Sider, Ronald J. "Karlstadt's Orlamünde Theology—A Theology of Regeneration." *MQR*, XLV (July, 1971), 191-218.

Siggins, I. D. K. *Martin Luther's Doctrine of Christ.* New Haven, 1970.

Siirala, Aarne. *Gottes Gebot bei Martin Luther.* Helsinki, 1956.

Smith, C. Henry. *The Story of the Mennonites.* 3rd ed., revised and enlarged. Newton, 1950.

Smith, Preserved. *The Life and Letters of Martin Luther.* Boston, 1914.

Smithson, R. J. *The Anabaptists. Their Contribution to Our Protestant Heritage.* London, 1935.

Stauffer, Ethelbert. "The Anabaptist Theology of Martyrdom." *MQR*, XIX (July, 1945), 179-214.

Stayer, James M. "Terrorism, the Peasants' War and the 'Wiedertäufer.'" *Archiv für Reformationsgeschichte*, LVI (1965), 227-229.

Steck, K. G. *Luther und die Schwärmer.* Zürich, 1955.

Steinmetz, David C. *Reformers in the Wings.* Philadelphia, 1971.

———. "Scholasticism and Radical Reform." *MQR*, (April, 1971), 123-144.

Stupperich, Robert. *Das Münsterische Täufertum. Ergebnisse und Probleme der neueren Forschung.* Münster, 1958.

Thiel, Rudolf. *Luther.* Wien, 1935.

Tillmanns, Walter G. *The World and Men Around Luther.* Minneapolis, 1959.

Torbet, Robert G. *A History of the Baptists.* Philadelphia, 1950.

Troeltsch, Ernst. *The Social Teaching of the Christian Churches.* Translated by Olive Wyon. 2 vols. London, 1931.

Tumbuelt, Georg. *Die Wiedertäufer. Die sozialen und religiösen Bewegungen zur Zeit der Reformation.* Bielefeld/Leipzig, 1899.

Vedder, Henry C. *Balthasar Hübmaier the Leader of the Anabaptists.* New York, 1905.

———. *The Reformation in Germany.* New York, 1914.

Verduin, Leonard. "The Chambers of Rhetoric and Anabaptist Origins in the Low Countries." *MQR*, XXXIV (July, 1960), 192-196.

———. *The Reformers and Their Stepchildren.* Grand Rapids, 1964.

Waltner, Erland. "The Anabaptist Conception of the Church." *MQR*, XXV (January, 1951), 5-16.

Wappler, Paul. *Die Täuferbewegung in Thüringen von 1526-1584.* Jena, 1913.

Warns, Johannes. *Baptism. Studies in the Original Christian Baptism, Its History and Conflicts, Its Relation to a State or National Church and Its Significance for the Present Time.* Translated from the German by G. H. Lang. London, 1957.

Watson, Philip S. *Let God be God! An Interpretation of the Theology of Martin Luther.* Philadelphia, 1949.

Wenger, John Christian. *Glimpses of Mennonite History and Doctrine.* 2nd ed., revised and enlarged. Scottdale, 1947.

Westin, Gunnar. *The Free Church Through the Ages.* Translated from the Swedish by Virgil A. Olson. Nashville, 1958.

Wicks, J. *Man Yearning for Grace.* Wiesbaden, 1969.

Wilbur, Earl Morse. *A History of Unitarianism. Socinianism and Its Antecedents.* 2 vols. Cambridge, Massachusetts, 1945.

Williams, G. H. "'Congregationalist' Luther and the Free Churches," *Lutheran Quarterly* (August, 1967), pp. 283-295.

——————. "'Congregationalist' Luther and Radical Reform." *Harvard Divinity Bulletin* (Autumn, 1967), pp. 9-12.

——————. *The Radical Reformation.* Philadelphia, 1962.

——————. "Studies in the Radical Reformation (1517-1618): A Bibliographical Survey of Research Since 1939." *Church History,* XXVII (March, 1958), 46-69; (June, 1958), 124-160.

Wiswedel, Wilhelm. *Bilder und Führergestalten aus dem Täufertum.* Kassel, 1952.

——————, and Friedmann, Robert. "The Anabaptists Answer Melanchton." *MQR,* XXIX (July, 1955), 212-231.

——————. "The Inner and the Outer Word: A Study in the Anabaptist Doctrine of the Scriptures." *MQR,* XXVI (1952), 171-191.

Wolf, Gustav. *Quellenkunde der deutschen Reformationszeit.* 3 vols. Gotha, 1914.

Wray, Frank J. "The Anabaptist Doctrine of the Restitution of the Church." *MQR,* XXVIII (July, 1954), 186-196.

Zeeden, Ernst Walter. *The Legacy of Luther.* Translated from the German by Ruth M. Bethell. Westminster, Maryland, 1954.

Zschäbitz, Gerhard. *Zur Mitteldeutschen Wiedertäuferbewegung nach dem grossen Bauernkrieg.* Berlin, 1958.

Zuck, Lowell H. "Anabaptism: Abortive Counter-Revolt Within the Reformation." *Church History*, XXVI (September, 1957), 211-226.

Index of Names

Abelard, Peter: 80
Adler, Clemens: 88
Agricola, Franz: 92
Agricola, John: 127-130, 133
Ambrose: 80
Arnold of Brescia: 80
Augustine: 13, 41, 42, 79, 80, 84, 131, 149

Barge, Hermann: 30, 44, 151
Bainton, Roland H.: 141, 152
Barth, Karl: 153
Bartholomew of Ahlfeldt: 105
Bax, Belford: 47
Bender, Harold: 74, 78, 143, 153
Beza, Theodore: 151
Blaurock, George: 67, 73
Boehmer, Heinrich: 13
Bornkamm, H.: 42
Brück, George: 38, 57
Brunner, Emil: 153
de Bruys, Peter: 80
Bugenhagen, Johannes: 117, 118, 141
Bullinger, Heinrich: 74, 144

Calvin, John: 130, 151, 153
Campanus, Johannes: 132, 183n
Carlstadt, Andreas Bodenstein von: 25; Wittenberg reformer, 29-37; Conflict with Luther, 37-45; Influence on Swiss Anabaptism, 70-77; 95, 102, 118, 128, 131, 136, 138, 141, 151, 158, 166n, 171n
Castellio, Sebastian: 151
Cellarius, Martin: 131
Cornelius, C. A.: 151
Coutts, Alfred: 91, 109
Cranach, Lucas: 48
Crautwald, Valentine: 115, 117, 118
Cyprian: 40

Denck, Hans: 22, 23, 26, 58, 67, 68, 102, 103; Person and teaching, 110-114; 124, 145, 146, 152, 170n, 178n, 183n
Duke Ernest of Mansfield: 58
Duke George of Saxony: 14, 35, 77
Duke John Frederick: 53, 106

Eck, Johann: 30, 86
Eckhard ("Meister"): 25
Egranus, Sylvius: 50
Elizabeth of Saxony: 92
Erasmus, Desiderius: 25, 60, 92, 133

Faber, Gellius: 27
Fischer, Hans George: 153
Franck, Sebastian: 22, 70, 110, 146-148
Frederick the Wise: 30, 35, 38, 43, 63

Grebel, Conrad: 67, 68 69, 70, 71; Letter to Müntzer, 73-80; 81, 88, 103, 144
Günther, Franz: 50

Hätzer, Ludwig: 23, 74, 99
Harbison, E. H.: 143
Hegenwalt, Erhard: 71
Heine, Heinrich: 157
Henry VIII: 102
Henry of Lousanne: 80
Hesse, Philip of: 70, 92, 106, 140, 142, 143, 149
Hofmann, Melchior: 26, 96, 102, 175n
Horsch, John: 153
Holl, Karl: 67
Hubmaier, Balthasar: 26, 61, 68, 70, 99, 103, 144, 146, 169n, 170n, 173n, 187n
Hughes, Philip: 152
Huss, John: 52
Hut, Hans: 67, 68, 99, 146

Ignatius of Antioch: 79
Irenaeus: 40

Joachim of Anhalt: 85
John of Leyden: 22, 97, 98, 102, 104
Jonas, Justus: 29, 43
Jones, Rufus: 112
Justin the Martyr: 79

Keller, Ludwig: 22
Knipperdolling, Hermann: 96-98
Knox, R. A.: 24, 102
Köhler, Walter: 25
Kramer, Michael: 90
Kreider, Robert: 25

Lang, John: 18
Lecler, Joseph: 138, 148
Leo X: 16, 20, 89
Lessing, G. E.: 143
Leonard von Liechtenstein: 146
Link, W.: 137
Littell, Franklin: 26, 143
Lösscher, Thomas: 137
Luther, Martin: Conversion, 13-14; *Sola fide* and *sola scriptura*, 14, 15, 21, 26, 28, 93, 109, 147, 154; Justification through faith, 14-16, 27, 154, 158; Reformation writings, 16-21; Ethics, 26-28, 89-93; Moderation, 30-40; Last supper, 19, 40-45, 117, 118; Scriptures, 53-54, 72, 109-110, 120-123, 156; Peasants, 59-66; Baptism, 19, 81-85; Church and state, 85-88, 157; Religious liberty, 17, 98-101, 106, 119, 124, 135-143, 151, 154; The Law, 126-130, 156; Trinity, 21, 130-133

Manz, Felix: 67, 69, 73
Marbeck, Pilgram: 144
Matthys, Jan: 96-98, 102
Melanchton, Philip: 29, 33, 34, 68, 90, 102, 118, 130, 132, 139, 141, 142
Metzsch, J. L.: 137
Mueller, Hans: 144
Müntzer, Thomas: 21, 22, 23, 25, 26, 27, 39, 42, 47; Person and teaching, 50-59; 63, 66, 67, 68, 70, 73; Possible influence on the Swiss Anabaptists, 74-77; 82, 85, 88, 91, 95, 99, 101, 102, 109, 110, 113, 128, 131, 136, 138, 140, 141, 142, 144, 152, 155, 157, 158, 166n, 189n

Newman, A. H.: 23
Nigg, Walter: 37, 152

Osiander, Andreas: 110
Oyer, John S.: 153

Payne, E. A.: 152, 153, 155
Peter the Venerable: 80
Pfeifer, Heinrich: 58

Plato: 50
Pruystinck, Eloy: 126

Rhegius, Urbanus: 68, 70, 99
Riegel, Hermann: 124
Roll, Heinrich: 96
Rothman, Bernt: 26, 96-98, 99, 102
Rühel, John: 63, 65
Rupp, Gordon: 171n

Sachs, Hans: 90
Schultz, Selina: 116, 123, 124, 126
Schwenckfeld, Caspar: 22, 110, 114-126, 148, 149, 152, 179n, 180n
Servetus, Michael: 132-133
Simons, Menno: 22, 27, 69, 84, 91, 104-105, 106, 144, 145, 146, 177n
Siirala, Aarne: 110
Smith, C. H.: 143
Smithson, R. J.: 143
Spengler, Lazarus: 113
Staupitz: 14
Storch, Nicholaus: 33, 34, 51
Stübner, Markus: 33, 34, 52
Suso, Heinrich: 25

Tauler, Johannes: 25, 53, 54
Tertullian: 79, 149
Troeltsch, Ernst: 26

Vedder, Henry: 32, 153
Verduin, Leonard: 153, 157

Wilbur, Earl M.: 130, 131, 152
Williams, G. H.: 124
Wüst, Michael: 69

Zasius, Ulrich: 60
Zuck, Lowell: 78
Zwilling, Gabriel: 29, 30, 38
Zwingli, Ulrich: 9, 68, 74, 99, 133, 142, 163n, 171n

www.ingramcontent.com/pod-product-compliance
Lightning Source LLC
Chambersburg PA
CBHW050635300426
44112CB00012B/1804